To:

From:

Date:

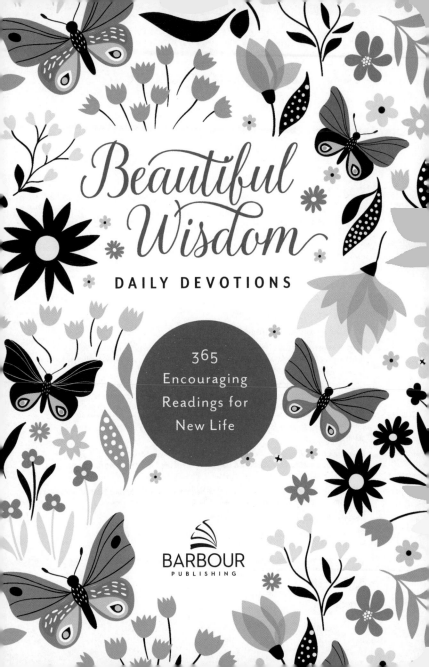

Beautiful Wisdom

DAILY DEVOTIONS

365
Encouraging
Readings for
New Life

BARBOUR
PUBLISHING

© 2018 by Barbour Publishing, Inc.

Print ISBN 978-1-63609-125-9

Adobe Digital Edition (.epub) 978-1-63609-401-4

Devotions previously appeared in *Whispers of Wisdom for Young Women*, *Daily Wisdom for Women 2015 Devotional Collection*, and *Daily Whispers of Wisdom for Busy Women*, all published by Barbour Publishing.

Scripture quotations are taken from the New Life Version copyright © 1969 and 2003. Used by permission of Barbour Publishing, Inc., Uhrichsville, Ohio, 44683. All rights reserved.

Cover Design: Greg Jackson, Thinkpen Design

Published by Barbour Publishing, Inc., 1810 Barbour Drive, Uhrichsville, Ohio 44683, www.barbourbooks.com

Our mission is to inspire the world with the life-changing message of the Bible.

Printed in China.

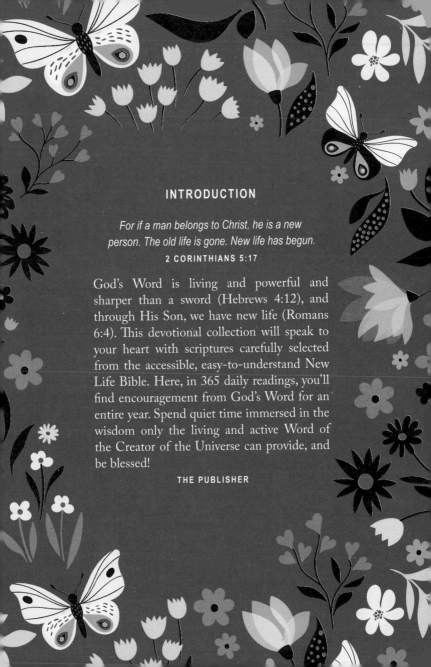

INTRODUCTION

*For if a man belongs to Christ, he is a new
person. The old life is gone. New life has begun.*
2 CORINTHIANS 5:17

God's Word is living and powerful and
sharper than a sword (Hebrews 4:12), and
through His Son, we have new life (Romans
6:4). This devotional collection will speak to
your heart with scriptures carefully selected
from the accessible, easy-to-understand New
Life Bible. Here, in 365 daily readings, you'll
find encouragement from God's Word for an
entire year. Spend quiet time immersed in the
wisdom only the living and active Word of
the Creator of the Universe can provide, and
be blessed!

THE PUBLISHER

Only One Thing

No, Christian brothers, I do not have that life yet. But I do one thing. I forget everything that is behind me and look forward to that which is ahead of me. My eyes are on the crown. I want to win the race and get the crown of God's call from heaven through Christ Jesus.

PHILIPPIANS 3:13–14

The start of a new year is filled with anticipation of what is ahead—a sense of getting to start over, make a fresh start—and with relief that some things are best left behind. Some make resolutions only to break them within a few days or hours. Some set goals both realistic and unrealistic. Many stay up New Year's Eve in order to welcome in the New Year; others value their sleep more and really couldn't care less.

Luke records a story in his Gospel illustrating our need to resolve to do only one thing. Jesus and His disciples came to Bethany and were invited to stay with Martha, Mary, and Lazarus. When Martha came to Jesus, complaining that her sister Mary wasn't helping her, Jesus spoke to her in loving concern: "Only a few things are important, even just one. Mary has chosen the good thing. It will not be taken away from her" (Luke 10:42).

Maintaining a close relationship with the Savior is the only goal Paul would set. He wasn't perfect at it, but he singlemindedly pursued it. And he encourages us to do so today. Life is much simpler when we choose to pursue only one thing—the race before us. Don't look back.

Heavenly Father, keep our eyes on the goal,
forgetting the successes and failures of this past year.

Run with Endurance

Let us put every thing out of our lives that keeps us from doing what we should. Let us keep running in the race that God has planned for us. Let us keep looking to Jesus.

HEBREWS 12:1–2

Running was the first and, for many years, the only event of the ancient Olympic games. So it is no wonder that the New Testament writers use the metaphor to describe the Christian life. The first races were 200-yard sprints. These gradually increased in length as the Olympic games continued to develop. The modern marathon commemorates the legendary run made by a Greek soldier named Pheidippides, who ran from the battlefield outside Marathon, Greece, to Athens to proclaim a single word: *victory!* Then he collapsed and died.

The Christian race lasts a lifetime, with Christ Jesus as our goal, the prize that awaits us at the finish line in heaven. It can't be run all-out as a sprint or no one would last the course. Though there was one race in the ancient games where the runners wore full armor, most of the time the ancient runners ran naked, stripping away anything that would slow them down. Obviously, the writer of Hebrews was familiar with the ancient sport of running when he advised believers to run with endurance the race God set before them.

Father, as we run the race You set before us this year,
let us run with endurance, not allowing anything
to distract us from the goal of Christ-likeness.

Life Is Short

Teach us to understand how many days we have.
Then we will have a heart of wisdom to give You.

PSALM 90:12

A pastor tried to illustrate the brevity of life to his congregation: "Think of a straight line stretching into infinity on either end. Anywhere on the line, place a dot smaller than a pinprick. That is your life, your 'threescore and ten' years Moses spoke of."

James 4:14 describes our life as "like fog. You see it and soon it is gone." In reality, given our finite minds trying to wrap around an infinite concept, these examples don't really come close to describing the brevity of life. But in spite of that, God does have a purpose for each one of us, a purpose He designed uniquely for each individual.

As a new year stretches ahead, many tend to procrastinate, thinking that time stretches into enough time to accomplish their goals and still "enjoy life." But Moses likens our lives to grass that springs up fresh in the morning but by evening it dries up and dies (Psalm 90:5–6). What seems a long time to us is really very little in the eyes of an eternal God. No wonder Moses' prayer was for wisdom to live a fulfilling and purposeful life in the brief time allotted to mankind. We would be wise to make this a daily prayer as we walk forward.

Father, teach us to number our days, to live
each day with purpose and wisdom as You lead
us to fulfill Your purposes through us.

Singing a New Song

He put a new song in my mouth, a song of praise to our God.
Many will see and fear and will put their trust in the Lord.

PSALM 40:3

For many, the New Year is a good time to reflect on the events of the past year, to review what God has done, to praise Him for deliverance and safety, and to thank Him for His provision—both individually and corporately. Some of the social networks online have software that will look at the posts and pictures an individual has made and put together a year in review, hitting the highlights and major events. But those "reviews" don't always pick up on the praise and thanksgiving to God that should result from such an accounting.

Take a moment to reflect on all that God has done in the previous months. Then proclaim the works of the Lord; be amazed at His outpouring of love, grace, and mercy. Break out in song, spontaneous and free. Praise God in hymns, praise songs, and scripture songs. Even those who can't "carry a tune in a bucket," as the saying goes, can praise God with a joyful noise. If God's people don't proclaim the glorious works of their God, how can they expect the world to ever have a right view of Him? Sing a new song of praise to God for His many and varied works, and renew your trust in Him for the new year ahead.

Father, thank You for the new song of
praise You have placed in my heart.

Strength of Heart

"Be strong and have strength of heart! Do not be afraid or lose faith. For the Lord your God is with you anywhere you go."

JOSHUA 1:9

Israel was on the verge of a new era in the life of their nation. Forty years before, God had delivered them from their four-hundred-year slavery to the Egyptian pharaohs. But when given the opportunity to enter the Promised Land, they instead saw the giants in the land and wouldn't trust God to give them the land in spite of the obstacles. Only Caleb and Joshua had the faith to believe God.

Now, after forty years of wandering in the wilderness, Joshua is tasked with the job of leading the children of those naysayers to take the land God promised long ago to Abraham. It's interesting to note that between Moses' charge and God's direct communication to the new leader, Joshua is told to "be strong" no less than seven times (Deuteronomy 31:6–7, 23; Joshua 1:6–7, 9, 18). And no wonder. Joshua faced a task that would be impossible to accomplish without God's help.

The challenges of a new year may seem impossible. Some may be old, familiar hurdles or battles; others may be hidden from view right now. Whatever is ahead, take courage from these promises given to Joshua, and claim them for whatever lies ahead. "Be strong and have strength of heart. . .for the Lord your God is with you anywhere you go."

Father, thank You for the promises of Your Word that You are always with us. We never need to face anything without Your presence and constant help.

Be Strong

"Do not be sad for the joy of the Lord is your strength."
NEHEMIAH 8:10

Nehemiah, Ezra, and other religious and civil leaders of their day had been given the job of leading the Jews back to Jerusalem after seventy years of exile. It hadn't been easy work for those who had made the long journey. Solomon's beautiful temple had been destroyed, and the attempts to rebuild it had resulted in something very inferior to what they remembered. Rebuilding the walls and reestablishing their homes were tasks made more difficult when they only had one hand with which to build. They held weapons in their other hand in order to defend their right to live in the land. At one point, the work of rebuilding was stopped after their enemies wrote a letter to the Persian king pointing out the unsuitability of the Jews to live out from under the immediate control of their captors.

Now the work was done, and the people wanted to hear what the Law of God said so they could avoid making the same mistakes again. All the Jews in the land came to Jerusalem and listened as Ezra read from the Law and Levites explained what they were hearing. The renewed understanding of God's Word caused them to weep. Finally, Nehemiah stood before the people he now governed and begged them not to be grieved and depressed. God was pleased with their desire to do what He commanded. It was a day for rejoicing for they were back in the land.

Father, joy gives us strength to do Your
will. Let us find our joy in You today.

Well-Watered Gardens

"The Lord will always lead you. He will meet the needs of your soul in the dry times and give strength to your body. You will be like a garden that has enough water, like a well of water that never dries up."

ISAIAH 58:11

Exhausted and weary to the bone, the writer walked into the prayer time barely able to summon any pleasure in the proceedings. The previous year had been grueling, and while she still clung to her faith in Jesus Christ, she had very little strength left. Empty and dry, she could barely make it through the motions of living. She came to the prayer room from a meeting with her agent, who had refused to drop her as a client. Frustrated at her lack of purpose and unable to write out of her desert-like existence, she sat facing the friend who had agreed to pray for her.

Soon after the prayer began, the dam holding her emotions hostage broke deep within. Tears flowed, and the Lord poured assurance after promise after confirmation over her head in the form of more life-giving water. God wasn't done with her yet. Hope pushed through the dry soil, turning lush and green in the showers of life-giving water.

Two months later, she stared in amazement at Isaiah 58:11. Almost word for word, the verse matched what her friend had prayed, proving once again that God's Word is living and powerful.

Thank You so much, Father, for sending Your Holy Spirit to wash us with the water of Your unchanging Word and to refresh us in the showers of blessings and mercies that are new every morning.

Confident Peace

*"I have told you these things so you may have peace
in Me. In the world you will have much trouble.
But take hope! I have power over the world!"*

JOHN 16:33

The apostle Paul said the peace Jesus spoke of in this passage was "greater than the human mind can understand" (Philippians 4:7). Part of the armor of God that Paul later describes in Ephesians 6 is the footwear, the sandals—the Gospel of peace. God has much to say about peace in the Bible. A quiet spirit, a peaceful spirit, is what God desires for each of His children. Yet worry in the midst of our busyness is much more common.

The scriptures tell us all we need to know in order to live a life of peace, of contentment, free from the worry and distraction of the world. Replacing the worry-thoughts with things that are true, honorable, right, pure, lovely, admirable, excellent, and worthy of praise (Philippians 4:8) will make room for the peace from God that transcends human understanding. Jesus gives it freely to all who desire to follow His example. Claim it today.

> Father, as I take every thought captive to the
> glory of Jesus Christ, help me to think on the
> things Paul listed in Philippians. May Your
> peace reign in my heart and life today.

Thirsting for God

O God, You are my God. I will look for You with all my heart and strength. My soul is thirsty for You. My flesh is weak wanting You in a dry and tired land where there is no water. So I have seen You in the holy place. And I have seen Your power and Your shining-greatness.

PSALM 63:1–2

David wrote many of the psalms in the middle of difficult times. Biblical scholars believe this one was written when David fled Jerusalem when his son Absalom took the throne from him. Even in the midst of David's breaking heart, he sought the Lord with a deep, soul-parched thirst. He was the deer being hunted by his son; he was the one longing to be filled, to be completely satisfied through the only source who truly satisfies.

Many years later, Jesus said, "Those who are hungry and thirsty to be right with God are happy, because they will be filled" (Matthew 5:6). The thirst Jesus describes is the same thirst David spoke of. Charles Spurgeon, a nineteenth-century pastor in London, explained it this way in his *Treasury of David*: This thirst is "the cry of a man far removed from the outward ordinances and worship of God, sighing for the long loved house of his God; and at the same time it is the voice of a spiritual believer, under depressions, longing for the renewal of the divine presence, struggling with doubts and fears, but yet holding his ground by faith in the living God."

> Father, I too thirst for You in the dryness
> of my soul. Thank You for Jesus, who
> alone is able to satisfy this thirst.

Perfect Rest

*"Come to Me, all of you who work and
have heavy loads. I will give you rest."*
MATTHEW 11:28

One day the crowds pushed against Jesus as He taught. So, instead of allowing them to push Him into the deeper waters of the Sea of Galilee lapping at His feet, He got into one of the fishing vessels His disciples owned. When the evening came, He asked His disciples to take Him to the other side of the lake. So they did. While the majority of the crowd couldn't follow Him, a few did who had boats.

Jesus, tired from the day's teaching, healing, and casting out demons, went to the back of the boat and fell asleep. Even when a severe storm blew up, He slept on. Finally, afraid the huge waves would swamp the ship, the disciples woke Jesus with their shouting: "Teacher, don't you care that we're going to drown?"

Jesus woke, heard the disciples' fear, and rebuked the wind and waves, and they instantly calmed. This is the kind of rest the Lord desires to give to His children when He said, "Come to Me, all of you who work and have heavy loads."

When we go to Him for rest, He eases, relieves, and refreshes our souls. He gives the best kind of refreshment we could ever wish for.

*Father, please remove the burden that weighs me down,
and give the rest that eases, relieves, and refreshes my soul.*

Trust God

Trust your work to the Lord, and your plans will work out well.
PROVERBS 16:3

Many people make resolutions at the beginning of a new year only to break them before the month is complete. Others set goals, then lay out detailed plans to accomplish them. In fact, January sees a plethora of self-help courses, webinars, blog posts, and other venues that emphasize how goals and/or resolutions will lead to success if we can manage not to break them or throw out the goals. There's nothing wrong with these things, except too many times we forget to include God in our plans.

In the first chapter of Joshua, we read of God's charge to Joshua after Moses was dead. It was time to lead the children of Israel into the Promised Land. God tells Joshua the secret to success: "Only be strong and have much strength of heart. Be careful to obey all the Law which My servant Moses told you. Do not turn from it to the right or to the left. Then all will go well with you everywhere you go. This book of the Law must not leave your mouth. Think about it day and night, so you may be careful to do all that is written in it. Then all will go well with you. You will receive many good things" (Joshua 1:7-8).

Solomon writes that we are to roll all our plans and goals onto the Lord. If they are in accordance with God's plan, then He will establish our plans and help us make them reality.

Father, I commit my plans to You today.

Renewed Strength

But they who wait upon the Lord will get new strength.
They will rise up with wings like eagles. They will run and
not get tired. They will walk and not become weak.
ISAIAH 40:31

Several times throughout scripture, the Lord had the writers use the eagle as a comparison to His people. Moses, speaking to the children of Israel just before his death, draws a beautiful picture of the eagle caring for its young. He then compares it to the Lord's leading in our lives. "He found him in a desert land, in the empty waste of a desert. He came around him and cared for him. He kept him as He would His own eye. Like an eagle that shakes its nest, that flies over its young, He spread His wings and caught them. He carried them on His wings. The Lord alone led him. There was no strange god with him" (Deuteronomy 32:10–12).

Isaiah carries that metaphor a bit further in Isaiah 40. Women seem to be most involved in nurturing their children, and as a result they tire easily. Starting in verse 27 in the Isaiah passage, Isaiah wonders how God's people can say that God is too busy or tired to care for His people. Instead he turns it around and says that even young men and children get tired. Only those who hope in the Lord will He carry on His wings, renewing their strength.

Father, thank You for these comparisons that show Your
loving heart in caring for Your children. I praise You for
enabling us to do the work You have called us to do.

God's Superabundant Work

God is able to do much more than we ask or think through His power working in us. May we see His shining-greatness in the church. May all people in all time honor Christ Jesus. Let it be so.

EPHESIANS 3:20–21

God is a lavish God who delights in doing much more than the human mind can dream or hope for.

A short time into his reign, King Solomon went to Gibeon to worship the Lord because the temple in Jerusalem wasn't built yet. One night the Lord came to Solomon in a dream and said, "Ask what you wish Me to give you" (1 Kings 3:5).

Solomon didn't hesitate: "Now, O Lord my God, You have made Your servant king in place of my father David. But I am only a little child. I do not know how to start or finish. . . . So give Your servant an understanding heart to judge Your people and know the difference between good and bad. For who is able to judge Your many people?" (vv. 7, 9).

God was pleased with Solomon's request and gladly granted it. But then He showed His superabundant nature. He gave Solomon wealth and honor and a long life (vv. 13–14). No other king in Solomon's time or even after has ever surpassed God's rich blessing on his life.

Father, keep my eyes fixed on You so I don't miss when You want to bless me in superabundant ways.

God's Joyful Love

The Lord your God is with you, a Powerful One Who wins the
battle. He will have much joy over you. With His love He will give
you new life. He will have joy over you with loud singing.
ZEPHANIAH 3:17

The first time a mom holds her newborn, a grandfather holds his grandchild, or an aunt holds her newborn niece or nephew, their hearts fill up with overwhelming love for that child. You look into the baby's eyes, check all the fingers and toes, and marvel over the perfection of this child. You can't imagine anything they do or say as the child grows up will lessen the love you have for them.

This scenario is just a tiny glimpse into how much God loves His children. Paul wrote in Romans 8:38–39: "For I know that nothing can keep us from the love of God. Death cannot! Life cannot! Angels cannot! Leaders cannot! Any other power cannot! Hard things now or in the future cannot! The world above or the world below cannot! Any other living thing cannot keep us away from the love of God which is ours through Christ Jesus our Lord."

Zephaniah says that God's love for His child is so over-whelming that He breaks into singing. Music is a spontaneous expression of many emotions but especially love.

Father, thank You for Your arms of
love holding me close to Your heart.

To Know Him Is to Trust Him

Those who know Your name will put their trust in You. For You, O Lord, have never left alone those who look for You.
PSALM 9:10

Names often reveal the character of a person. This is true in biblical times, especially when it comes to the names of God. A study of His names often brings a deeper awareness of God and who He is. Isaiah 9:6, in predicting the birth of Christ, listed several of His names: "For to us a Child will be born. To us a Son will be given. And the rule of the nations will be on His shoulders. His name will be called Wonderful, Teacher, Powerful God, Father Who Lives Forever, Prince of Peace."

In other places, He is referred to as Lord Jehovah, Almighty God, Shepherd, Priest, King of kings, and Lord of lords. He is the God who Sees, the Righteous One, Master, Redeemer, the All-Sufficient One. Each name describes a little different attribute or includes the many sides of His character. All are perfectly true about Him.

A study of the names of God, Jesus, and the Holy Spirit not only gives us a deeper insight into the nuances of who He is, but it also strengthens our ability to trust Him implicitly with every detail of our lives. He has promised to reveal Himself to those who truly seek Him out, who truly desire to "know Him. I want to have the same power in my life that raised Jesus from the dead. I want to understand and have a share in His sufferings and be like Christ in His death" (Philippians 3:10).

Father, reveal Yourself to me through
Your names so I will trust You more.

The Lord Gives Victory

"See, God saves me. I will trust and not be afraid. For the Lord God is my strength and song. And He has become the One Who saves me."

ISAIAH 12:2

The first time we see the phrase "the Lord God is my strength and song" is in the book of Exodus in the song Miriam and the women danced to as Moses and Miriam and the children of Israel sang. The reason for their rejoicing was their deliverance from Pharaoh and his army. When the Israelites left Egypt, they came to the Red Sea. They realized the army of Egypt had followed them. Then the Lord opened the Red Sea, and the Israelites crossed on dry land. The Egyptians followed. But once the last Israelite was safe on the other side, the Lord closed the waters over the Egyptians who had followed them. It was a great deliverance, and the people celebrated.

Later, Isaiah not only predicted God's judgment on the people of Israel because of their sin and desire to go their own way, he also predicted that God would send salvation and deliverance once their time of judgment was complete. As God had delivered the nation of Israel in ancient times, so would He deliver His people in the future. All would know His name; all would trust Him and not be afraid; all would find strength in praise and rejoicing. And therein lies true victory.

Father, faith in You brings victory in the battle against sin. May we sing praises to You for Your salvation.

Be Quiet and Know

*Be quiet and know that I am God. I will be honored
among the nations. I will be honored in the earth.*

PSALM 46:10

September 11, 2001. A day Americans will remember forever.
Terrorists took over passenger planes and ran two of them into
the World Trade Center towers in New York City. Another
crashed into the Pentagon in Washington D.C. Yet another
plane headed to the nation's capitol crashed into a Pennsylvania
field when the passengers took out the hijackers, refusing to let
them fulfill their purpose.

While the whole world watched the horrible events unfold,
many turned to the Word of God to find comfort in this unprec-
edented carnage. Psalm 46 is one of the passages promising
peace in the midst of cataclysmic events. The psalmist starts the
song with "God is our safe place and our strength. He is always
our help when we are in trouble. So we will not be afraid, even
if the earth is shaken and the mountains fall into the center of
the sea" (vv. 1–2). No matter what happens, God is standing
ready to help. Later in the psalm, the reader is invited to "see
the works of the Lord" (v. 8), to watch as the Lord destroys all
those who stand in opposition to Him.

Then the reader sees the command: "Be quiet and know that
I am God." No matter what happens, God has it all under His
control. There is no need for fear.

Father, quiet my spirit before You today
so I may know who You are.

All You Need

God can give you all you need. He will give you more than
enough. You will have everything you need for yourselves.
And you will have enough left over to give when there is a need.

2 CORINTHIANS 9:8

Maybe you cringe every time you hear that God wants to bless you. Perhaps you think that message is overblown by television evangelists or positive thinkers. Here's a biblical truth: We serve a God who owns the cattle on a thousand hills. He has more than enough for every situation. Does that mean He's going to shower down excessive heavenly blessings on you every day? Maybe not, but there will definitely be days—and seasons— when the blessings flow.

Whether you're in a season of plenty or lack, remember that God hasn't forgotten you. Today's scripture is a promise you can take to the bank. He can give you more than you need. When He does, you will have plenty of everything. Specifically, you will have enough to do the work that He has called you to.

So, brace yourself! Maybe those TV preachers are on to something. God loves you so much and wants to give you what you need, not so that you can gloat in your possessions but so that you are equipped to do His work.

Lord, I get it. You don't want to bless me just for the sake
of spoiling me. You long to give me the things I'm lacking
so that I'm well-equipped to carry forth Your message
to my friends and loved ones. Thank You, Father!

God Is the Boss

Whatever work you do, do it with all your heart.
Do it for the Lord and not for men.
COLOSSIANS 3:23

Over the centuries, many men and women have accomplished amazing things—things that have won them recognition from the world in the form of Nobel Prizes, Olympic medals, literary awards, books on the bestsellers lists, honorary doctorates, and much more. Most pursue these awards and titles to bring glory to themselves; a few make their accomplishments less known, seeking God's direction, following His leading. Earthly medals and awards, recognition and acclaim only last a few years at best.

Jesus said, "Do not gather together for yourself riches of this earth. They will be eaten by bugs and become rusted. Men can break in and steal them. Gather together riches in heaven where they will not be eaten by bugs or become rusted. Men cannot break in and steal them. For wherever your riches are, your heart will be there also" (Matthew 6:19–21).

It's so easy to fall into performance and/or approval traps, but they usually suck the joy out of the job. When we recognize that we work for the Lord, not for the approval of man, we are freed from man's laws and expectations. We are free to be the people God created, fulfilling the purposes He had in mind for us. Remember something C. T. Studd, British cricketeer and missionary, wrote: "Only one life, 'twill soon be past. Only what's done for Christ will last."

Father, help me put aside any desire for man's approval,
but only seek to do those things that will last for eternity.

Knowing God's Will

Christian brothers, I ask you from my heart to give your bodies to God because of His loving-kindness to us. Let your bodies be a living and holy gift given to God. He is pleased with this kind of gift. This is the true worship that you should give Him. Do not act like the sinful people of the world. Let God change your life. First of all, let Him give you a new mind. Then you will know what God wants you to do. And the things you do will be good and pleasing and perfect.

ROMANS 12:1–2

Frank Sinatra popularized the song "My Way," written by Paul Anka. The lyrics tell the story of an old man looking back on his life. He's satisfied with how he lived. He has no regrets for anything, even when he failed, because he alone controlled his life and he "did it my way."

It's a sad song, really, when the lyrics are analyzed in the light of God's Word. Paul wrote to the church in Rome, laying out in the first part how all people are born with a sin problem, one about which they can do nothing. Their only hope is in Jesus' work on the cross. Finally, he comes to the last section of the letter, and he pleads with his readers to give themselves entirely over to God's control. Because He has done so much for us, total surrender—a living sacrifice—is the only way to truly worship Him.

God's will is clear: turn away from the world's behavior and customs, and let God transform our thinking.

Father, I desire Your way over "my way."
Transform my thinking. Godly actions will follow.

Approach God with Trust

Let us go with complete trust to the throne of God.
We will receive His loving-kindness and have His
loving-favor to help us whenever we need it.

HEBREWS 4:16

The dictionary defines *trust* as the "assured reliance on the character, ability, strength, or truth of someone or something." This definition fits the admonition written by the author of Hebrews.

In this passage, Jesus' work on the cross and a description of why He is our great High Priest gives us the means to "go with complete trust to the throne of God." Jesus—100 percent God, 100 percent man—is the only one who fulfills God's demands for holiness and righteousness in those who approach Him. When we accept Christ's sacrifice on the cross, we believe that He paid the blood ransom required to remove our sins from us, making a relationship with God a reality. We do not have to adhere to a set of dos and don'ts or jump through a lot of hoops that man requires in order to gain an audience with our Father God. We have complete trust in Jesus Christ's ability to make us able to stand before a holy God.

With that restored relationship, we are also certain that when we approach God's throne in need of grace and mercy, we will receive it. What a great and precious promise we can cling to as we run the race set before us.

Father, thank You for the confidence that
is ours because of the work of Your
Son, Jesus Christ, on the cross.

Content in Christ's Strength

*I am not saying I need anything. I have learned to be happy with whatever
I have. . . . I can do all things because Christ gives me the strength.*

PHILIPPIANS 4:11, 13

Sometimes Paul seems like a giant of a man, way above everyone else on the spiritual scale. Granted, it is a man-made scale, certainly not one God uses.

Paul wrote his letter to the Philippian church from a prison in Rome. Prisons in the ancient world were nothing compared to those in our country today. In chapter one, we learn that Paul was guarded day and night by the emperor's own elite guards—the praetorians. Because Paul never backed down from sharing the Gospel with whoever crossed his path, many among the guards believed in Christ and then carried the Gospel into Nero's palace. Because of this unique opportunity to spread the Gospel, Paul rejoiced.

In the latter part of the letter, he declared that the gift the Philippians sent him was welcomed with rejoicing. But even without it, he could rejoice because he had learned to be content in whatever situation and condition he found himself. So how was Paul able to do this when so many of God's people today never learn his secret? Before Paul ended the paragraph, he told us: "I can do all things because Christ gives me the strength." Paul couldn't generate contentment in all situations, but Christ in him could. The same "secret" enables God's people to do the same nearly two thousand years later.

Father, thank You for enabling us to live joyful,
contented lives through Jesus Christ.

Trust God, Be Blessed

*"Good will come to the man who trusts in the
Lord, and whose hope is in the Lord."*
JEREMIAH 17:7

The believer's hope is founded on Jesus Christ alone, for He alone was able to pay the sin price for all mankind. Implicit trust in God's provision should be a natural result if a person has trusted in Christ for salvation. But sadly, it isn't always. In Jesus' parable of the sower, He tells of four different kinds of ground the seed falls on and compares it to sowing the seed of the Gospel on human hearts.

Jesus told the parable of the wise man and the foolish man, saying all people go into one of those categories. The wise person listens to Jesus' teachings and follows Him. Their life is built on a solid foundation so that when the storms come with the high winds and floodwaters, they will not collapse and wash away. They stand firm in the hope of the Lord. But the foolish person is the one who hears Christ's words but doesn't obey them. Their foundation is laid on shifting sand, so that when the winds and storms come, their house collapses and they have nothing to hope for.

Determine to be the wise person and be blessed because you place your confidence in Jesus Christ alone for salvation and a future.

Father, I thank You that my hope is built on
the firm foundation of Jesus Christ.

With God, Why Fear?

*When I am afraid, I will trust in You. I praise the Word
of God. I have put my trust in God. I will not be
afraid. What can only a man do to me?*

PSALM 56:3–4

God chooses the most improbable people to do His work
(1 Corinthians 1:27–29).

Gideon was threshing wheat in a winepress when an angel
from the Lord spoke to him: "The Lord is with you, O powerful soldier" (Judges 6:12). Gideon worked alone, but he may
have looked around to see if there was anyone else who'd
sneaked in. Now Gideon knew he was the epitome of fear.
After all, who threshes wheat in a winepress when he needs
the winds of the hills to blow the chaff away? But fearful
Gideon listened to what God had to say and gathered an
army to fight the Midianites. But then God told him to
pare his army down to 300. Three hundred against the vast
Midiante army? But by this time, God had shown Himself
trustworthy, and Gideon obeyed. Because he trusted God,
he put his fear aside and relied on God for the outcome.

God wants followers who will obey His leading in spite
of fear.

> Father God, sometimes my fears threaten to
> overwhelm me and shut me down. Help me
> give my fears to You as I obey Your will.

God's Word Accomplishes His Purposes

"The rain and snow come down from heaven and do not return there without giving water to the earth. This makes plants grow on the earth, and gives seeds to the planter and bread to the eater. So My Word which goes from My mouth will not return to Me empty. It will do what I want it to do, and will carry out My plan well."

ISAIAH 55:10–11

Farmers and ranchers settled this country, especially in the move to the West. Many immigrants came into the country looking for land, which was plentiful here. With a general population shift to the cities, where people can find jobs, farming and ranching aren't as prominent. For many, the experience of planting a field with seed, waiting on God to send the rain at the right times, giving the plants the moisture they need to bud and flourish, and seeing the crop through harvest is only something they read about.

The Lord uses this analogy to describe what happens when God's Word goes out in a sermon, in verses memorized, or in the written word. God promises that when His Word is planted in someone, it doesn't go to waste. It may take a long time to see it take root and grow and be harvested, but it will. For it will not return to God until it has achieved the purpose for which He sent it. So moms of wayward children, take heart. God is still working.

Father, thank You for the promises of Your Word that we can hang on to when life gets hard.

God Goes with You

"Be strong and have strength of heart. Do not be afraid or shake with fear because of them. For the Lord your God is the One Who goes with you. He will be faithful to you. He will not leave you alone."

DEUTERONOMY 31:6

In *The Horse and His Boy*, one of the books in the Narnia series by C. S. Lewis, we see a beautiful picture of how the Lord gives us strength and courage to do His will. The boy, Shasta, runs away from home. Along the way, he meets up with a talking horse from Narnia and a nobly born girl, Aravis, with her talking horse. They decide to take their horses to Narnia, but their plans fall apart when they have to go through the Calormene capital city, Tashbaan.

Several times as they travel, they are chased by lions, harassed by cats, and generally persecuted by various members of the cat family. Finally, on one particularly dark night, Shasta crosses over a mountain pass alone. In the dark and fog, Shasta senses rather than sees a creature walking along beside him. And he's terrified.

Later, when he meets Aslan, Shasta learns that all the cats were Aslan, guiding them, pushing them, and yes, terrifying them into doing what they needed to do. Aslan was also his protector as he crossed the steep and dangerous mountain pass in the dark. Shasta is angry until he realizes that Aslan did everything out of love, even hurting Aravis when her pride was keeping them from the mission they'd been given.

Father, thank You for the beautiful picture of Your protection and courage to those who are Yours.

Nothing Is Impossible with God

"For God can do all things."

LUKE 1:37

Gabriel, the archangel tasked with telling Mary that she would be the mother of the promised Messiah, spoke these words to her when she asked how such a thing could happen when she wasn't married. She responded with humility and submitted to the Lord's will.

Two other times in scripture an angel announces a birth to couples who in human years were too old for such a thing to happen. When the angel told Abraham that Sarah would conceive and have a son within the year, Sarah laughed. When the angel asked why she laughed, she denied it at first and then said she was too old. The angel responded that nothing was too hard for God. And it happened as God said it would. Then Sarah's laughter of unbelief turned into joy.

Several months before Gabriel appeared to Mary, he showed up in the temple where a priest named Zechariah was sacrificing the daily offering. Gabriel told him that he and his wife, Elizabeth, would have a son in their old age. The child would be the forerunner to the promised Messiah. Zechariah's unbelief led to losing his voice for the next nine months until his son was born and he gave him the name the angel had said.

God delights in doing the impossible, waiting until the perfect time to fulfill His Word.

> Father, give me faith to believe Your Word
> as Mary received the news of Jesus' birth,
> knowing that nothing is too hard for You.

God's Grace in Weakness

"I am all you need. I give you My loving-favor. My power works best in weak people." I am happy to be weak and have troubles so I can have Christ's power in me. I receive joy when I am weak. I receive joy when people talk against me and make it hard for me and try to hurt me and make trouble for me. I receive joy when all these things come to me because of Christ. For when I am weak, then I am strong.

2 CORINTHIANS 12:9–10

The apostle Paul had many amazing experiences over the years after his conversion, and he saw God bring him through many trials, each designed to draw him ever closer to his goal to be like Christ. One such experience was getting to visit heaven, whether in the Spirit or out of the Spirit—either in reality or in a vision—he didn't know. But in order to keep Paul humble, the Lord sent a "thorn in the flesh."

Scripture doesn't say exactly what that "thorn" was, but it caused Paul enough pain and trouble that he asked the Lord to take it away, not once but three times. Finally God told him, "I am all you need. I give you My loving-favor. My power works best in weak people." In other words, "No. All you need is My grace to help you cope with this thorn. For in your weakness you are forced to depend on Me for strength to get you through and still be able to proclaim My Gospel. Others can see Me in you, when your 'thorn' should keep you from doing anything at all."

Father, help me to rely on Your grace as
Paul did, knowing You allow weakness to
keep me from working independently.

God's Provision

And my God will give you everything you need
because of His great riches in Christ Jesus.

PHILIPPIANS 4:19

Sometimes the littlest words in our language pack a lot of meaning into them. *All* is one of those words. Three letters encompass the total extent of the whole. Everything is in the word *all*.

In the letter to the Philippians, Paul is wrapping up a discussion of how God had used the church to provide for Paul's need while he was in prison, even though many of them didn't have much to give. Paul spoke out of experience when he told them God would supply all their financial needs because they gave sacrificially to help another person with a greater need.

But God meeting their financial need isn't all that is encompassed in the meaning Paul intended to convey when he chose this particular word. When Jesus taught this principle to His disciples, Luke recorded it in his Gospel: "Give, and it will be given to you. You will have more than enough. It can be pushed down and shaken together and it will still run over as it is given to you. The way you give to others is the way you will receive in return" (6:38). Jesus indicated that whatever a person has to give, when they give it, they will receive as they have given. Emotional, spiritual, physical, material—whatever the need, God will supply it abundantly.

Father, thank You for this promise that You
will abundantly supply for every need I have
through the riches of heaven in Christ Jesus.

God Has a Plan

"For I know the plans I have for you," says the Lord, "plans for well-being and not for trouble, to give you a future and a hope."

JEREMIAH 29:11

When Jeremiah wrote this, Israel was already in captivity in Babylon. Things looked pretty bleak, and many held no hope of returning to the land God had given them generations before under Joshua's leadership. It was because they refused to listen to the prophets, telling them to repent of their sin of consistently turning away from God's plan and living the way they wanted to, that they were in this predicament.

After the majority of the Jews were taken to Babylon, Jeremiah wrote them a letter telling them to accept where they were. Since they were going to be there the full seventy years God had predicted, they were to settle down, build houses, establish communities, plant gardens, marry, die, celebrate their special days—in other words, live life to the fullest while they were there. The sooner they accepted God's punishment, the sooner they could begin living again. The letter concluded with a reminder that God had not forgotten them. He still had plans for His people. Good plans, not evil. He wanted to give them hope that this punishment wasn't for forever.

God still has a plan for each one of His children. They are still plans for peace and good, hope-filled plans.

Father, thank You for the thoughts and plans You
have for each of Your children. Help us to live
life to the fullest in the hope of those plans.

Jesus Never Forsakes

Keep your lives free from the love of money. Be happy with what you have. God has said, "I will never leave you or let you be alone." So we can say for sure, "The Lord is my Helper. I am not afraid of anything man can do to me."

HEBREWS 13:5–6

What a wonderful "comfort" verse, filled with the promise of God's protection, help, and provision—God assures His people He has everything under control. Because of what God does, we have no reason to be dissatisfied with anything God allows into our lives—either good or bad.

Study the book of Job. Listen to Job's statements of faith throughout the book. But none are so convincing as his statements in chapters one and two, refusing to sin against God with his words. Even after his wife—his closest companion here on earth—urged him to curse God and die, Job refused to comply. He acknowledged that God had the right to give and to take away. And he blessed the Lord throughout, accepting that God never revealed the whys to him.

Father, I don't need to know the whys.
You are in control no matter what happens.
Thank You for this promise.

Stop Analyzing

My eyes are on the crown. I want to win the race and get the
crown of God's call from heaven through Christ Jesus.

PHILIPPIANS 3:14

Judy lay awake recounting all the conversations she'd had at the office that day. *Was I too harsh when I made that comment? What if Jerry misunderstood what I said? What about the decision to move forward on the Tyson account? Was that too. . . ?* Judy's mind was racing with questions, overanalyzing the decisions and commitments she made at work and in her personal life that week.

Suddenly, her sister's words came back to her. "You pray every day for God to help you do the very best you can. Don't you trust Him to complete that work?" Her sister was right, and she was wasting precious time when she could be getting some much-needed sleep. She slipped down beside her bed and kneeled to ask God to help her let go of thoughts that seemed to hold her captive each night.

We often want to cover our bases, assuring ourselves that our decisions are right, but we must not lose ourselves in the analysis. Find your strength in the leadership of the Holy Spirit, and then relax and enjoy peaceful sleep.

Lord, help me to trust You in the decisions I make
throughout my day. Help me to stop second-guessing
myself and trust who You created me to be. Amen.

Emptiness

*"You have shown me the ways of life.
I will be full of joy when I see Your face."*

ACTS 2:28

Imagine you're looking at a full-to-the-brim rain barrel. You've been in a season of abundant rain. It never occurs to you that a dry season might be around the corner.

Now picture yourself, weeks later, staring down into the barrel, noticing that it's bone dry. Drought has taken its toll. Now you have a picture of what it's like when you go through a season of spiritual wholeness and spiritual drought. Your rain barrel—your heart—is only as full as what's poured into it.

Did you realize that God can refill your heart with just one word? When He sees that your well is running dry, it breaks His heart. The only solution is to run to His arms and ask for a fresh outpouring of His holy water, the kind that will replenish your soul and give you the nourishment you need to move forward in Him.

It's up to you. God is waiting to meet with you. His everlasting water is prepped and ready to be poured out on you. All you need to do. . .is run to Him.

Father, I've been blaming my dry spell on so many different things: Exhaustion. Frustration. You name it, I've pointed the finger at it. Lord, I need the kind of water that You provide–the kind that will never run dry. Today, Lord, I run into Your arms, ready to be refreshed!

Trust Test

Hear my prayer, O Lord! Let my cry for help come to You.
PSALM 102:1

Have you had days when your prayers seemed to hit the ceiling and bounce back? Does God seem distant for no reason you're aware of? Chances are good that if you've been a Christian for more than a short time, you've experienced this.

The psalmist experienced it as pain and suffering became his lot. At night, insomnia plagued him. During his tired days, enemies taunted him. His was a weary life, and in earthly terms, he hardly could see the outcome.

But once the psalmist described his plight, his psalm turned in a new direction, glorifying God. Suddenly, life wasn't so bad anymore because he trusted in the One who would save him.

When prayer hits the ceiling, it's time to remind ourselves of God's greatness, not complain about what we think He hasn't done. As we face trials that threaten to undo us, let's remind ourselves that He has not forgotten us, and our ultimate security is never at risk.

As we feel the dangers of life, let's trust that God is still listening to our prayers. He will never fail us. All He asks is that our reliance on Him remains firm. At the right hour, we'll feel His love again.

> Even when I don't feel Your presence, Lord,
> You have not deserted me. Keep me trusting
> and following You, O Lord. Amen.

A Small Deal

Everyone should look at himself and see how he does his own work. Then he can be happy in what he has done. He should not compare himself with his neighbor.

GALATIANS 6:4

Do you have a tendency to overreact to life's challenges? Do you make a big deal out of things? If so, it's time to accept a challenge. For a full week, make up your mind to "make a small deal" out of your challenges. When you're tempted to panic, take a deep breath, count to ten, and make the smallest possible scenario out of it that you can. Will this be difficult? Absolutely. Is it possible? Definitely.

When you decide to create "big deals" out of everyday situations, you find yourself facing relationship strains, high blood pressure, and other woes. These things morph and grow to crazy proportions when you overreact. When you choose "small deals," you will experience forgiveness, peace, and the ability to bounce back without holding bitterness. It's your choice!

When you opt to make a "small deal" out of things, you will also have the satisfaction of knowing that you are pleasing your heavenly Father's heart. Now, that's a very big deal!

Lord, I don't want to be seen as someone who overreacts to things. I acknowledge that I've done this at times. Please remove this tendency from me so that I can live at peace with others. I want to please Your heart, Father.

Leaving a Legacy

*But the loving-kindness of the Lord is forever and
forever on those who fear Him. And what is right with
God is given forever to their children's children.*

PSALM 103:17

Have you given any thought to the legacy you will leave behind
after you're gone? If you're a parent or grandparent, you surely
have pondered the generations coming up behind you. Maybe
you've wondered what, specifically, they will remember about
you. If you're not yet married or don't have children of your
own, perhaps you could give thought to the legacy you will leave
behind to your friends, coworkers, and/or neighbors.

It's an amazing thing to think about God's goodness carrying
on from one generation to another and another. If you really
pause to think it through, the original twelve disciples left a
legacy for the early church. Those dedicated believers—in spite
of persecution and pain—left a legacy for the next generation,
and so on. Without the seeds they planted, the church would
surely not have survived.

It's so important to press through. Be a seed planter, no matter
how difficult your life. Others are watching and gleaning from
your example.

Father, I can see how important my seed-planting is!
I want to leave a legacy, Lord. Above all else, I want
people to remember me for my walk with You.

Joy Is Jesus

You have never seen Him but you love Him. You cannot see Him now but you are putting your trust in Him. And you have joy so great that words cannot tell about it. You will get what your faith is looking for, which is to be saved from the punishment of sin.

1 PETER 1:8–9

As children, we find joy in the smallest things: a rose in bloom, a ladybug at rest, the circles a pebble makes when dropped in water. Then somewhere between pigtails and pantyhose, our joy wanes and eventually evaporates in the desert of difficulties.

But when we find Jesus, "all things become new" as the Bible promises, and once again, we view the world through a child's eyes. Excitedly, we experience the "joy so great that words cannot tell about it" that salvation brings.

We learn that God's joy isn't based on our circumstances; rather, its roots begin with the seed of God's Word planted in our hearts. Suddenly, our hearts spill over with joy, knowing that God loves and forgives us and that He is in complete control of our lives. We have joy because we know this world is not our permanent home and a mansion awaits us in glory.

Joy comes as a result of whom we trust, not in what we have. Joy is Jesus.

Dear Jesus, thank You for giving me the joy of my salvation. Knowing You surpasses anything and everything else the world offers. Never allow the joy in my heart to evaporate in the desert of difficulties. Amen.

DAY 38

A Creative God

In the beginning God made from
nothing the heavens and the earth.
GENESIS 1:1

Did you realize that you are made (designed, created) in the image of a very creative God? It's true! He breathed life into you, after all. It stands to reason that some of His creativity would have spilled over into you, His creation.

The same God who created the heavens and the earth—who decided a giraffe's neck should be several feet long and a penguin should waddle around in tuxedo-like attire—designed you, inside and out! And He gifted you with a variety of gifts and abilities, all of which can be used to His glory.

So, what creative gifts reside inside of you? Have you given them a stir lately? Maybe it's time to ask God which gifts are most useable for this season of your life. He's creative enough to stir the ones that can be used to reach others. He will bring them to the surface and prepare you to use them—much like He did during Creation—to bring beauty out of dark places.

So, brace yourself! Your very creative God has big things planned for you!

Lord, thank You for creating me in Your image. I get so excited when I think about the fact that Your creativity lives inside of me. Just as Your Spirit moved across creation in the book of Genesis, I ask You to move across the creative gifts in my life and stir them to life!

Say No to Blabbermouths

He who goes about talking to hurt people makes secrets known. So do not be with those who talk about others.

PROVERBS 20:19

If you're like most people, every day you're surrounded with the temptation to gossip. Whether it's at work, at school, in a circle of close friends, or simply out in the community, the rumor mill is always turning.

The wisdom in Proverbs spells plainly its warning: a gossip can't be trusted to keep their mouth shut, so don't share secrets with them!

As Christians, we need to take this attitude a step further and stand up against gossip. Don't be afraid to voice your displeasure—in love, of course—when your friends talk about others. Introduce encouragement and uplifting words into your conversations, and resist the temptation to fall into old habits.

Words are powerful. If you've ever been the victim of having your secrets blabbed behind your back, you know the pain they cause. Commit yourself to cutting gossip from your life, and your relationships will be strengthened.

Father, please forgive me for talking about others behind their backs. I don't want to be known as a blabbermouth. Help my words to always be encouraging to others. Amen.

A Roaring Fire

*God's Word is living and powerful. It is sharper than a sword
that cuts both ways. It cuts straight into where the soul and spirit
meet and it divides them. It cuts into the joints and bones. It tells
what the heart is thinking about and what it wants to do.*

HEBREWS 4:12

The world is filled with books on every topic and in many languages. You can find pages at your fingertips on a computer keyboard and can explore volumes of information that provide you with entertainment and knowledge, but only the Bible—the Word of God—can truly speak to you.

No matter what you are facing, there is always something in the Bible to help you find your way. There is simply no other book like it. Other books can encourage, inspire, and motivate—but the Bible gives life. The Word of God can infuse you with strength, sustain you in battle, and uphold you during the darkest days you'll ever face.

Maybe for you the fire of God's Word starts out as a small glowing ember. You could read for days, and then suddenly you stumble upon that scripture—those amazing words—written so many years ago that seem written specifically to you. You know it the moment the Word comes alive as it ignites your heart. It comforts you, provides an answer to the questions you've been asking, and consumes you with a hunger for the truth.

Lord, I want to read Your Word and hear
Your voice as it speaks to me. Ignite me
with a passion for the Bible. Amen.

The Truth about the Holy Spirit

*"Then I will ask My Father and He will give you another Helper.
He will be with you forever. He is the Spirit of Truth. . . . You
know Him because He lives with you and will be in you."*

JOHN 14:16–17

To some Christians, the Holy Spirit is a mystery. To others, He is a frightening part of the Trinity. And for even mature believers, the Holy Spirit is often misunderstood.

Jesus called the Holy Spirit a comforter, counselor, and friend. In Acts, the Messiah-promised Spirit fell on the early church with power. He made the new Christians bold, authoritative, and fearless. And the Spirit longs to do the same for us.

Are you lonely? Let Him be a friend to you. Are you grieving? The Holy Spirit will comfort you. He can guide you to the perfect scriptures for your grief, and He will pray to the Father for you when you don't have the words. Do you want to make a difference for Christ? Pray for the Spirit to give you opportunities to share your faith with seekers.

Our Father wants to make the Spirit less of a mystery. Jesus longs for you to understand the One who came to be with the church after He ascended to heaven. And instead of frightening you, the Holy Spirit wants to be as second nature to you as your next breath.

Will you let Him?

> Father, thank You for providing the Holy Spirit.
> Make me aware of His promptings, and help me
> to understand the Spirit's dealings with me.

Just Do It

Be happy in your hope. Do not give up when trouble comes. Do not let anything stop you from praying.
ROMANS 12:12

The words seem to readily roll off our tongues, "I'll be praying for you." Words may come easy, yet are we faithful to actually pray? Praying for someone is different than simply thinking about them or wishing them well. Prayer is hard work because it requires time and discipline. Prayer is spiritual warfare.

Whenever we commit to pray for someone, the enemy schemes to prevent it. Why? Even Satan knows that prayer unleashes God's power. Prayer is a spiritual weapon at our disposal. It has the power to demolish strongholds and defeat Satan. Prayer gives us access into the spiritual realm so we can communicate with our heavenly Father through Jesus Christ, His Son. We claim the promises and victory we have been given. We submit our hearts and ask that God's will be done.

Nothing draws us closer to other people than praying for them. Asking for God's intervention in their lives is an awesome privilege. We experience matchless rejoicing when our prayers are answered. We may not understand how, yet we realize that somehow our prayers have made a difference. Let's not just promise to pray for someone. Let's be faithful to do it!

Dear Lord, often I have good intentions to pray for others but fail to follow through. Help me to be faithful in prayer so that I may see Your power at work. Amen.

An Exhortation

Then David said to his son Solomon, "Be strong. Have strength of heart, and do it. Do not be afraid or troubled, for the Lord God, my God, is with you. He will not stop helping you."

1 CHRONICLES 28:20

In 1 Chronicles 28:20, King David has just given his son Solomon and the people of Israel detailed instructions for building the Lord's temple. Can you imagine how awed and overwhelmed the people felt as they heard the plans for the temple's design? First Kings 6 tells us that it took *tens of thousands* of skilled workmen *seven years* to complete the temple! No wonder David exhorted his people to be strong and courageous! No wonder he urged them to resist discouragement and fear!

God knew His people could complete the undertaking He had set before them, but He also knew they would be overwhelmed by the enormity of the task. Perhaps you too are feeling disheartened by the sheer size of your responsibilities. Maybe you feel like giving up. David's words still offer us encouragement in the face of the seemingly insurmountable: Be strong and courageous! Do the work! Don't be afraid or discouraged by the size of the task. The Lord God is with you, and He will not fail you or forsake you!

Dear Lord, give me strength and courage to do the work You have called me to do. Take away my fear and discouragement, and help me to lean on You. Amen.

Are You Getting Squeezed?

*He gives us everything we need for life and for holy
living. He gives it through His great power.*

2 PETER 1:3

Does your schedule ever get so full you feel like you can't
breathe? Maybe your boss demands meeting on top of meeting,
or your children's extracurricular activities have you going in
circles. Somehow you keep moving forward, not always sure
where the strength comes from but thankful in the end that
you made it through the day.

In those situations, you're not just stretching your physical
body to the limit but your mind and emotions as well. Stress
can make you feel like a grape in a winepress. The good news is
that God has given you everything you need, but it's up to you
to utilize the wisdom He has provided. Don't be afraid to say no
when you feel you just can't add one more thing to your to-do
list. Limit your commitments, ask someone to take notes for
you in a meeting you can't make, or carpool with someone who
shares your child's extracurricular activity.

Alleviate the pressure where you can, and then know that
God's power will make up for the rest.

*Lord, help me to do what I can do; and I'll trust You
to do for me those things that I can't do. Amen.*

Outside of Time

> *"I tell from the beginning what will happen in the end. And from times long ago I tell of things which have not been done, saying, 'My Word will stand. And I will do all that pleases Me.'"*
>
> **ISAIAH 46:10**

Time ticks away, fleeting past as we go about our busy day. How often have you wished time would stop—stand still for moments, hours, or even days? It's normal to want to capture the good times in our lives and hold them tightly.

As an eternal being, God stands outside of time. He *was*, *is*, and always *will be*. We live in the moment—the sliver of time we call today, and that is where our focus often stays. But what if we looked at our lives from God's perspective? He created us to live for all eternity with Him. He didn't intend for us to live our lives here on earth, die, and *then* begin eternity with Him.

Eternity is now! It starts with the realization that your salvation has granted you a never-ending story—a life without end. Sure, you'll leave this earth at some point, but you'll carry on as a child of God with Him forever and ever. You can live outside of time knowing there is really no end to your time with Him.

God, help me to live each day
with an eternal focus. Amen.

An Unchanging Boss

The sleep of the working man is pleasing, if he eats little or much.
But the full stomach of the rich man does not let him sleep.

ECCLESIASTES 5:12

God created work to be good! Even before the Fall, Adam and Eve worked. God told them to care for the Garden of Eden, name the animals, and even rule over the area. Only after sin entered the picture did Adam and Eve come to realize that their work was no longer 100 percent enjoyable but quite difficult at times.

The earth's soil refused to cooperate, and weeds immediately sprang up. Pain from childbearing intensified, and later Cain would kill his brother, Abel. With an ancestral history such as this, how are present-day Christians supposed to enjoy and profit from the work we do?

A key factor behind our work is not our identity but our motivation. When Adam and Eve worked, they were working for God. Just because sin entered the world doesn't mean we have a different boss. God doesn't require us to be slaves. In fact, He allows us to take a righteous pride in the work we do for Him. Our projects and daily tasks are a reflection of what we can give back to Him.

> Lord, thank You for giving me the work I have.
> Give me a passion for reflecting You in it. Amen.

Checklist

I receive joy when I am weak. I receive joy when people talk against me and make it hard for me and try to hurt me and make trouble for me. I receive joy when all these things come to me because of Christ. For when I am weak, then I am strong.

2 CORINTHIANS 12:10

The apostle Paul suffered from an unknown "thorn in the flesh." He begged God to take it away. He didn't stop asking until God revealed an important spiritual truth: God's strength is made perfect in weakness.

Paul searched for words to explain this principle to the Christians at Corinth. *What things keep them from serving God? How can I help them understand that God will use those very weaknesses to make them strong?* He came up with a checklist.

Weaknesses. What area do we struggle with constantly, whether it is physical, mental, or emotional?

Insults. What hurtful things do others say about us, whether true or not?

Hardships. What physical and financial catastrophes have happened to us recently?

Persecutions. Do others make fun of our faith?

Calamities. What natural or man-made disasters have impacted our world?

Paul stopped struggling against his thorn in the flesh when he realized it was God's gift to make him rely on God's strength. God wants us to do the same with our weaknesses. Each day we should check where we feel weak. When we turn that area over to Him, God will demonstrate His strength.

Christ Jesus, You are all-powerful. We pray
that You will step into our weaknesses, take over,
and demonstrate Your power and care on our behalf. Amen.

Clear Vision

*Know that wisdom is like this to your soul. If you find it,
there will be a future, and your hope will not be cut off.*

PROVERBS 24:14

If you've ever worn glasses, you know what it's like to try to go without them. Talk about a fuzzy world! You take tentative steps, cautiously moving forward, knowing that, at any minute, you might trip over something or knock something down.

Clarity of vision is a wonderful gift. Once you put those glasses on, you can clearly see the road ahead and take bold, big steps. Confidence rises inside you as you focus on the path set before you.

In this same way, God can bring clarity/vision to your path when you ask for His wisdom. Picture yourself in a rough situation. You don't know which way to go. You ask for the Lord's wisdom. He offers it, and the road ahead of you is suddenly clear. It's as if you've put on spiritual glasses! That's what His wisdom does—gives definition. Boldness. Confidence. Makes clear the path.

What are you waiting for? No need for a fuzzy road ahead. Put on those glasses, then take a bold step forward!

Father, I'm so excited that I don't have to walk
around confused and blinded. No fuzzy roads for me,
Lord! Today I pause to ask for Your wisdom so that
the road ahead will be clear. Thank You for great
vision and the confidence to move forward.

Listening vs. Talking

"My sheep hear My voice and I know them. They follow Me."
JOHN 10:27

It has been said that the Lord gave us two ears and one mouth for a reason: we need to listen twice as much as we speak. However, talking seems to come easier for most of us. Our interaction with others becomes the model for our relationship with the Lord. We can become so busy talking to Him during our prayer time that we forget He has important wisdom to impart to us!

Jesus is our Good Shepherd. As His sheep, we have the ability to distinguish His voice. But are we taking the time to listen? It seems much of our prayer time is devoted to reciting our wish list to God. When we stop and think about it, doesn't God already know our needs before we utter one word? We need to learn to listen more instead of dominating the conversation. God is the One with the answers. He knows all things and possesses the wisdom we yearn for.

Learning to listen takes time. Do not be afraid to sit in silence before the Lord. Read His Word. He will speak softly to your heart. He will impart truth to your hungry soul. He will guide you on the path you should take. Listen.

Dear Lord, help me learn how to listen and distinguish
Your voice. Grant me time to be silent in Your presence.
Speak to my heart so that I may follow You. Amen.

Available 24-7

*I have called to You, O God, for You will answer
me. Listen to me and hear my words.*

PSALM 17:6

No one is available to take your call at this time, so leave a message and we will return your call—or not—if we feel like it. . .and only between the hours of 4:00 and 4:30 p.m. Thank you for calling. Have a super day!

We've all felt the frustration of that black hole called voice mail. It is rare to reach a real, honest-to-goodness, breathing human being the first time we dial a telephone number.

Fortunately, our God is always available. He can be reached at any hour of the day or night and every day of the year—including weekends and holidays! When we pray, we don't have to worry about disconnections, hang-ups, or poor reception. We will never be put on hold or have our prayers diverted to another department. The Bible assures us that God is eager to hear our petitions and that He welcomes our prayers of thanksgiving. The psalmist David wrote of God's response to those who put their trust in Him: "He will call upon Me, and I will answer him" (Psalm 91:15). David had great confidence that God would hear his prayers. And we can too!

Dear Lord, thank You for always being there for me.
Whether I am on a mountaintop and just want to
praise Your name or I am in need of Your comfort
and encouragement, I can count on You. Amen.

Margin

The man who goes into God's rest, rests from his own work the same as God rested from His work. Let us do our best to go into that rest or we will be like the people who did not go in.

HEBREWS 4:10–11

Imagine a busy person's planner or calendar. More often than not, it is bursting with notes and reminders and is well-worn from frequent use. Seldom is there an opening in the day's schedule for unexpected things that may arise, let alone a few minutes set aside for rest. But God instructs us to plan for rest in our schedule and to leave ourselves some breathing room in order to accommodate last-minute things.

Hebrews 4 refers to the final, eternal rest that we will enter into with Christ. But in the meantime, we are called to lead an uncluttered life so we are ready for service to God. We are not to busy ourselves with the cares of the world, completely filling our margins.

Does your life have a clean margin, or have you filled your page completely, leaving no room for additions or corrections? Is there room in your life for the plans God has for you?

Lord, correct my thinking and clear my clutter. Help me to work a margin into my day so that Your plans, last-minute notes, corrections, and additions can find a place in my life. Let me not be so busily focused on my own agenda that I miss Yours. Amen.

Heavenly Riches

"Your heart will be wherever your riches are."

LUKE 12:34

Where is your greatest treasure? Do you own something so valuable it sits in a safe-deposit box in your bank? Maybe you take it out once in a while then return it for safekeeping.

If that's really your life's greatest treasure, you're in trouble, for according to this verse, your heart is locked up in a narrow, dark safe-deposit box, where it's awfully difficult to love others and enjoy the world God has given you.

Maybe you don't own that kind of valuable, but you're inordinately proud of the vehicle you drive. Would you really want your heart to sit out in all weather, where it could eventually rust away? Even the best care will never make a car last forever. Hide it in a garage, but it still has a limited life.

But when your best treasure is your relationship with Christ and His eternal reward, you don't have to worry about where your heart is. It's safe with Jesus, free to love others, and valuable to both you and the people with whom you share Christ.

Are you gathering earthly riches or eternal ones? Those on earth won't last. Sending treasures before you to heaven is the wisest thing you can do. Worldly goods fade, but not those in Jesus' treasure vaults.

> Lord, help me send riches ahead of me
> into eternity instead of grabbing all
> the earthly items I can get. Amen.

Do Foxes Make You Fume?

"Catch the foxes for us, the little foxes that are destroying our grape-fields, for the flowers are on the vines."
SONG OF SOLOMON 2:15

What makes you fume? You know, those bothersome little annoyances that drive you up the wall? We all have them—like losing our keys when we're in a hurry, missing the train home from work, or losing five pounds only to gain back six over the weekend.

The Bible teaches us it is the "little foxes" in life that "spoil the vine." The real joy-robbers aren't the big catastrophes but the trivial, petty annoyances we encounter daily. One or two consecutive foxes have been known to hurl the best of us into an all-out tailspin, ruining an otherwise perfect day.

So how do we harness little foxes? The psalmist said, "When my worry is great within me, Your comfort brings joy to my soul" (Psalm 94:19). God understands our human frailty. Wherever we are, whatever we are doing, He is eager to administer calm, peace, and joy! As we turn to the Lord in prayer and praise, He begins to "catch for us the foxes."

God's antidote to our flaying emotions is simple: prayer plus praise equals peace.

Still fuming?

Dear God, please give comfort to my disquieted soul, and drive away the little foxes of aggravation. When I'm tempted to fret and fume, remind me of Your antidote to keep my emotions in balance. Amen.

Futile Faith?

"For the one right with God lives by faith. If anyone turns back, I will not be pleased with him."

HEBREWS 10:38

We clean the windows and wash the car, and a day later it rains. We sweep the kitchen floor, and hours later the crunch of cookie crumbs resounds under our feet. Some tasks seem so futile.

So it is with our spiritual life. We pray unceasingly and no answers seem to come, or we work tirelessly and problems entrench us. In frustration we wonder, *Why did this happen? What purpose is there to all of this?* It all seems so pointless.

To the skeptic, logic must pervade every situation. If not, there is no basis for belief. But to the person of faith, logic gives way to faith—especially during the most tumultuous, nonsensical times.

So even when our prayers remain unanswered, we continue to pray. Even when God is silent, we continue to believe. And though we grope for answers, we continue to trust.

When our chaotic lives turn upside down and we labor to find rhyme and reason, God asks us to hold fast to our faith. For no labor of love is pointless, no prayer is futile.

Dear Lord, please forgive me for allowing my problems
to undermine my faith. I trust in You, knowing
that my faith in You is never futile. Amen.

Called to Rest

Then He went away by Himself to pray in a desert.
LUKE 5:16

Christians often make the mistake of believing the Lord wants us to be busy about His work constantly. We sign up for everything and feel guilty saying no to anything that is asked of us.

Certainly, we are called to be about God's work. We are His hands and feet in this world, and He can use us in mighty ways. But we are also called to rest and pray. Jesus put a priority on this, frequently leaving the crowd to seek solitude. He encouraged His followers to do the same. One day when they had been busy meeting the needs of people all day, Christ insisted that the disciples come away with Him to rest and to nourish themselves.

There is no denying that our lives are busy. All sorts of demands are placed on us today. You may find yourself in a station in life that pulls at you from every angle. Make time to rest. Find a place that is quiet where you can pray. Jesus modeled this for us. He wants us to find rest in Him.

Father, show me the importance of rest. Allow me
to say no to something today in order that I might
say yes to some quiet time with You. Amen.

A Day of Rest

"You will work six days and rest on the seventh day. So your
bull and your donkey may rest. And the son of your female
servant, and the stranger, may get their strength again."

EXODUS 23:12

If there is one scriptural principle that we routinely abandon, it
is that of the Sabbath. Because Christ has become our rest, and
because we now worship on the Lord's Day, we often disregard
the idea of a Sabbath rest.

Rest was at the heart of the Sabbath. One day out of seven,
God's people were not to work or to make others work, so they
could all be refreshed.

God Himself started the work-rest pattern before the earth
was a week old. God didn't rest because He was tired; He rested
because His work of creation was finished.

But our work is never done! How can we rest?

It's not easy. There are always more things that can be done.
But most of those things can wait a day while you recharge.

God's design for the week gives rest to the weary. Let's not
neglect His provision.

Father, help me to rest from my labor as You
rested from Yours. Refresh me this day. Amen.

Knowing Who You Are in Christ

*Men become right with God by putting their trust
in Jesus Christ. God will accept men if they come
this way. All men are the same to God.*

ROMANS 3:22

Sometimes we measure our value by "what we do" (our work or our talents), but this should never be. Who you are is more than a name. More than a face. More than the job/work you do. You are uniquely created, a true one of a kind. You are God's kid. His. Loved. Cherished. Blessed.

What does the Bible say about you? You are: a new creation. A royal priesthood. A holy nation. The righteousness of God. A holy temple. A member of the body. A citizen of heaven. Saved by faith. Raised up by Him. The aroma of Christ. Filled with heavenly gifts. Delivered from the domain of darkness. Capable of doing all things through Him who strengthens you. On and on the descriptions go.

Wow! When you read all of those things, you begin to see yourself as God sees you. You're not "just" another person. You're a child of the One True King, and He delights in you! Today, take a close look in the mirror. Don't stare at your reflection in the usual way. Get God's perspective. Then begin to see yourself the way He does.

Lord, I needed this reminder that I'm all of the
things You say I am. First and foremost, I'm Yours!
So, no putting myself down, Father! Give me
Your eyes to see myself the way You see me.

A Coffee Filter

*Watch your talk! No bad words should be coming
from your mouth. Say what is good. Your words
should help others grow as Christians.*

EPHESIANS 4:29

A coffee filter serves an important role in the brewing of a fine
cup of coffee. It holds back the bitter grounds while allowing
the soothing, aromatic drops of rich coffee to flow into the pot.
When you remove the filter, it contains nothing but soggy, dirty
coffee grounds that no longer serve any good purpose.

Imagine what would be found if a filter were placed over your
mouth to capture all that is distasteful before it left your lips.
How full would that filter become before the day ended?

Our Father desires that our words be soothing and inspiring,
never bitter or distasteful. In fact, His message of love cannot
flow from a bitter mouth. We can ask the Holy Spirit to be our
filter in order to keep the bitter grounds out of the tasty brew
that God intends to come forth from our mouths. With the
filter of the Holy Spirit in place, He can use us to bring His
message of love to those around us.

Heavenly Father, please forgive my harsh and bitter
words of the past. Help me to use a fresh filter on
my tongue each day so I may bring Your comfort
and joy to those whose lives I touch. Amen.

Persistence

"These twenty-three years. . .the Word of the Lord has come to me.
And I have spoken to you again and again, but you have not listened."
JEREMIAH 25:3

The Bible is full of persistent people, people who persevered despite problems and difficulties, long after the time most people would consider such persistence wise. Noah spent one hundred years building the ark. Abraham waited twenty-five years for Isaac, the son of promise. And by the end of his life, Jeremiah had preached God's message to an unbelieving audience for forty years. Israelites called him a traitor, threw him in prison, and left him to die, but he continued preaching God's message. Nothing slowed him down.

Jeremiah's faith enabled him to persevere. The writer of Hebrews could have had Jeremiah in mind when he wrote, "Others were talked against. Some were beaten. Some were put in chains and in prison. . . . They were too good for this world" (Hebrews 11:36, 38).

God expects the same persistence of us. He calls for persistence, also known as perseverance, over a dozen times in the New Testament. He means for the trials that come our way to increase our perseverance. When we successfully pass small hurdles, He may put bigger ones in our way. Why? Because He doesn't love us? No—because He does.

Persistence results in faith that is pure, molten gold.

Lord, we can only persist because You are
unchanging. We pray that we will keep our
eyes fixed on You and keep moving forward,
regardless of what happens around us. Amen.

DAY 60

Convenient Love

*Jesus said to him, " 'You must love the Lord your God with
all your heart and with all your soul and with all your mind.'
This is the first and greatest of the Laws. The second is like
it, 'You must love your neighbor as you love yourself.' "*

MATTHEW 22:37–39

Christians have been given two assignments: love God and love
each other.

People say love is a decision. Sounds simple enough, right?
The fact is that telling others we love them and showing that
love are two very different realities. Let's face it—some people
are harder to love than others. Even loving and serving God
seem easier on a less stressful day.

Think about convenience stores. They're everywhere. Why?
Because along the journey, people need things. It's nearly
impossible to take a long road trip without stopping. Whether
it's gas to fill our vehicles, a quick snack, or a drink to quench
thirsty lips, everyone needs something. Gas station owners realize this—and we should too.

It may not always be convenient to love God when the to-do
list stretches on forever or when a friend asks us for a favor
that takes more time than we want to give. But God's love is
available 24-7. He never puts us on hold or doles out love in
rationed amounts. He never takes a day off, and His love is
plentiful.

> Lord, I promise to love You and my
> neighbor with my whole heart. Amen.

Owning Your Faith

"The Helper is the Holy Spirit. The Father will send Him
in My place. He will teach you everything and help
you remember everything I have told you."

JOHN 14:26

Is your faith deeper and stronger than when you first accepted Jesus? Or are you stuck back in the early, childlike days of your faith?

We each must make our own personal choice to continue to build our faith. Rather than just taking things at face value, we need to wrestle with issues so that we can own God's truths and share them with others. No longer a simple "Because the Bible says so." It now becomes a matter of "Where does the Bible say it and why?" Instead of expecting others to lead us, we each need to nurture a personal desire for deepening our relationship with God.

While we are responsible for choosing to grow in faith, we don't do it on our own. Jesus promises that the Holy Spirit will teach and guide us if we allow Him to. He will help us remember the spiritual truths we've learned over the years. Fellowship with other Christians also helps us to mature as we share our passions and are encouraged.

God wants you to own your faith. Make it real with words and actions.

Jesus, I want to know You intimately. Help me
to mature in my walk with You daily. Guide my
steps as I seek You through Your Word. Amen.

Run the Race

All these many people who have had faith in God are around us like a cloud. Let us put every thing out of our lives that keeps us from doing what we should. Let us keep running in the race that God has planned for us.

HEBREWS 12:1

Running a marathon isn't for sissies. Months of rigorous training are required in order to run 26.2 miles. Even stellar athletes can succumb to dehydration, muscle cramps, or sheer exhaustion. Runners dress lightly so they are unencumbered. Cheering spectators encourage them throughout the course. Runners are also spurred on by one another. Running a marathon requires training, discipline, and determination. The cost is great, but the reward is well worth it.

A Christian's journey is much like a marathon. The road isn't always easy. Spiritual training is required to endure and finish the race triumphantly. Train by reading and obeying God's Word. Discipline yourself to keep your eyes on Jesus at all times. Be determined to spend time in prayer.

The writer of Hebrews reminds us that others are watching. Perhaps saints in heaven can observe our course. Most definitely other Christians and nonbelievers witness how we live our lives. Let their cheers bring encouragement. Let their presence inspire and motivate. Be quick to confess sin in order to run the race unhindered. Persevere. Jesus waits at the finish line. The reward will be well worth it!

> Dear Lord, help me run this Christian
> race with perseverance. Amen.

My Rights

Do not work only for your own good.
Think of what you can do for others.
1 CORINTHIANS 10:24

Everyone is concerned with their own rights these days: women's rights, animal rights, workers' rights. . .the list goes on. Society tells us to be our own advocates. "If you don't fight for yourself, nobody will" is a common philosophy.

While taking care of yourself is necessary and good, it's easy to get carried away. Through God's power, we need to reprogram our minds to think of others first—before we insist on what is best for ourselves. The Bible tells us not to even be concerned about ourselves. Why? Because God promises to take care of us, and He will never leave us or forsake us.

So what rights do you have as a son or daughter of the King? You have the right to approach God's throne with confidence (Hebrews 4:16) because of what Jesus did for us on the cross. Trust Him to take care of you, and ask Him to help you focus less on yourself and your rights in society and more on those who are hurting, lonely, and poor who may cross your path each day.

> Father, help me to get my mind off myself
> and my own rights. I thank You that I can
> come to You with confidence, knowing that
> You will take care of all my needs. Amen.

Trust and Obey

*Then they would put their trust in God and not forget
the works of God. And they would keep His Law.*

PSALM 78:7

From the time we were children, we knew the song "Trust and obey, for there's no other way to be happy in Jesus than to trust and obey."

It's one thing to talk about trust, another to live it. And here's the problem: if you don't trust God, you probably won't obey His commands. So, these two things go hand in hand. Don't believe it? Here's an example: Imagine the Lord asked you to take a huge step of faith, something completely outside of your comfort zone. You would likely hesitate. But would you eventually take the step, even if it made no sense to you? If you trusted God—if you had seen Him work time and time again in your life—you would eventually take the step of faith, even if it made no sense. Why? Because you trust that He's got your best interest at heart. (And you've probably figured out that He has something pretty remarkable up His sleeve!)

God is trustworthy. He won't let you down. When you settle that issue in your heart once and for all, obedience is a natural response.

Father, I know I can trust You. Sure, there will be
faith journeys ahead. I know that. But Lord, I want
to obey, to step out boldly. When I do, You take
me to new, exciting places I've never been before.
Thank You for leading and guiding, Father!

You Are What You Hold on To

Hate what is sinful. Hold on to whatever is good.

ROMANS 12:9

The invention of superglue was revolutionary because the glue had the ability to bond immediately with a variety of materials. That is wonderful news if your grandmother's porcelain vase breaks in half. But superglue must be used with extreme caution. Accidents can happen in a split second. If the tiniest drop falls in the wrong place, two items will unintentionally and permanently bond.

What are we cemented to? Bonding takes place as we draw close to something. Choose to cling to what is good and avoid evil at all costs. We should not even flirt with sin, because it can quickly get a foothold in our lives. Like superglue in the wrong place, we could unintentionally find ourselves in bondage by embracing temptation. What may seem innocent at the time could destroy us.

Beware of your temptations. Know your areas of vulnerability, and avoid them. If you struggle with unhealthy eating habits, do not buy tempting foods. If gossip is a temptation, avoid the company of friends who enjoy passing on tidbits about others. If overspending is an issue, stay away from the mall. Instead, draw close to the Lord. Allow Him to satisfy your deepest longings. When we cling to good, evil loses its grip.

Dear Lord, help me avoid temptation. May I
draw close to You so I can cling to good
and avoid evil in my life. Amen.

Ask for Joy

Bring joy to Your servant. For I lift up my soul to You, O Lord.
PSALM 86:4

The psalmist buried a nugget in this verse, showing us the source of joy and how to be joyful. All we have to do is ask, then look to God to "rejoice our soul."

So often we get stuck in frustration, depression, ingratitude, or anger. We go about our days feeling defeated, without the hope and joy the scriptures promise us. But have we asked our Lord for joy? Have we lifted our soul to Him?

Psalm 16:11 tells us, "Being with You is to be full of joy." When we draw near to God, confessing our sin and our need of Him, we are met by His mercy, His forgiveness, His perfect love that casts out all fear. In the presence of that love, our joy is found, regardless of our circumstances. He is a father. He desires to love and care for His children.

Just as we want our children to come to us when they hurt, our heavenly Father longs to hear your voice crying out to Him. Sure, He already knows your need, but He also knows there is benefit for each of us in the confession, in crying out to Him. When we hear ourselves verbally lifting our souls to Him, we are reminded of our need of Him. Confession is good for the soul.

Father, help me to lift my soul to You, the source of joy. Only You can make me rejoice. Forgive my pride, which keeps me from confessing my sins. Draw me into Your loving presence where there is fullness of joy.

Reflections of Light

"Rise up and shine, for your light has come.
The shining-greatness of the Lord has risen upon you."

ISAIAH 60:1

God said, "Light, be," and light came into existence. Light appeared from the lips of God so He could see all He was about to create—and His creation could see Him.

When you gave your heart to God, His light came on inside your heart. Christianity lives from the inside out. When your heart is right, then your actions truly portray the influence that God and His Word have in your life.

Your life should then begin to reflect the character and nature of the One who created you and oppose all darkness. You are a reflection of His light to everyone around you. From within, you shine on the lives of others around you and become a light to the world.

As you point others to God, to His light—His goodness, mercy, and love—your light shines, repelling darkness and giving comfort to everyone God brings across your path.

How encouraging to know your life can brighten the whole room. You have the power to open the door of people's hearts for the Holy Spirit to speak to them about their own salvation. Don't miss a moment to let your life shine!

Jesus, show me what I can do and say
to let my light shine brightly. Amen.

What's in Your Heart?

Be happy in the Lord. And He will
give you the desires of your heart.
PSALM 37:4

What is it that you most desire? Is it a successful career or large bank account? Do you wish for someone with whom you can share romantic dinners or scenic bike rides? It really doesn't matter. What does matter is that you are fully committed to God. When that is the case, the desires in your heart will be the ones He places there. He will grant them because they honor Him.

Too many times we look at God's promises as some sort of magic formula. We fail to realize that His promises have more to do with our own relationship with Him. It begins with a heart's desire to live your life in a way that pleases God. Only then will fulfillment of His promises take place.

The promise in Psalm 37:4 isn't intended for personal gain—although that is sometimes a side benefit. It is meant to glorify God. God wants to give you the desires of your heart when they line up with His perfect plan. As you delight in Him, His desires will become your desires, and you will be greatly blessed.

Lord, I know You want to give me
the desires of my heart. Help me live
in a way that makes this possible.

No Fear

"When you pass through the waters, I will be with you. When you pass through the rivers, they will not flow over you. When you walk through the fire, you will not be burned. The fire will not destroy you."

ISAIAH 43:2

Can you imagine standing at the edge of the Mississippi River and having the waters part so you could walk across on a dry riverbed? To call it a miracle would be an understatement.

Scripture tells us over and over again of God's mighty acts. He parted the Red Sea so thousands of Israelites could cross on dry land. Daniel spent the night in the company of hungry lions and emerged without a scratch. Three of his friends were unscathed after hours in a blazing furnace.

These are more than Sunday school stories. They are real miracles performed by *your* God. These miracles were not included in scripture merely for dramatic effect, because God's power wasn't just for the Israelites, Daniel, and Shadrach, Meshach, and Abednego. One of the reasons God recorded His mighty acts was so we would have the assurance His power is available to us as well. When you are facing what seems to be impossible odds, return to scripture. Recount His marvelous deeds. Then remember that this promise in Isaiah is *yours*.

Heavenly Father, when I am facing an impossible task, help me to remember all the miracles You have performed. Thank You for the promise that this same power is available to me whenever I need it.

Learning as We Grow

"But I am only a little child.
I do not know how to start or finish."

1 KINGS 3:7

When babies are born, they cannot do anything for themselves; they cannot walk or talk or feed themselves. As children grow, they slowly begin to learn new skills, like sitting up, crawling, and walking. Later, children will be expected to put their toys away, make their beds, dry the dishes, or walk the dog. But children do not innately know how to perform these duties—they must be learned.

When King David died, Solomon became the king of Israel. Just like a child who does not yet know how to put away his toys, Solomon confesses that he does not know how to carry out his duties as king of Israel. Instead of sitting down on his throne in despair, though, Solomon calls on the name of the Lord for help.

As Christians, we are sometimes like little children. We know what our duties as Christians are, but we do not know how to carry them out. Just like Solomon, we can ask God for help and guidance in the completion of our responsibilities. God hears our prayers and is faithful in teaching us our duties, just as He was faithful to Solomon in teaching him his.

Dear Lord, thank You for being willing to
teach me my Christian responsibilities. Help
me to learn willingly and eagerly. Amen.

Equipped for the Task

May God give you every good thing you need so you can do what
He wants. May He do in us what pleases Him through Jesus Christ.
HEBREWS 13:21

God knew Paul the apostle would face hard times in his life. This distinguished, well-educated Pharisee went through an intensive training period for more than seven years, living obscurely in his hometown. God equipped Paul because He knew the price he would pay for following Christ: lashed five times, beaten three times with rods, stoned once, shipwrecked three times, adrift alone in the sea a night and day, robbed, rejected by his own countrymen, hungry, cold, naked, and resigned to a relentless thorn in his flesh. Through it all, many Gentiles came to know Jesus.

Hopefully, we aren't being equipped for a rigorous life like Paul's. But whatever He's called us to do, He will give what we need to accomplish it. You may not feel you are equipped, but God keeps His word. Scripture plainly states He's given you everything good for carrying out His work. When you are discouraged in ministry and you want to quit, remember He promises to work in you what pleases Him. The Spirit empowers us, making us competent for our tasks.

Lord, help me to draw on Your resources that I
might be fully equipped for accomplishing Your
tasks. Work in and through me to touch the
lives of others as only You can do. Amen.

Commune with Me

When we give thanks for the fruit of the vine at the Lord's supper,
are we not sharing in the blood of Christ? The bread we eat at
the Lord's supper, are we not sharing in the body of Christ?

1 CORINTHIANS 10:16

Oh, what a blessed privilege, to commune with the Lord. To spend time with Him. To break bread together. To remember the work that Jesus did on the cross. Yet how often do we do this without really "remembering" the depth of its meaning?

The night that Jesus was betrayed—the very night before some of His closest followers turned on Him—He sat down for a special meal with them. He took the bread and broke it, then explained that it, symbolically, provided the perfect picture of what was about to happen to His very body on the cross. Then He took the cup of wine and explained that it too had pertinent symbolism, for it represented His blood, which was about to be spilled on Calvary.

The disciples surely couldn't comprehend fully what Jesus was talking about, but less than twenty-four hours later, it was abundantly clear. And now, two thousand years later, it's clearer still. And Jesus still bids us to come and commune with Him. He longs for us to remember—to never forget—the price that He paid on the cross that day.

Commune with me. Such simple words from God to mankind. Run to Him today. Spend time in holy, sweet communion.

Father, I get it! It's not just about breaking bread
together. It's all about spending time with You. Being
with You. Remembering all You did for me. I long
to curl up next to You and hear Your heartbeat
today, Lord. I choose to commune with You.

All You Need

*"Your Maker is your husband. His name is the Lord of All.
And the One Who saves you is the Holy One of
Israel. He is called the God of All the earth."*

ISAIAH 54:5

Are you without? Do you find yourself longing for a certain relationship in your life? Maybe you never knew your earthly father, and there is a void in your heart for a daddy. Perhaps you are single and longing for a mate, or married but your mate seems absent even though they are there with you. Do you wish for a child? Is your relationship with your mother or brother or friend constantly draining you?

God is the great "I Am." He is all things that we need. He is our maker. He is our husband. He is the Lord Almighty, the Holy One, the Redeemer, the God of all the earth—and these are just the names found in one verse of scripture.

God is the Good Shepherd, your Provider, your Protector, your Comforter, your Defender, your Friend.

He is not a god made of stone or metal. He is not unreachable. He is present. He is near, as close as you will let Him be, and He will meet your needs as no earthly relationship can. Seek the fullness of God in your life. Call upon Him as your Prince of Peace and your King of Glory. He is all that you need—at all times—in all ways.

> O Father, be close to me. Fill the empty
> spots in my heart. Be my husband,
> my redeemer, and my best friend. Amen.

A Clear Focus

*Hope that is put off makes the heart sick, but a
desire that comes into being is a tree of life.*

PROVERBS 13:12

We all have dreams and a desire to pursue them. But then life gets busy, and we become distracted with the choices we have to make on a daily basis. Do you go right or left, choose this way or that? Too much too fast is overwhelming, and looking for balance can leave us lost, not knowing which way to turn. The best way to gain your balance is to stop moving and refocus.

Jesus is your hope! He stands a short distance away bidding you to take a walk on water—a step of faith toward Him. Disregarding the distractions can be hard, but the rough waters can become silent as you turn your eyes, your thoughts, and your emotions on Him.

You can tackle the tough things as you maintain your focus on Jesus. Let Him direct you over the rough waters of life, overcoming each obstacle one at a time. Don't look at the big picture in the midst of the storm, but focus on the one thing you can do at the moment to help your immediate situation—one step at a time.

Lord, help me not to concentrate on the
distractions but to keep my focus on which
step to take next in order to reach You. Amen.

Follow the Leader

O Lord, lead me in what is right and good, because of the
ones who hate me. Make Your way straight in front of me.
PSALM 5:8

Modern culture is full of enemies of righteousness. We seek instant gratification instead of practicing patience. Rudeness is seen as strength, while gentleness is devalued as weakness. Indulgence is promoted, but self-control is not. Greed and deceit are excused as part of competition. Image seems more important than honesty. Rationalization has become an accepted form of making excuses for bad behavior.

Yet the psalmist offers us hope for learning to live as a Christian in an environment that does little to help us. He reminds us to ask the Lord to lead us in righteousness. Too often we believe in Him for our eternal salvation but go about trying to live our daily lives as if being righteous is something we have to figure out on our own. Christ is the righteousness of God embodied for us. In Him, we have been accepted by the Father and given the Spirit, who enables us to live in right relationship to God and others. Daily and hourly, we can pray for Christ's leading, asking Him to keep us focused on Him and mindful that we are following Him. He has a path that He desires to walk with each of us, guiding us each step of the way.

Lord, help me remember to ask for Your
leading. Show me the path You have designed
for my life, and give me clear direction.

Growing Up

As you have put your trust in Christ Jesus the Lord to save you from the punishment of sin, now let Him lead you in every step. Have your roots planted deep in Christ. Grow in Him. Get your strength from Him. Let Him make you strong in the faith as you have been taught. Your life should be full of thanks to Him.

COLOSSIANS 2:6–7

When we reach out to the heavenly Father and choose to accept Him into our hearts, our journey has just begun. We want to walk on the pathways He has chosen for us, and to do that, we must learn to follow the map: His Word. The foundation of our faith must be built on Christ's presence in our lives. Building a strong foundation takes time, so don't become fainthearted when you walk forward a few steps only to slide back. Our God understands our struggles.

In Him we are planted so that our roots grow strong. In Him we are built up, by studying and hearing the Word and fellowshipping with other believers. In Him we are established, as the foundation is dug deeper and cemented firmly.

This is not a quick process; it is a journey, and we cannot say one day we will arrive. For these are lifelong lessons, and we are guided by the Holy Spirit. Each time we open His Word and hear His voice, we experience something new. He is an awesome God. Let us give thanks to the great Teacher.

> Dear Jesus, we love You and are so grateful You sacrificed Your life for us. Teach us what we should know to become close followers of You.

The Purpose of My Life

I have much desire for Your saving power, O Lord.
Your Law is my joy. Let me live so I may praise
You, and let Your Law help me.

PSALM 119:174–175

We each have so many plans and goals and dreams for our lives, but our main mission should be to live each day to please God. Our purpose here on earth is to worship the God who created us and calls us His children.

Praise and worship isn't just about singing songs to God every Sunday morning. Praise and worship should be an everyday activity. Praise is about putting God first in our lives. It's about doing our daily tasks in a way that honors Him.

Can you really do laundry or mow the yard to please God? Can you really go to work to please God? Can you really pay the bills and make dinner to please God? The answer is a resounding *yes*! Doing all the mundane tasks of everyday life with gratitude and praise in your heart for all that He has done for you is living a life of praise. As you worship God through your day-to-day life, He makes clear His plans, goals, and dreams for you.

Dear Father, let me live my life to praise You.
Let that be my desire each day. Amen.

No Matter What

In everything give thanks. This is what God
wants you to do because of Christ Jesus.
1 THESSALONIANS 5:18

Sometimes being thankful seems almost impossible. How can I be thankful when I'm working as hard as I can and I'm still unable to pay off all my debt? How can I be thankful when my car dies, my water pump breaks, or my wallet is stolen? How can I be thankful when my parents split up or my friend betrays me or my children refuse to behave?

Living in today's world is difficult, and we often experience hardships that make being thankful extremely difficult. When Paul wrote this verse, however, you can bet that he did not write it lightly. He knew what it was to experience hardships and suffering. But Paul also knew the wonderful power and blessing that comes from having a relationship with Christ.

Jesus enables us to be thankful, and Jesus is the cause of our thankfulness. *No matter what happens,* we know that Jesus has given up His life to save ours. He has sacrificed Himself on the cross so that we may live life to the fullest. And while "to the fullest" means that we will experience pain as well as joy, we must *always* be thankful—regardless of our circumstances—for the love that we experience in Christ Jesus.

Dear Lord, thank You for Your love. Please let me
be thankful, even in the midst of hardships. You
have blessed me beyond measure. Amen.

Abide in the Vine

*"I am the Vine and you are the branches. Get your
life from Me. Then I will live in you and you will give
much fruit. You can do nothing without Me."*

JOHN 15:5

Fruit is the tangible evidence of life. Only live plants can produce fruit. Nourishment travels from the roots to the branches, sustaining the fruit. Jesus refers to Himself as the vine and to us as branches. Unless we are attached to the vine, we are not receiving spiritual nourishment. We become grafted into the vine by faith in Jesus Christ as Lord and Savior. His power then flows through us, producing spiritual fruit.

The fruit we bear is consistent with His character. Just as apple trees bear apples, we bear spiritual fruit that reflects Him. Spiritual fruit consists of God's qualities: love, joy, peace, patience, kindness, goodness, faithfulness, gentleness, and self-control. The fruit of the spirit cannot be grown by our own efforts. We must remain in the vine.

How do we abide in Him? We acknowledge that our spiritual sustenance comes from the Lord. We spend time with Him. We seek His will and wisdom. We are obedient and follow where He leads. When we remain attached to Him, spiritual fruit will be the evidence of His life within us. Abide in the vine and be fruitful!

*Dear Lord, help me abide in You so that I may produce
fruit as a witness to Your life within me. Amen.*

I Surrender

*I will have joy in the Lord. I will be glad in the God Who saves
me. The Lord God is my strength. He has made my feet like
the feet of a deer, and He makes me walk on high places.*

HABAKKUK 3:18–19

Sometimes life seems like an uphill battle, and we certainly
don't feel like celebrating. We find ourselves frustrated by the
demands of the day and worried about the future. It's just
too difficult to stay the course—keep on keeping on. We're
tempted to throw up our hands in frustration and quit. That's
when we must realize we're in the perfect position: hands raised
in surrender.

Learn that God's promises are true. When we relax in His
care and focus on Him, He will be with us in all our difficulties.
He didn't promise a life with no problems. He did promise to
carry us through. In Proverbs 3:5 it reads, "Trust in the Lord
with all your heart, and do not trust in your own understanding."
Are we trusting in the Lord with *all* our hearts? Do we trust
Him with our future and the future of those in our care? Have
we become confident in His Word?

Surrender and *trust*. Two words that lead to life and joy.
Choose to surrender and trust this day. He'll then bring you
safely over the mountains.

> Dear Lord, surrendering and trusting don't
> come naturally. Gently guide me so I might
> learn of You and become confident in Your care.
> Enable me to live life to the fullest. Amen.

God Cares for You

"Think how the flowers grow. They do not work or make cloth. Yet, I tell you, that King Solomon in all his greatness was not dressed as well as one of these flowers. God puts these clothes on the grass of the field. The grass is in the field today and put into the fire tomorrow. How much more would He want to give you clothing? You have so little faith!"

LUKE 12:27–28

Take a look at God's creation. He has created this world with such intricate detail. He designed every tree, the majestic mountains, a glorious sun, and a mysterious moon. Each animal has been given unique markings, parts, and sounds. Consider the long-necked giraffe, the massive elephant, the graceful swan, and the perfectly striped zebra!

If God makes the flowers, each type unique and beautiful, and if He sends the rain and sun to meet their needs, will He not care for you as well?

He made you. What the Father makes, He loves. And that which He loves, He cares for. We were made in His image. Humans are dearer to God than any of His other creations. Rest in Him. Trust Him. Just as He cares for the birds of the air and the flowers of the meadows, God is in the business of taking care of His sons and daughters. Let Him take care of you.

Father, I am amazed by Your creation. Remind me that I am Your treasured child. Take care of me today as only You can do. Amen.

Ups and Downs

We break down every thought and proud thing that puts itself up against the wisdom of God. We take hold of every thought and make it obey Christ.

2 CORINTHIANS 10:5

Living according to our fickle feelings is like riding a roller coaster: one day up, one day down. It's easy to fall into the trap of believing those thoughts more than what God says in His Word. Don't let every emotion that surfaces dictate the direction of the day. Capture loose thoughts with a Christ-centered net.

To begin this process, we should latch on to God's promises and steady our course. We need to line up our feelings with what we know the Bible says. The apostle Paul said, "We walk by faith and not by sight." Sometimes we won't sense God's presence, but because He's promised He'll never leave us, we must believe He's there. Jesus said, "My peace I leave you." Accept that peace. Let it rule in your heart. Concerned about having enough? "My God shall supply all your needs." Proven promises to stand on. Promises we can live by. Search the scriptures for promises. They are there.

God is a God of faithfulness, and He works in ways that faith, not feelings, can discern. Trust Him. We must—even when we don't feel like it.

Dear heavenly Father, I choose to accept Your promises as a child of the King. Thank You for all You've done for me. Amen.

Seek Him

One thing I have asked from the Lord, that I will look for: that I may live in the house of the Lord all the days of my life, to look upon the beauty of the Lord, and to worship in His holy house.

PSALM 27:4

David understood what it takes to dwell with God. He continually gazed at His beauty. At the time he composed this psalm, David was living on the run, not in the lavish palace of a king. He was finding beauty and richness in the starkest of environments, stripped of amenities.

Do we seek God's beauty in our environment, which is not quite so bleak? Isn't His beauty reflected in the smiling toddler in the grocery store line? What about the elderly married couple's hand-holding throughout the service? Don't these reflect our Creator?

When we bite into an apple—crisp, sweet, and naturally packaged for freshness—or observe the grace and agility of a dancer or listen to the intoxicating notes of a flute, don't they reveal more about God? Where did it all originate? Whose power and creativity is behind it all? Life reveals glimpses of His power and awesomeness. These everyday things draw us into His presence where we can praise Him, enjoying His beauty and greatness all the days of our life.

Magnificent Creator, Your greatness and beauty surround me. May my eyes gaze at You, seeking You, that I might dwell in Your presence continually. Amen.

A Better World

Help each other. Speak day after day to each other while it is still today so your heart will not become hard by being fooled by sin.

HEBREWS 3:13

First, the good news: You have been saved by Christ. You can live in His power. You can revel in the joy of this life. And in the end, you will be with Him in heaven.

Now for the bad news: There's still a lot of sin in this world. People hurt each other, countries are at war, and at times, even the godly give the Christian faith a black eye. So how can we live with the right perspective? How can we make this world a better place?

Begin by encouraging at least one person every day. Find something encouraging to say to someone you love. Do something special for an absolute stranger. Stretch out your hand and touch someone else's life. And do these things selflessly, without expecting anything in return.

Need ideas? How about buying a coworker a cup of iced coffee with a shot of hazelnut creamer? Or pray for a loved one before he or she walks out the door to begin the day. Write out a word of encouragement, and place it in someone's mailbox at church. Pay the toll for the car behind you.

Make this a better world by doing something nice for someone else. Start today.

Father God, I want to make this world a better place. Show me whom You want me to bless today. Allow me to be Your conduit of love. And I'll praise You for it! Amen.

What's Your Motive?

Each man's work will become known. There will be a day when it will be tested by fire. The fire will show what kind of work it is.

1 CORINTHIANS 3:13

Churches offer many places for God's children to serve. There are areas in children's ministries—nurseries, classrooms, music programs, or vacation Bible school—that are often strapped for willing workers. Maybe volunteering to clean the building or help with upkeep is more your style. Does your church have a nursing home ministry or food pantry ministry? Are you involved?

Do you genuinely wish to help in some of these areas to bring glory to God? If you get involved, you will be blessed beyond measure. We are all called to be useful for Christ. When we do so willingly and with a servant's heart, the joy that fills us will be indescribable and lasting.

On the other hand, if our service is merely to receive praise and recognition from our peers, we'll receive our reward, but it won't be the blessing of God that it could have been. God knows our hearts. He recognizes our motives and rewards us accordingly.

Lord, I want to serve You with a pure
heart. Let all I do bring glory to You.

Justice and Mercy

"O my God, turn Your ear and hear! Open Your eyes and see our trouble and the city that is called by Your name. We are not asking this of You because we are right or good, but because of Your great loving-pity."

DANIEL 9:18

Being merciful is not as popular as being just. There are plenty of commercials and billboards for law firms saying they'll "get you what you deserve." And the phrase "It's not fair!" is never far from our lips. Sometimes we have a good idea of what we deserve, but most of the time we think we deserve more than we actually do.

As Christians, we must resist the temptation to think and talk about the ways in which our lives are not fair. Instead, we should remember the words of Daniel and humble ourselves before the God of creation. The world tries to tell us that we deserve to be treated well; we deserve money, success, and possessions; we deserve happiness and an easy life. But Daniel knew the world's sense of justice was not God's justice.

We do not deserve help from God. We don't *deserve* anything from God. But our God is merciful and loving, and He delights in us. God helps us, listens to us, and *loves* us because He is merciful. Praise Him for His mercy today!

Dear Lord, thank You for Your mercy. Thank You for Your love. Teach me to humble myself before You and look for Your mercy rather than for the world's justice. Amen.

More Than an Email

*You are as a letter from Christ written by us. You are not written
as other letters are written with ink, or on pieces of stone. You
are written in human hearts by the Spirit of the living God.*

2 CORINTHIANS 3:3

Most of us can't go a day or even a few hours without checking
our email. It's fast, it's free, and it's practical. But don't you just
love it when you go to the mailbox and stuck between a bunch
of bills is a letter from a good friend or loved one? Doesn't that
just make your day? A real letter is special because you know the
other person took the time to think about you and went to the
trouble to purchase a stamp and handwrite a precious note just
for you. That beats an email any day!

We've all heard it said that sometimes we are the only Bible
a person will ever read. We are a letter from Christ. When
you are sharing your faith or even in your everyday relationships, always try to go the extra mile with people. Go beyond
"fast, free, and practical." Be more than an email: be a precious
letter from Christ, and take the time to let them know how
loved and treasured they are by you and by the Lord!

Father, help me to make the people in my life feel
loved and cherished. Help me to remember that I am
a letter from You as I interact with others. Amen.

Choose Happy

A glad heart is good medicine,
but a broken spirit dries up the bones.
PROVERBS 17:22

Feeling gloomy, blue, out of sorts? Do you have an Eeyore personality, always "down in the dumps"? Scripture exhorts us to choose joy, to choose happy. And it's not always an easy task.

When a person is ill, a gloomy spirit can make it difficult for God's healing power to work. William J. Parker, a theologian, stated, "Let the patient experience an inward awareness of [God's] healing force and let him overcome his heaviness of heart and he will find his new outlook to be like medicine." Despite the sickness, we look to our heavenly Father for encouragement and strength, a heavenly tonic. A smile and a glad heart heal us from within and also help those who come into the circle of its influence. At times it might seem impossible to cultivate a cheerful outlook on life, but in our Christian walk, it should become an intentional act as much as learning to control our temper or be kind. This new spirit within grows from a faith that all things can work together for good when we walk in God's light and look to Him for everything.

Dear Lord, today my spirit is heavy, my heart
downtrodden. Help me lift my eyes to You and
choose to believe You are at work in my life. Create
in me a happy, clean heart, O Lord. Amen.

Our Secret Life

"Then your Father Who sees in secret will reward you."
MATTHEW 6:6

We live two lives. Our visible life is lived before others. Our secret life is lived solely before the Lord. Are they consistent? Many times, the motives behind our actions are to impress others. Our real heart is revealed by what we do in secret, when only the Lord is watching.

How do we choose to spend our time and money? Do we pray aloud to look spiritual in the eyes of others? Are we generous to attain a certain reputation? Do we mention tithing and fasting to appear devout? When we look closely at our motives, we must admit that sometimes we are more concerned about gaining the applause of people than of God.

Perhaps your behind-the-scenes sacrifices are going unnoticed by the world. Do not be discouraged. God knows. He hears your prayers and sees what you are doing in secret to serve Him. Eternal treasures are being stored up in heaven. Your selfless acts will be rewarded. Do not give up and think it doesn't matter. It matters to God. Seek to please Him above anyone else. Live before an audience of One so that your life will honor Him.

Lord, help me walk consistently in Your truth. May
what I do in secret bring glory to You. May I not
seek man's approval but Yours alone. Amen.

Be Still

"You will keep the man in perfect peace whose mind is kept on You, because he trusts in You."

ISAIAH 26:3

If you watch the news on a regular basis, you'll find that our world is full of chaos and despair. And while most newscasts only focus on bad news, there's no denying that much of the world is in turmoil. Hurricanes, terrorism, school shootings—it's enough to make hibernation an attractive option.

During the prophet Isaiah's time, the Israelites faced their own reasons for discouragement and fear. They had been taken from their homes, forced into captivity, and persecuted for their faith. And although much of their suffering stemmed from their disobedience to God, He had compassion on them. Longing for His children to know His peace, God sent prophets like Isaiah to stir up faith, repentance, and comfort in the hearts of the "chosen people."

God's message is just as applicable today as it was back then. By keeping our minds fixed on Him, we can have perfect, abiding peace even in the midst of a crazy world. The path to peace is not easy, but it is simple: focus on God. As we meditate on His promises and His faithfulness, He gets bigger while our problems get smaller.

> God, when I focus on the world, my mind and heart feel anxious. Help me to keep my mind on You so that I can have hope and peace.

Comfort in Sadness

*You have seen how many places I have gone. Put my
tears in Your bottle. Are they not in Your book?*

PSALM 56:8

In heaven there will be no more sadness. Tears will be a thing of the past. For now, we live in a fallen world. There are heartaches and disappointments. Some of us are more prone to crying than others, but all of us have cause to weep at times.

Call out to God when you find yourself tossing and turning at night or when tears drench your pillow. He is a God who sees, a God who knows. He is your "Abba" Father, your daddy.

It hurts the Father's heart when you cry, but He sees the big picture. God knows that gut-wrenching trials create perseverance in His beloved child and that perseverance results in strong character.

Do you ever wonder if God has forgotten you and left you to fend for yourself? Rest assured that He has not left you even for one moment. He is your Good Shepherd, and you are His lamb. When you go astray, He spends every day and every night calling after you. If you are a believer, then you know your Good Shepherd's voice.

Shhhh. . .listen. . .He is whispering a message of comfort even now.

Father, remind me that You are a God who sees my pain.
Jesus, I thank You that You gave up Your life for me. Holy
Spirit, comfort me in my times of deep sadness. Amen.

God's Joy

Ezra said to them, "Go, eat and drink what you enjoy, and give some to him who has nothing ready. For this day is holy to our Lord. Do not be sad for the joy of the Lord is your strength."

NEHEMIAH 8:10

The beginning of each month brings a daunting mound of things to accomplish. However, looking back to God's provision during the past month gives His children hope. Nehemiah encouraged the Israelites after they finished rebuilding the walls of Jerusalem to enjoy themselves (in a godly manner). They endured scorn, weariness, and threats from the nations around them as they were rebuilding their homes, but God protected them and blessed their work. When they were tempted to wallow in regret over past wrongs, they were told not to be burdened by guilt but to go forward doing what is pleasing and joyous to God. God's joy is in the faith of His children, and staying close to God is what gives His creation joy and strength no matter what may come in the future. The Israelites were also told to give to those in need as part of their celebration so that everyone could share in the joy. The passage says that when the people understood what they were told—God's message of hope—they rejoiced greatly. This month is another opportunity to repent of wrongdoings and enjoy the Father's ever-present goodness.

Father God, thank You for the redemption hope You give through Jesus. Help us to leave the burdens of the past and the worries of the future in Your hands. In Your joy we find true joy and lasting strength.

He Chose

The Lord did not give you His love and choose you because you were more people than any of the nations. For the number of your people was less than all nations. But it is because the Lord loves you and is keeping the promise He made to your fathers.

DEUTERONOMY 7:7–8

In the book of Deuteronomy, God tells the people of Israel that they are unique. Who else has "heard the voice of God speaking out of the midst of the fire" and lived? What other nation could claim that Jehovah was on their side as they saw all the miracles God did for them? However, God says that this special treatment, this unique relationship with the one true God, is not a result of anything done by the Israelites. They did nothing to deserve this love; it was freely given to them. They were actually a terribly rebellious and ungrateful people. However, God still reached down to them and constantly assured them of His love and presence. Many people today seek to do things to gain acceptance or affection. They judge their worth by their accomplishments, looks, possessions. But God says He loves His people, and it is nothing they do that makes them right with God. It is only God's grace, evidenced most powerfully through the death and resurrection of Jesus, that produces the Maker's love. He chose to love and to save. What's more, He chose to love the least.

Father, humble us when we think we can reach You
by our own strength. When we are discouraged and
weary, let us remember that You love us still.

I Am

And God said to Moses, "I AM WHO I AM." And He said,
"Say to the Israelites, 'I AM has sent me to you.'"
EXODUS 3:14

The words "I am" ring out in the present tense. These words are used some seven hundred times in the Bible to describe God and Jesus. When Moses was on the mount and asked God who He was, a voice thundered, "I Am." In the New Testament, Jesus said of Himself, "I am the bread of life; I am the light of the world; I am the Good Shepherd; I am the way; I am the resurrection." Present tense. Words of hope and life. I Am.

Who is God to you today? Is He in the present tense? Living, loving, presiding over your life? Is the Lord of Lords "I Was" or "I've Never Been" to you? Have you experienced the hope that comes from an everlasting "I Am" Father? One who walks by you daily and will never let go? "I Am with you always."

We are surprised when we struggle in the world yet hesitate to turn to our very Creator. He has the answers, and He will fill you with hope. Reach for Him today. Don't be uncertain. Know Him. For He is, after all, I Am.

Father, we surrender our lives to You this day.
We choose to turn from our sins, reach for
Your hand, and ask for Your guidance. Thank
You for Your loving-kindness. Amen.

Thank You

But as for me, I will always have hope and I will praise You more and more. My mouth will tell about how right and good You are and about Your saving acts all day long. For there are more than I can know.

PSALM 71:14–15

Those in the workplace, be it an office or at home, really appreciate a "thanks—well done" every now and then. Kudos can make the day go smoother. And when others brag on us a tad, it perks up the attitude. Think then how our heavenly Father loves to hear a hearty "thank You" from His kids.

Our lives should be filled with praise to the Living Lord and King of Kings. He is a mighty God who created us and watches over us. We ought to tell others of the deeds He has done in our lives. For the power of our testimony is great. Tell how He is our Savior and our hope. The psalmist exhorts us to hope continually because we know even in the darkest days, He has given us a promise to never leave our sides.

Synonyms for praise include: *admire, extol, honor, glorify, honor,* and *worship.* This day take one or two of these words and use them to thank your heavenly Father. Don't take Him for granted. Give Him the praise He deserves.

Father God, how good You are. You have blessed us
immeasurably, and for that we choose to glorify
Your name. Let us shout it from the mountain:
our God is good, forever and ever. Amen.

Bitterness

She said to them, "Do not call me Naomi. Call me Mara. For the All-powerful has brought much trouble to me. I went out full. But the Lord has made me return empty. Why call me Naomi? The Lord has spoken against me. The All-powerful has allowed me to suffer."

RUTH 1:20–21

God has unseen beauty hidden in the midst of trials. Naomi, whose name means pleasant, poured out her sorrow to the women of Bethlehem, her hometown, in the scripture reference above. She lost her husband, two sons, and her home for a second time. However, God shows throughout history that He heals both physically and spiritually. He gives beauty for ashes and joy for the spirit in distress. For Naomi, the answer was right beside her: her loyal daughter-in-law Ruth. Naomi, this old and tired woman, did not realize what happened would be used by God in His great rescue plan for humanity. In her confusion and despair, she was bitter; but El Shaddai, God Almighty, had everything under control. He used the death of Naomi's sons and her return to Bethlehem to bring Ruth and Boaz together. Otherwise, God would have used another family to be the ancestors of Jesus. God once again brought pleasantness to Naomi by giving her a new home and hope. Although she did not personally see the blessing of kingship that came to Boaz's great-grandson David, Naomi was an important part of God's great plan for the little town of Bethlehem.

El Shaddai, give me perseverance to trust in Your greater plan. Turn bitter and angry hearts to see Your work of redemption and reconciliation.

Strength

Then Hannah prayed and said, "My heart is happy in the Lord. My strength is honored in the Lord. My mouth speaks with strength against those who hate me, because I have joy in Your saving power. There is no one holy like the Lord. For sure, there is no one other than You. There is no rock like our God."

1 SAMUEL 2:1–2

Hannah was filled with sorrow because she could not have children, and her husband's other wife taunted her because of this. Even though Hannah was the favorite wife (her name means favored), she still longed to be a mother. So she brought her suffering heart before God in prayer, and God graciously answered. He gave her a son whom she named Samuel and who became one of the greatest judges and prophets of the Old Testament. God did not stop there. He also gave her five other children after Samuel. Hannah acknowledges that Jehovah God is her strength. In her deepest pain and overwhelming despair, she first turned to God. His answer filled the longing in her heart and drew her to a deeper worship of God. He is the only one who can give strength to overcome the worries of this world. God calls His children to seek deliverance from their burdens only in Him because any other option is futile and fleeting.

Rock of Ages, help Your children to rejoice in You as their strength. Keep us from trusting in ourselves, and remind us that You answer prayers often in unexpected ways.

Written on Him

"Can a woman forget her nursing child? Can she have no pity on the son to whom she gave birth? Even these may forget, but I will not forget you. See, I have marked your names on My hands. Your walls are always before Me."

ISAIAH 49:15–16

God's people, during the life of the prophet Isaiah, were under threat of captivity, and they saw impending doom. They knew their dark and rebellious hearts brought this about, and they feared that Jehovah would forget or forsake them. God responded by likening Himself to a mother—the ultimate symbol of love and devotion. Mothers care for their children to guide and protect them. However, in this fallen world, there are also women who abandon their children. God says that unlike weak and broken earthly parents, He will remain steadfast. He can do no less when He says that He marked His children on the palms of His hands. Carved into His hands! This image comes to life when Jesus took nails through His hands to save sinners and make them children of God. What a powerful promise: He will never leave us nor forsake us.

Holy God, thank You that we can call You Abba, or Daddy. Thank You that Jesus suffered, died, and rose again so that people of all tribes and nations could know You as Father. Thank You that You never forget Your children. Help us to never doubt Your compassion, provision, and love.

Free at Last

*The heart is free where the Spirit of
the Lord is. The Lord is the Spirit.*
2 CORINTHIANS 3:17

Rules exist to keep order in our lives and to establish boundaries. Parents have rules for their children; the police have rules for drivers. All are necessary for humans to get along with each other, to cooperate. And when people operate completely outside of the rules, chaos can ensue. So when we begin life as a Christian, we learn that Jesus did not come to bring chaos—He came to bring each of us a new life.

In scripture, Paul was speaking to the church in Corinth, but he certainly wasn't telling them to throw caution to the wind and live completely outside the box. What he was saying was once the Spirit of the Living God lives inside you, there is freedom, an emancipation from bondage, a release from sin. What a cause for rejoicing! Free indeed.

But we cannot live this way in our own power. When we form this covenant with God and are saved, then with Jesus and the Holy Spirit, we can defeat the enemy who is trying to steal and destroy. Put on this armor to face the world. Be ready for the fight. Look to the Word to provide you with the needed tools to walk through each day.

Father God, thank You for the Holy Spirit
that You have placed inside my heart.
Quicken me to hear Your voice. Amen.

Cleaning Up

*Come close to God and He will come close to you. Wash your
hands, you sinners. Clean up your hearts, you who want to
follow the sinful ways of the world and God at the same time.*

JAMES 4:8

Picture a muddy, unshorn sheep. A shepherd would have a job
before him to clean up that animal because the fleece is quite
deep. He must dig down with the shears layer by layer, tugging
at the wool as he goes. In order to shear the sheep, he has to
have hold of it, a firm grasp on a wiggling, uncooperative animal.
Whatever it takes, the shepherd cleans the sheep.

Now picture us. Uncooperative, squirming, with insides
that need to be cleaned. Our thoughts and actions have not
been pure. Maybe we have lost our temper, taken advantage of
another, or gossiped. Actions that are not what God wants of
us. Actions that are called sin. Sin that blackens the heart. Like
the sheep, we must be gathered in and cleaned.

Our most glorious God has promised He will do that for us
when we ask. If we draw near to God and ask for His forgiveness, He will cleanse our hearts and make us part of His fold.
Hallelujah. What a magnificent and overwhelming plan He
has for us!

> Dear Lord, is gaining a new life truly as simple
> as that? I reach out my hand in surrender and
> ask You to become the King of my life. Thank
> You for all You have done for me. Amen.

Life in the Light

Of what great worth is Your loving-kindness, O God! The children of men come and are safe in the shadow of Your wings. They are filled with the riches of Your house. And You give them a drink from Your river of joy. All life came from You. In Your light we see light.

PSALM 36:7–9

David packs so many beautiful metaphors in the verses above that reveal to readers important aspects of God's character. His love is unfailing, and no price could ever be put on this love.

People find comfort and protection when they turn to God's love and when they seek to do everything according to God's will—this is what it means to be in the shadow of His presence.

It is in the presence of God that people have a veritable feast for the soul, which is evidenced materially or physically. God fills the spiritual thirst of people by giving them of Himself— knowledge of Himself, instilling in them His love, and giving them His characteristics.

Just as Jesus preached in the Sermon on the Mount in Matthew 5 (where he also provided physical bread): God will bless and fill those who hunger for and thirst after the goodness and purity of God. The Creator God is the source of all life, and it is only through Him that humans can understand the meaning and purpose of existence. It is His Light—Christ— that gives us life.

Great Refuge, illuminate our minds and hearts to see the light that is Christ and to be beacons from which this light shines onto others who are in darkness.

Fragrant Prayers

May my prayer be like special perfume before You. May the lifting up of my hands be like the evening gift given on the altar in worship.

PSALM 141:2

Coming before God in honest prayer is often difficult. There are many distractions offered by the world. Prayer is also easily corrupted into something it should not be, which is why Jesus spends so much time emphasizing the need to dispel previous conceptions of prayer. He presents prayer as a very personal and intimate conversation with the Father. The Bible is filled with examples of the importance of heartfelt and sincere prayers. God asks His children to bring Him something beautiful in their prayers; and if His children love Him, they long to give Him sweet-smelling prayers. What makes prayers beautiful? Throughout the Bible, God reveals that prayers should be a mixture of praise, confession of sins, and petitions. The humble heart of the one praying, who lets the Holy Spirit work in them, makes the most beautiful of prayers. It is not the use of clever words that draws God's ear, but words that show a desire to know Him at a deeper level. When His children pray with their whole being, the position of the heart, mind, and body are all affected. The beautiful fragrance of Christ will follow His children wherever they go.

Father, we echo the voice of the psalmist in saying that we want our prayers to be drenched in Your Word and to be like sweet-smelling incense before You. Let us continue both day and night to fellowship with You in prayer.

Seriously?

I ask you from my heart to live and work the way the Lord expected you to live and work. Live and work without pride. Be gentle and kind. Do not be hard on others. Let love keep you from doing that. Work hard to live together as one by the help of the Holy Spirit. Then there will be peace.

EPHESIANS 4:1–3

Do you have a friend, relative, or coworker who you feel is trying to drive you crazy? At times, do you think you need to throw your hands in the air and walk away, or maybe get in that person's face and tell it like it is? While there are times for confrontation and discussion of conflicts, often at the center of the problem is "me." I am my problem. Perhaps we need to look in the mirror and evaluate the situation to see where we can improve.

Scripture encourages us to be humble, gentle, and patient. Then to bear one another in love. Wow! Huge directions. Doesn't the Lord get it? Doesn't He see how. . . Wait. Yes, He does. He understands full well we cannot accomplish these tasks in our own strength. That's why He has given us the Holy Spirit. So we can lean on Him to guide us to peace.

As we walk through the days ahead, let us keep our eyes lifted, which removes the problems from our sight. Maybe not from our lives, but the focus isn't necessarily on the difficulty—be it human or otherwise. Our focus is on Jesus. And with His help, we can conquer all.

> Father God, refresh the Holy Spirit within
> me. Let me feel His presence. Amen.

The Comparison Trap

Everyone should look at himself and see how he does his own work.
Then he can be happy in what he has done. He should not com-
pare himself with his neighbor. Everyone must do his own work.

GALATIANS 6:4–5

In John 21, the apostle John records a conversation Jesus had with Peter shortly after His resurrection. Jesus prepared a breakfast for His disciples after a night of fishing. Then Jesus invited Peter to go for a walk. Just days before, Peter had denied knowing Jesus. Now, three times Jesus asked Peter if the fisherman-turned-disciple loved Him. By asking this question, Jesus not only let Peter know that he was forgiven for his lapse of faith, but also He let Peter know that God still had a purpose and plan for Peter. He also spoke of how Peter would eventually die for His Gospel.

Peter, maybe a little embarrassed by all the attention he was getting, looked over his shoulder and saw John following them. Peter asked the Lord, "What about him? How will he die?" Peter fell into the comparison trap.

Jesus answered, "What does it matter to you what I have planned for another? Live your life according to My plan. That's all you need to be concerned about."

And that's all Jesus still requires of His followers. God has a unique plan and purpose for each one, equipping them as they keep their eyes on Him and follow Him daily.

> Father, show me Your plan for today, and help
> me not to compare my path with others. Amen.

Just the Pits

*"You planned to do a bad thing to me. But God planned
it for good, to make it happen that many people
should be kept alive, as they are today."*

GENESIS 50:20

We can speak of ourselves as "being in the pits," which is symbolic of deep, difficult experiences in life. Many times, we are in the pits because of our mistakes, our wrongdoings. But sometimes there's no explanation. Sometimes it's an emotional pit; we are discouraged or depressed. And while in that pit, we can become comfortable. The pit makes us bitter, or we can let it make us better.

In Genesis, Joseph's brothers threw him into a pit to end his life. Instead, he was rescued, and that life experience transformed him into a godly man. He experienced extremes in life, literally from rags to riches. Yet his character shined through because whether in the pits or the palace, his faithfulness to God never wavered. He defined his success as doing God's will. Then he was able to see the evil turned into good.

It might take some time to get to a mountaintop when we're in the valley, but we can struggle out of the murky depths with God's help. The Holy Spirit within can enable us to turn things around so we are at least on level ground.

Dear Lord, help me. I'm so down I don't know
which way is up. Please, Father, take me by
the hand and pull me from this pit. Amen.

Where Is Your Treasure?

"Gather together riches in heaven where they will not be eaten by bugs or become rusted. Men cannot break in and steal them. For wherever your riches are, your heart will be there also."

MATTHEW 6:20–21

Treasure maps show up regularly in children's stories and pirate movies. What is so intriguing about a treasure map? It leads to treasure! People have gone to great lengths in search of treasure, sometimes only to find in the end that the map was a hoax and no treasure existed.

Imagine a treasure map drawn of your life, with all its twists and turns. Where do you spend your time? How do you use your talents? Would the map lead to heaven, or is your treasure in earthly things?

Each day consists of twenty-four hours, regardless of how we use them. We make choices about the priorities in our lives. The world sends messages about how we should spend our time; however, if we listen to the still, small voice of God, we will learn how to "gather riches in heaven."

Nurturing relationships and sharing Christ with others, as well as reading God's Word and getting to know Him through prayer, are examples of storing up treasures in heaven. Using our gifts for His glory is also important. The dividends of such investments are priceless.

Eternal God, help me to store up treasures in heaven with the choices I make today. Give me opportunities to show Your love. Remind me of the importance of time spent with You. Amen.

What Next?

*Even if the fig tree does not grow figs and there is no fruit on the vines,
even if the olives do not grow and the fields give no food, even if there
are no sheep within the fence and no cattle in the cattle-building, yet
I will have joy in the Lord. I will be glad in the God Who saves me.*

HABAKKUK 3:17–18

Have you ever had a day when everything has gone wrong? The neighbor's dogs bark all night, so you don't get any sleep. You spill coffee on your favorite shirt. The car has a flat tire. You're running late, so you get a ticket for speeding. You end up wondering what next—what else can go wrong?

On days like this, it's hard to find any reason to be joyful. How can we be happy when every time we turn around another disaster strikes? Instead of greeting everyone with a smile, on these down days we tend to be cranky or snarly. We tell anyone willing to listen about our terrible lot in life.

Rejoicing in the Lord is not a matter of circumstances but of will. We can choose to remember the God of our salvation and be content with His love for us. No matter how much goes awry, we have so much more to be thankful for because of the grace of God.

God is sovereign. With His help we can rise above the worry of our circumstances to find peace and contentment. Then, no matter what is happening in our lives, other people will see the joy of God.

*Thank You, God, that You have provided for my
salvation and my joy. Help me to look to You instead
of dwelling on my momentary troubles. Amen.*

Consider This

*When I look up and think about Your heavens, the work of Your
fingers, the moon and the stars, which You have set in their place,
what is man, that You think of him, the son of man that You care for him?*

PSALM 8:3–4

When we reflect on the world around us—the beauty of trees, mountains, streams—it staggers the imagination. Looking up into the heavens, gazing at planets and stars light-years away, we are humbled. Just think: God, in His infinite wisdom, has created all these things with His mighty hands, just as He created us.

Viewing and considering such magnificence puts everything into perspective. Our problems seem miniscule in comparison to the heavens above, the majesty of the mountains, and the grandeur of the trees. Knowing that God has favored us with His grace, mercy, and love and has given us the responsibility to care for those things He has put into our hands fills us with songs of praise.

If life is getting you down, if your problems seem insurmountable, take a walk. Look around, below, and above you. Take a deep breath. Draw close to a tree and touch its bark, examine its leaves. Look down at the spiders, ants, and grass. Feel the wonder of the earth. Thank Him for the heavens—the sun, moon, and stars—above you. This is what God has created for us, for you. Praise His worthy name.

Lord, the beauty of this earth is so awesome. In the glory of
all You have created, thank You for caring so much about
me, for creating the magnificence that surrounds me, and
for giving up Your Son Jesus for all our sakes. Amen.

All by Myself

"Be careful not to say in your heart, 'My power and strong hand have made me rich.' But remember the Lord your God. For it is He Who is giving you power to become rich."

DEUTERONOMY 8:17–18

Little Logan set up a lemonade stand. He stirred the mixture into a pitcher of water and floated ice cubes with lemon slices his mom cut. Logan designed a sign with brightly colored pasteboard and markers: ICE COLD LEMONADE—75 CENTS. Now he was ready for business!

At first, only Mom came. Soon members of a neighboring family each bought a glass. Grandma and Grandpa came! Grandpa said he was awfully thirsty and drank two glasses. Aunt Shelly drank a couple of glasses too.

By lunchtime, Logan had sold ten glasses of lemonade. He yelled, "Mommy, I'm rich! And I did it all by myself!"

Logan did not consider his mother's investment in lemons, lemonade mix, napkins, cups, and pasteboard—or her time. It never crossed his mind that she tipped off his customers on the phone about the stand while he waited for business to magically appear!

We smile at a little boy's self-centeredness, but sometimes we adults act as if financial accomplishments live and die with us. God showers us with health, intelligence, education, and opportunity. Every breath and heartbeat are gifts from Him! Like Logan, we never suspect the roles He plays behind the scenes to encourage and prosper us.

Father, please forgive me when I take credit
for blessings You give because of Your generous
heart. Help me use them for Your glory. Amen.

Thunder Roars

It will be that whoever calls on the name of the Lord
will be saved from the punishment of sin.

JOEL 2:32

Do you ever tremble with fear? Whether it be from dangers
without or emotional distress within, fear can paralyze people.
It is as though a hand grips us by the throat and we are pinned
in place with nowhere to go. Yet the Lord our God has said do
not be afraid, He will save us.

The book of Psalms reveals a man who quivers and hides in
caves to escape his enemies. Time and again David calls out to
the Lord because he has been taught God will calm his fears.
The circumstances do not always change, the thunder may still
roar, but just like David, we can know our lives are secure in the
hand of the Almighty Creator of the Universe. He *will* save us.
It's a promise.

Today make a list of those things that cause you to quake in
your boots. Read the list out loud to the Lord, and ask Him to
provide the necessary bravery to overcome each one. Ask Him
to see you through the deep waters and to hold you tightly over
the mountaintops. For when you call on His Name, He hears
and answers. Listen closely and remember He saves.

Father, I'm scared. Please hold me close and
calm my anxious heart. Tune my ears to hear
Your Word and know what to do. Amen.

Hunger for God's Word

Your words were found and I ate them. And Your words became a joy to me and the happiness of my heart. For I have been called by Your name, O Lord God of All.

JEREMIAH 15:16

Why does God tell people to read His Word? He commands this because it is His primary means of communication with His children. Believers are inexorably bound to Him, and because of this great bond, only the will of the Father gives the greatest comfort. Jeremiah's words may seem extreme, but God wants to give a startling picture of what it means to hunger for His words. While on earth, Jesus knew the Old Testament scriptures by heart; Paul as a Pharisee may have spent years poring over the books of the law (the first five books of the Bible written by Moses). The disciples too, although mostly poor, came to a deep and saving knowledge of God's words as they listened to Jesus. If people are God's children, then they also should find delight in reading His Word. They should wrestle with it, analyze it, let it convict and change them; it should be their sustenance just as food and water. Just like earthly hunger cannot be satisfied by eating once a day, His children also continually desire more spiritual growth until they are finally united with Jesus in heaven.

Great Provider, let Your words be sweet as honey to Your children. Give us diligence to read—to eat—from the scriptures daily, even when we are tired or our spirit rebels. Thank You for the peace You fill us up with when we spend time with You.

DAY 112

A Repentant Heart

"Yet even now," says the Lord, "return to Me with all your heart, crying in sorrow and eating no food. Tear your heart and not your clothes." Return to the Lord your God, for He is full of loving-kindness and loving-pity. He is slow to anger, full of love, and ready to keep His punishment from you.

JOEL 2:12–13

One of the most dangerous things about religion is how easily one can pretend to be faithful. Jesus spoke to the religious leaders of His day, saying that they were beautiful goblets on the outside, but on the inside, they were dirty and broken. God's children need to have truly repentant hearts to avoid becoming spiritually dead on the inside. It does not matter if people put on a facade of holiness and of feeling sorry for their sins. If their hearts are not truly changed, then their lives will remain unchanged and far from God's blessings. Believers are told to break their hearts of sin so that God can fix them and make them work properly. When His children show remorse for the bad they committed, God is gracious to forgive and compassionate to heal and to restore. People can only begin to understand God's colossal love when they understand the depth and darkness of their own sin. Confess the brokenness and then rejoice in God's salvation.

Gracious Abba, reveal to Your children even the most subconscious of wrongs, and let them confess their sins, knowing You are the Father who forgives. Thank You for Your great patience and Your abounding love.

Are You Sure?

*Abraham did not doubt God's promise. His faith in
God was strong, and he gave thanks to God.*

ROMANS 4:20

Doubt and uncertainty can upend us if we let them. When we are unsure of something, our steps falter, our words stutter, and our hearts rattle in our chests. Fear can set in. We must guard against this anxious spirit and trust the word God has spoken. To protect against an onslaught of concern, we must learn to lean on Him and allow the Holy Spirit to flow within us.

Paul wrote about doubting God's promises and said that feeling can only be combated by rejoicing. He who was chained, in prison, shipwrecked, and often in danger speaks of singing praises and being full of joy! But how, in our world, are we able to overcome our moods and rejoice? It is difficult, most certainly, and has to be a conscious choice. Steeping your heart in the Word of God, knowing verses that will comfort you, is a great beginning.

A doubting spirit is not of God, for He is not the author of confusion. Theologian Matthew Henry stated, "God honours faith; and great faith honours God." To truly give Him the glory, we must trust. Of this we are sure.

Lord, help us in our unbelief. Our very human nature
causes us to look to the right and to the left. Help us to
keep our focus on You and to trust implicitly. Amen.

Let the Light Judge

Do not be quick to say who is right or wrong. Wait until the Lord comes. He will bring into the light the things that are hidden in men's hearts. He will show why men have done these things. Every man will receive from God the thanks he should have.

1 CORINTHIANS 4:5

Dr. Helen Roseveare served as a medical doctor and missionary in the Congo from 1953 to 1973. When civil war erupted, she refused to leave the country and endured horrific treatment including rape at the hands of rebel soldiers. It could have been easy for her to doubt God's goodness, but she instead looked to her pain as sharing in the suffering of Jesus. How simple it is to jump to conclusions about certain situations or certain people. However, God says that creation is to wait for His judgment. Since Jesus is the Light of the world, only He can make things clear and judge justly. Christians should not remain passive but should wisely seek justice through the guidance of God's Spirit. Love should replace the spirit of judgment. God's love is the strongest of weapons, and when this dwells in and flows from His children, then they can endure times of uncertainty and darkness without falling into the trap of judging God or others. When they endure, they will in the end also reign with Jesus, just as Paul tells Timothy (2 Timothy 2:11–13), and they will receive praise from God.

Light of all creation, give us patience to wait for You to
expose the darkness and to bring Your perfect justice.
Keep us from pride and from wrongly judging others.

Simple Disciplines

Do you not know that your body is a house of God where the Holy Spirit lives? God gave you His Holy Spirit. Now you belong to God. You do not belong to yourselves. God bought you with a great price. So honor God with your body. You belong to Him.

1 CORINTHIANS 6:19–20

In the first century, life was quite different than it is today. The required tasks of the day were so physically demanding that it was unnecessary to set aside periods for concentrated exercise. Meals consisted of homegrown and gathered fruits, vegetables, and meat.

Today we are not nearly as naturally healthy. We avoid physical exertion by using cars, escalators, elevators, moving sidewalks, riding lawn mowers—the list goes on. We have turned a once-healthy diet into an overprocessed, sugar-laden diet, high in sodium, fat, and other unthinkable chemicals.

God, in His infinite wisdom, created us with certain bodily needs to teach us discipline. We need to institute simple, physical disciplines like exercise, diet, and rest to properly care for the temple of the Holy Spirit—our bodies. While those actions will attend to the needs of the body, spiritual disciplines such as prayer, fasting, and fellowship will attend to the spirit.

Father, forgive me for not caring for Your temple
as I should. Help me to make time in my life
for those simple disciplines that You require
for a healthy body and spirit. Amen.

The Great Wealth of the Poor

Listen, my dear Christian brothers, God has chosen those who are poor in the things of this world to be rich in faith. The holy nation of heaven is theirs. That is what God promised to those who love Him.

JAMES 2:5

The great phenomenon of this era is the explosion of Christianity in the developing world. There are many more poor Christians than there are rich Christians. Jesus said that it is easier for a camel to pass through a needle's eye than for a rich man to go to heaven. Trusting God is a lot more difficult for a woman or a man when they are surrounded by comfort and material wealth. Amazingly, when one is in a dry place—physically, emotionally—that person is more likely to have a sincere and total dependence on God. The marginalized followers of Jesus often see their various forms of poverty as a blessing. They are following in the steps of their Rescuer, who also lived in poverty. Jesus had little in the world's eyes, but He had the Father. In His Sermon on the Mount, Jesus blessed the poor in spirit by saying that they will have the kingdom of heaven. God not only gives endurance and rich faith to His children who are poor here on earth, but they have assurance of a final reward—being in the presence and fellowship of the One they love—their Maker, Father, and Friend—for eternity.

Father, thank You for Your love and provision
for Your needy children. Help us to always
remember our greatest wealth is Christ.

Trust the Good News

All this helps us know that what the early preachers said was true.
You will do well to listen to what they have said. Their words are as
lights that shine in a dark place. Listen until you understand what they
have said. Then it will be like the morning light which takes away the
darkness. And the Morning Star (Christ) will rise to shine in your hearts.

2 PETER 1:19

The beauty of the Old Testament is that it foreshadows the coming of Jesus through the histories that depict humanity's great need for God as rescuer. The apostle Peter knew that God's message was true. Like any good Jewish boy, he had learned the Torah, the first five books of the Bible, and then he actually saw Jesus as the One who made all those images and promises come true. However, there was a time when Peter doubted the role of Jesus as Savior. His denial was the darkest moment of his life. Peter's letters were most likely written to other Jews of his time who also were well acquainted with the Old Testament prophecies about the Messiah. Peter tells the readers to believe the good news of Jesus Christ. It is completely reliable. In the darkest moment of Peter's despair, Jesus—as the incarnate Word of God, Divinity in the flesh—broke the chains of sin holding humans captive since the fall of Adam and Eve. In Jesus' death and resurrection, the awesomeness of God's mysterious rescue plan was revealed. Light came into the hearts of humankind and gave them Life.

Indelible Light, guide us to trust and live
out Your message so that Jesus can fight
the darkness within and give us life anew.

Finding God Real

The fool has said in his heart, "There is no God." They are sinful and have done bad things. There is no one who does good. God has looked down from heaven at the children of men to see if there is anyone who understands and looks for God.

PSALM 53:1–2

"I used to be an atheist. Now, I'm not." The congregation clapped and cheered this young man's story at a baptismal service celebrating several new believers in Christ. One lady shared how lost and empty she had become and how her friends' faith walks drew her to church and then to Christ Himself. Story after story brought hope to life.

One woman and her husband shared how hopeless they had each come to feel. Their marriage was falling apart. Some costly decisions caused him to lose his job. For some time, she had been considering divorce, just like those in her family had chosen. She thought she had made up her mind to leave him. That was, until some neighbor friends from church came alongside them.

They sought God. He answered. It was a process, of course, this journey of faith, but trusting God with their struggles was life changing. He has been a very real presence in helping them work through things.

> Lord, thank You for being not only alive
> and well, but active in my life. Show me
> what You have for me today. Amen.

Quick and Slow

*My Christian brothers, you know everyone should listen
much and speak little. He should be slow to become angry.
A man's anger does not allow him to be right with God.*

JAMES 1:19–20

Kindergartners learning traffic signals know that yellow means
"slow down." James 1:19–20 also is a yellow light!

Have you wished, after a conversation with a friend, that you
had not given that unsolicited advice? Your friend needed a listening ear, but you attempted to fix her problem instead.

Have you raced through a hectic day, only to end it by taking
out your frustrations on family members or friends? Or perhaps you have borne the brunt of someone else's anger and
reacted in the same manner, thus escalating the situation. Later,
when tempers calmed, you found yourself regretting the angry
outburst.

Too often words escape before we know what we are saying.
Like toothpaste that cannot be put back in the tube, once words
are spoken, it is impossible to take them back. Words, whether
positive or negative, have a lasting impact.

Practice being quick and slow today—quick to listen, slow to
speak, slow to become angry.

God, grant me the patience, wisdom, and grace
I need to be a good listener. Remind me also,
Father, to use my words today to lift others up
rather than to tear them down. Amen.

God Is Sovereign

I will come in the strength of the Lord God. I will tell about how right and good You are, and You alone.

PSALM 71:16

God is sovereign. Think about those words for a minute. This means He has the ultimate authority. Supreme power. The highest rank. There is no one else we can run to whose opinion is higher—or holier—than the Lord's. He alone has the answers to what we face, and His sovereignty assures us that we can trust Him, even when everything around us is whirling out of control. Sure, it's not always easy, but it's always the right choice.

Have you acknowledged God's sovereignty in your life? If so, it might be time to take your hands off the situations you're dealing with and trust that He—out of His great love for you—will offer the best solution. No trying to fix things on your end! Relax. Your sovereign Lord has everything under control in His time and His way.

Dear Lord, I have to admit, I don't always trust Your sovereignty. I trust my own instincts first. Help me to let go and trust You in every situation with Your timing and Your answers. Today I choose to let go, releasing my troubles into Your capable hands.

Mondays

*Our hope comes from God. May He fill you with joy and
peace because of your trust in Him. May your hope
grow stronger by the power of the Holy Spirit.*

ROMANS 15:13

Ah, Monday! How we love it! (Not!) Most of us dread Mondays
because they represent "getting back to work." We live for the
weekends, but the Lord doesn't want us to dread our work week.
We need to be excited, hopeful, as each new week approaches.
After all, each new day provides an opportunity to love others
and share the Gospel message.

Think about that for a moment. You are an ambassador of
Christ, spreading His love to those you come in contact with.
Whether you're headed to the classroom, the workplace, or
you're homeschooling your kiddos, Monday can be a fun day,
a fresh new start, a chance to pray for God-encounters. When
you spend time praying for those fun, divine appointments,
God always comes through, surprising you with people in your
path. . .usually people who need to see the smile on your face or
the song in your heart.

So, don't despise Mondays! They are a special gift from your
heavenly Father, who happens to believe that every day of the
week is pretty awesome because He created them all!

Father, I don't always look forward to Mondays.
Sometimes I dread them. Remind me that each
new week is a fresh chance to share Your love.

Spring

*There is a special time for everything. There is a
time for everything that happens under heaven.*

ECCLESIASTES 3:1

Don't you love the four seasons? They represent change, and change can be a good thing. Springtime is delightful because it's filled with images of new life. Rebirth. Joy. All you have to do is look around you and your heart can come alive. Flowers budding. Trees blossoming. Dry, brown grass morphing to green. This season is a true do-over, isn't it?!

The Bible teaches us that God ordained the seasons. He set them in place and wants us to enjoy them. In the same way, we go through different "seasons" in our spiritual lives too. Think about it. Our hearts can get frozen over (winter). Then God breathes new life into us and a thawing begins (springtime). From there, we move into full blossom, a season of productivity (summer). Then, as with all things, we slow down, preparing for change (autumn).

Yes, God surely ordained the seasons, but springtime is one with a remarkable sense of expectation, so enjoy it!

Father, I love springtime! Everything feels so new,
so fresh. I'm ready to put yesterday behind me. The
heaviness of the "winter" seasons in my life evaporates
on a warm breeze. I appreciate the lessons learned over
the past several months, but I'm so happy it's spring!

Second Chances

If we tell Him our sins, He is faithful and we
can depend on Him to forgive us of our sins.
He will make our lives clean from all sin.

1 JOHN 1:9

Ever had a really bad day, one where you wished you could crawl back in bed, pull the covers over your head, and start over? Sure, we've all had days—or weeks—like that. Maybe we've said something or done something we regret. Perhaps we've been wounded by the words or actions of someone we thought we could trust and returned injury for injury. We've slipped up. . . in a big way. Oops!

If you're in an "Oops!" season, don't give up. God can redeem any situation you're going through by offering a second chance. There's no mistake you've made that's too big, too bad for Him to handle. Just confess your mess-up to Him, and watch what happens next. Today's scripture assures us that He is faithful (won't leave you) and just (sure) to forgive us our sins. He offers a do-over. Not only that, He cleanses us from the inside out of all our wickedness. Whew! Talk about a fresh start!

So, what's stopping you? Your do-over awaits!

Lord, I'm so grateful for second chances. I've messed
up so many times and in so many ways. Sometimes
I want to hide in the corner. But You're a God
of do-overs. Thank You for redeeming even the
worst situation and offering me new chances.

Others Focused

*"Do for other people what you
would like to have them do for you."*
LUKE 6:31

We live in a "me, myself, and I" time, don't we? Turn on the
television and you see commercials focused on improving self
with makeup, perfume, or health products. Check out the latest,
greatest books and you'll find a zillion self-help titles, guaran-
teed to bring you great success and happiness. Not that focus-
ing on self brings happiness. Not at all. Glance in the mirror
and you'll see a dozen reasons to complain about how you look
or to wish you could trade lives with someone else. Such are the
woes of hyper-focusing on yourself, after all!

It's time to turn our gaze off "self" and on to those around
us. When we're "others" focused, there's very little to complain
about. Our own needs and wants take a backseat. Oh, it's hard
at first. Turning your eyes from self to others is never easy. But
the rewards? They're out of this world!

Dear Lord, I'm so glad that You are turning my focus.
I don't want to be self-absorbed. When my gaze is
turned to those around me, I see Your heart for
mankind, not my wants and wishes for myself. Thank
You for offering me this God-focused perspective.

Perfect Peace

*"You will keep the man in perfect peace whose mind
is kept on You, because he trusts in You."*
ISAIAH 26:3

Peace is an elusive thing. We allow our emotions to control us
and then wonder why peace rarely follows. Strangely, peace has
nothing to do with emotions. Ponder that for a moment. Your
peace—or lack thereof—isn't controlled by an emotional pup-
peteer. You can choose peace in the middle of the storms of life.

What's robbing you of your peace today? Take that "thing"
(situation, person, etc.) and write it down on a piece of paper,
then pray over it and shred it. Release it to God. Keep your
mind steadfast on God, not what was written on the paper. It's
no longer the driving force in your life. Your trust is in God, and
He cares even more about your situation (or that person) than
you do, anyway.

Letting go. . .taking your hand off. . .will bring peace. It's
never easy to release something that's had a hold on you, but
you will be blessed with supernatural peace once you do.

O Lord! I've been holding on to things I should
have let go of ages ago. Please forgive me, Father!
Today I release those things into Your hands. As I
let go, flood me with Your peace from on high!

Sabbath Rest

The same promise of going into God's rest is still for us. But we should be afraid that some of us may not be able to go in.

HEBREWS 4:1

We move at such a rapid pace. Life tugs and pulls at us, and we respond, sprinting toward goal after goal. What overachievers we are!

The Lord never intended for us to go around the clock. He didn't design our bodies to run in "energizer bunny" mode 24-7. We can live like this for a little while, sure, but eventually something's gotta give, and it's usually our health. Or our emotions. Or our relationships. Or—worst of all—our times of intimacy with God.

We are created in the image of God, and He is always on the move! Still, He instigated the Sabbath for a reason, because He knows mankind's tendency to go, go, go. Sure, we have work to do. Yes, we have people to care for and souls to reach. But if we're broken down from lack of sleep or from over-extending ourselves, there won't be anything to offer others. So, slow down! Take a breather. For that matter, take a nap. And don't apologize for it! Moments of respite are precious.

Lord, thank You for the reminder that You want me to rest. It's not always easy. I'm such a go-getter, but I have to confess that taking a break feels really, really good. Draw me away to Your side for a special time of rest, I pray.

Corporate Worship

Praise the Lord! Sing a new song to the Lord!
Praise Him in the meeting of His people.
PSALM 149:1

Worship is so powerful in a private, intimate setting, but there's something equally as powerful in corporate worship. There, side by side with other Christians, we lift our hearts, our voices, our words of praise in a mighty, thunderous chorus. What bliss! And what a wonderful way to prepare for heaven, where we will gather around the throne of God and sing, "Holy, holy, holy!" together with all His people.

When we come into the house of God, like-minded and ready to focus on Him, we are a force to be reckoned with! The gates of hell cannot prevail against us. Two or more (in this case, often hundreds) are gathered together in unity. And unity is the key. Like-minded. Together.

When we enter into corporate worship, we aren't focused on self. The problems of the day wash away. We aren't focused on others, though they are surrounding us on every side. We are solely focused on God, the One we adore. Our eyes, our hearts, our thoughts are on Him alone.

Father, I love worshiping with fellow believers. What a blast to stand alongside my brothers and sisters in Christ to lift my voice in song and to hear Your Word preached. Whether we're singing, praying, or hearing a life-changing message, we do it all for You.

Joy for the Journey

The Lord is my strength and my safe cover. My heart trusts in Him, and I am helped. So my heart is full of joy. I will thank Him with my song.
PSALM 28:7

There are times when joy seems impossible. When you're going through a rough season, for instance, or when you're face-to-face with a proverbial Goliath. The enemy of your soul would like nothing more than to rob you of your joy. He's skilled at tripping you up, creating havoc.

But, guess what? It's possible to praise—to be joyful—even in the middle of the battle. There's a great story in the Old Testament about a man named Jehoshaphat who was facing a mighty opposition—an army, no less! He sent the Levites (the praise and worshipers) to the front lines. In other words, he led the way into the battle with praise on the lips of his warriors. And they prevailed!

The same is true in our lives. We must lead the way with praise. If we will maintain the joy in our hearts, even in the midst of our battles, we will be triumphant in the end. So, don't let the enemy steal your joy, even if you're walking through a difficult season. There are plenty of victories ahead if you don't give up.

Lord, I must confess, I don't always feel like singing a song of praise when I'm facing a huge battle. In fact, I usually just want to curl up in a ball and give up. Thank You for this reminder that I can be joyful even when I'm in the middle of a struggle.

A Healthy Body

Dear friend, I pray that you are doing well in every way.
I pray that your body is strong and well even as your soul is.
3 JOHN 2

If you've ever faced a health crisis or watched a loved one go through a catastrophic illness, you realize the value of good health. There's nothing like almost losing it to realize what you've had all along! In spite of modern technology, great doctors, and the advance of research, health issues persist.

We face seasons where our bodies refuse to cooperate with us. During those times, we have to remember who our healer really is. Doctors are great, but ultimately God is our healer. He longs for us to turn to Him—to trust Him—during our seasons of physical and emotional weakness. He also longs for us to take care of the bodies He's given us. How can we do this? By watching what we put in it and by getting the proper amount of rest and exercise. Our vessels are precious gifts, and we can't afford to wreck them with excessive food or poor nutrition.

If you're in a rough place health-wise, pour out your heart to the Lord. Ask Him to show you the foods that you should be eating and the ones you should avoid. Visit your doctor and get their input as well. Working as a team, focus on turning your health issues around.

Father, I don't want to abuse this precious vessel
You've entrusted to me. I need to take better care of
my body. Show me Your plan for my health, Lord,
then guide me as I take steps toward better health.

Heart and Soul

"But from there you will look for the Lord your God. And you will
find Him if you look for Him with all your heart and soul."
DEUTERONOMY 4:29

Have you ever put something aside as a gift to give someone and then when the occasion came, you were unable to find it? You searched through every drawer, rifled through all your closets, checked and rechecked your cabinets, and finally, just as you were ready to give up, you found the gift.

Luckily for us, God has provided us with exact directions on how to seek and find Him. He offers us His Word as His manual for daily Christian living—if we are devoted to study and meditation. God promises that we will find Him if we look for Him with all our heart and soul.

If you had stopped looking after a cursory search for the gift, you would have never found it. It took serious searching to find that gift again, and it took determination and a willingness to not give up. In the same way, reading our Bibles once in a while and saying an offhanded prayer when we think about it is not a satisfactory way to seek God. Only with serious commitment— commitment with all our heart and soul—will we truly find and know God.

Dear Lord, thank You for Your promises.
Please teach me to seek You with
all my heart and soul. Amen.

The True Love

"You must love each other as I have loved you."

JOHN 13:34

In a society that has distorted the concept of love, it's reassuring to know that God loves us with a deep, limitless love. He is, in fact, love itself. He gave His Son to die for people who didn't love Him in return. God the Father even had to turn His face from His Son when He died, as He took the sin of mankind upon Himself. What incredible love that is!

We Christians tell Jesus we love Him, and His response is "I love you more." We cannot comprehend that kind of love, yet we are the recipients of it. And He loves us not because of anything we've done but because of His goodness. 1 John 4:19 says, "We love Him because He loved us first."

Jesus also commands us to love others in the same way that He loves us. We all have unlovable people in our lives. But Jesus doesn't see anyone as unlovable. Look at that difficult-to-love person through new eyes today, and love them as God has loved you.

Heavenly Father, thank You for Your love for me. Forgive me for not loving others in that same way. Give me the ability to love others as You have instructed. Amen.

Bad Company

*Do not let anyone fool you. Bad people can make
those who want to live good become bad.*
1 CORINTHIANS 15:33

The young nurse began her career with stars in her eyes. However, her naive bubble quickly burst during her first lunch break. Other nurses gossiped viciously about coworkers and then pretended to be best friends when reunited on the floor. She vowed to avoid the gossip she had just witnessed. But as the weeks passed, she began chiming in during similar conversations. What was happening to her?

We are like sponges, absorbing the contents of our environment. We become like the people we spend time with. Others influence us—for better or for worse. For that reason, we must choose our friends wisely. Decide what kind of person you would like to become. Spend time with people who exhibit those qualities. Good character produces good character. The opposite is also true.

Bad character is contagious. It is subtle. It doesn't happen overnight. Choose to surround yourself with positive role models that foster good character.

Dear Lord, help me choose my friends wisely so
that I will be positively influenced. Amen.

Made to Laugh

Then we laughed with our mouths,
and we sang with our tongues.
PSALM 126:2

Comedians live their lives to make people laugh. From famous actors on the movie screen to the class clown at a local high school, we take a moment to celebrate with them. Sometimes the many worries in life keep us from letting our guard down, relaxing, and enjoying the little things in life that bring us great joy and laughter.

It feels good to laugh—from a small giggle that you keep to yourself to a great big belly laugh. It is a wonderful stress reliever or tension breaker. How many times have you been in an awkward situation or in a stressful position and laughter erupted? It breaks the tension and sets our hearts and minds at ease.

As children of the Creator Himself, we were made to laugh— to experience great joy. Our design didn't include for us to carry the stress, worry, and heaviness every day. When was the last time you really had a good laugh? Have you laughed so hard that tears rolled down your cheeks? Go ahead! Have a good time! Ask God to give you a really good laugh today.

Lord, help me rediscover laughter. Help me to take every opportunity You bring to see the joy in life and the comedy that it brings to my world every day. Amen.

Joyful Perseverance

Make a clean heart in me, O God. Give me a new spirit that will
not be moved. Do not throw me away from where You are. And
do not take Your Holy Spirit from me. Let the joy of Your saving
power return to me. And give me a willing spirit to obey you.

PSALM 51:10–12

Perseverance. Some days that word sounds so difficult. Maybe you dread Mondays, knowing that a full week of work and errands and demands await you. Maybe mornings in general are tough, each day holding burdens of its own.

Do not grow weary. Strive each day to keep a pure heart. Don't complain or dwell on small annoyances. Recognize your own worth in God's eyes, and recognize the worth of others as well. Be joyful even when you are not particularly happy.

This world will do all it can to pull you down, to tell you to give up. When you're tempted to grow discouraged, remember that you stand in the presence of God and that He has given you the gift of His Spirit for times such as these.

Ask God for the power to press forward when your own spirit grows tired. Turn to other Christian believers for encouragement. Know that you are not alone—that you will never be alone. God craves your devotion. Turn to Him, and persevere.

Lord, forgive me for being shortsighted and feeling
overwhelmed by the worries of this world. Remind
me of Your grace and salvation. Remind me of Your
love for me, so that I might better love others.

A Peaceful Home

*Then my people will live in a place of peace, in
safe homes, and in quiet resting places.*
ISAIAH 32:18

Home is where you should feel safe and most free to be yourself—a place of refuge from the outside world. Your home should reflect a strength and quiet confidence welcoming to your family, friends, and God.

The atmosphere of your home starts with you. It takes a conscious effort and true discipline to leave the world's cares at the threshold of the front door and stay committed to the pursuit of a peaceful home.

Perhaps you've been running all day and you need to slow down. Take a few minutes before you enter your home, and find your focus. Let go of the day. Shake off the frustration of work, school, relational, and financial concerns. Make a decision to be proactive and peaceful instead of reactive and defensive.

Then step across the threshold into a place of peace. Put a smile on your face, and make a deliberate effort to relax. Speak to your family in a soft, positive, encouraging voice. You set the tone of your home, and you control the pace within it. Make it a place of peace today.

Lord, thank You for reminding me to cast off
the cares of the day. Help me to bring peace,
harmony, and unity into my home. Amen.

Get a Life

Life began by Him. His Life was the Light for men.
JOHN 1:4

Do you have a life?

You've probably been asked that more than once. Having a life usually means you have a busy social calendar, lots of places to go, things to do, and friends to hang out with. The world tells us that those are the things that bring happiness and fulfillment. The Bible defines having a life a bit differently.

In John 14:6, Jesus tells us that He is the way, the truth, and the life. He is our only way to our Father in heaven. Jesus is the light of the world and the only One who can fill us with life. Real life. Deep fulfillment. A life that makes a difference and lasts for eternity.

So, do you have the light of Christ living inside you or do you need to get a life? A place to go, things to do, and people to see don't mean a whole lot at the end of your life here on earth. You will never look back and wish you could have attended one more social event.

Jesus is the only way to eternal life. Make sure you've got a life before you leave!

> Dear Jesus, I want You to light up my
> soul and give me eternal life. Help me
> to live my life for You. Amen.

Are You a Mary or a Martha?

Martha had a sister named Mary. Mary sat at the feet of Jesus and listened to all He said. Martha was working hard getting the supper ready. She came to Jesus and said, "Do You see that my sister is not helping me? Tell her to help me."

LUKE 10:39–40

Are you a Mary or a Martha? Are you sitting at Christ's feet or busying yourself with His work? Aren't both necessary? How do we live and strike a balance between the two?

As you read the rest of this Bible story, you find that Jesus does not tell Mary to help Martha. Instead, He points out that Martha is worried and upset about many things. He is pleased with Mary's choice to sit and listen to Him.

Certainly it is necessary to work. Work must be completed, meals must be made, the house must be kept clean. But beware of becoming so much like Martha that you forget to sit still and listen to your Savior as Mary did. Set aside time in each day to read the Word and pray. You will find Him in a new way as you quiet yourself before Him.

> Father, often I seek to please You through my acts
> of service. I work hard. Calm my spirit and show
> me the value of resting in Your presence. Speak to
> me as I still myself before You now. Amen.

A Time for Sadness and a Time for Joy

There is a time to cry, and a time to laugh;
a time to have sorrow, and a time to dance.

ECCLESIASTES 3:4

Solomon has been declared the wisest man who ever lived. The third chapter of Ecclesiastes, which Solomon authored, tells us that there is a time for everything. Do you find yourself in a time of weeping or a joyful time today? You may be mourning a deep loss in your life. You may ache to your very core with disappointment and sorrow. There is a time to be sad. You don't have to put on a show or an artificial happy face. It is okay to grieve. It is appropriate even. There are times in our lives when we must rely on God's grace just to see us through another day. We may need to lean on other believers and let them carry us for a time. But the good news is that there are also joyful occasions. Psalm 30:5 says that weeping may last for a night but that joy comes in the morning. If you are in a sorrowful period, know that joy is just around the corner. You may not be able to imagine it today, but you will smile and even laugh again. If you are joyful today, know that even when you face sad days, the Lord will be there walking with you. He never leaves us alone.

Thank You, God, for the knowledge that sadness does not last forever. There are highs and lows in life, and as Your Word declares, there is a time for everything. Amen.

Creative Image-Bearer

*And God made man in His own likeness. In the likeness of
God He made him. He made both male and female.*

GENESIS 1:27

As children, we learned we are different from animals because we reason, but much more than that sets humans apart. We are made in God's image. We can reason because God reasons. But what else do we do that bears His likeness?

Is bearing God's image limited to demonstrating character qualities like love, forgiveness, hope, or honesty? Is it doing good deeds and acts of kindness? Does it mean every conversation should be peppered with spiritual language? Or is there a larger sense in which we bear God's image?

In the context of Genesis 1, when we imagine, create, and bring order to our world, we are bearing God's image. To bake a beautiful cake or design a quilt is to reflect God's creativity. To put a budget together in a systematic fashion, write a report, or bring organization to a pile of dirty laundry is to show God's ability to make order and beauty out of chaos.

As we work on projects and do our jobs, we reveal the Creator God to a world that doesn't recognize Him. When we get stuck, when no idea will come to mind, we can ask the One whose imprint we bear. The Creator who made us and loves us puts every good, true, and lovely thought in our minds.

Father, may we bear Your likeness better today
than yesterday. Cause us to remember that
You are the source of creativity, imagination,
and organization. Help us do Your will.

For Such a Time as This

"For if you keep quiet at this time, help will come to the Jews from another place. But you and your father's house will be destroyed. Who knows if you have not become queen for such a time as this?"

ESTHER 4:14

Esther was between the proverbial rock and a hard place. If she approached the king without being invited, she risked losing her life. If she kept silent, she and her family would die. Her wise cousin Mordecai helped put the situation into perspective. He explained that God's plans and purposes would prevail— whether Esther cooperated or not. Esther merely had to choose whether she wanted to experience the joy of participating in God's plan of deliverance for the Jewish people.

Can you imagine the honor of being chosen to help God in this way? God has placed each of us on this earth for a purpose. When we cooperate with Him, we get to experience the blessing of being a part of His plans. If we choose not to participate, there will be consequences. Don't be mistaken—God's purposes will still unfold. But we won't get to be a part of it. Like Esther, the choice is ours. Will we cooperate with God or keep silent and miss out on our place in history?

Heavenly Father, thank You for placing me on earth at this time in history. Thank You for the opportunity to be a part of Your plan. Help me to choose to cooperate with You.

The Perfect Reflection

"Think about your ways!"
HAGGAI 1:7

You probably know how it feels to have a bad hair day or a huge zit on your face. On days like these, we try to avoid the mirror. The last thing we want is to keep running into a reflection of ourselves when we look less than our best.

Our Christian lives often have a similar feel. Instead of facing our imperfections as followers of Christ, we work hard to avoid any mention of or allusion to them. God's command to give careful thought to our ways may fill us with dread because the reflection can be so unattractive.

As we give careful thought to our ways, we should first look back to where we have come from and reflect on God's work in our lives. We are on a journey. Sometimes the road is difficult; sometimes the road is easy. We must consider where we were when God found us and where we are now through His grace. Even more importantly, we must think about the ways our present actions, habits, and attitude toward God reflect our lives as Christians. Only when we are able honestly to assess our lives in Christ can we call on His name to help perfect our reflection.

Dear Lord, help me to look honestly
at the ways I live and make changes
where necessary. Amen.

No Liars Allowed

"God is not a man, that He should lie. He is not a son of man, that He should be sorry for what He has said. Has He said, and will He not do it? Has He spoken, and will He not keep His Word?"

NUMBERS 23:19

Have you ever let someone else down? Or have you experienced disappointment when others didn't follow through with what they said they'd do? As imperfect humans, we've all been on the giving and receiving ends of such circumstances.

But God is different. It's not just that He's upstanding and reliable; instead, God, by His very nature, is incapable of lying, indecision, manipulation, or going back on His Word.

What does this mean for His children? First, it means that we never have to wonder if God is planning to follow through with His promises. It means we can count on Him to do what He says, never wavering or being wishy-washy. God's truth will remain true now and forever.

No matter what frustrations or disappointments are happening in your life, take comfort in the fact that God remains constant. Praise Him for His very nature of stability and support, and thank Him for His everlasting goodness.

I am amazed by You, dear Lord. When I am
surrounded by the sins of the world, still Your
awesome perfection shines through. You are my rock,
my redeemer, and ever-faithful friend. Amen.

His Healing Abundance

"See, I will make it well again, and I will heal them.
I will let them have much peace and truth."
JEREMIAH 33:6

Our health—physical, mental, emotional, and spiritual—is important to God. He longs to see us whole in every area of our lives. As believers in His grace and goodness, we ought to be diligent about seeking health so that we can be good stewards of His gifts.

If we confess our sins to God, He will bring relief to our souls. When we're distressed, we have Jesus, the Prince of Peace, to give us peace. When our emotions threaten to overwhelm us, we can implore Jehovah Rapha—the God Who Heals— to calm our anxious hearts. When we're physically sick, we can cry out to Jesus, our Great Physician. While He may not always heal us in the ways we might like, He will always give us strength, courage, and peace.

So whether our problems affect us physically, spiritually, mentally, or emotionally, we can trust that God will come to us and bring us healing. And beyond our temporal lives, we can look forward with hope to our heavenly lives. There we will be healthy, whole, and alive—forever.

Jehovah Rapha, thank You for healing me.
Help me do my part to seek health and the
abundance of peace and truth You provide.

Contentment

The Lord is my Shepherd. I will have everything I need.
PSALM 23:1

Probably the most familiar passage in the Bible, the twenty-third Psalm is a picture of contentment. If the Lord is our shepherd, then we are His sheep. Sheep are fragile animals, easily lost and injured and in need of constant care. They are vulnerable to predators, especially if separated from the flock, and need to be guarded and led to places of safety.

A shepherd spends all his time with his sheep. Theirs is a close relationship, and He is always guarding them. He is responsible for nourishment, rest, places of safety, and care for the injured. The sheep do not have to seek these things; it is the shepherd's job to know what they need and provide it.

Though it's not very flattering to be thought of as sheep, it does help to describe our relationship with God. Because we are sheep, with Christ as our shepherd, we do not have to worry, strive, want, or lack. We are never alone. As Philippians 4:19 says, "My God will give you everything you need because of His great riches in Christ Jesus."

> Lord, cause me to remember that I am a sheep
> and You are my shepherd. In times of loneliness,
> anxiety, need, or pain, help me to turn to You.

Count the Cost

*"If one of you wanted to build a large building, you would sit down
first and think of how much money it would take to build it."*

LUKE 14:28

What might it have been like to be one of Christ's first followers?

Christ empowered His twelve disciples and sent them out
to do miracles (Mark 6:7, 13, 30). When the Lord sent out
seventy-two of His closest followers, they returned, exploding
with joy and excitement (Luke 10:1–17).When the church
began after the resurrection, the public liked the disciples
(Acts 2:47).

But all too soon, the novelty wore off. Persecution began.
Christians were hunted, imprisoned, murdered. Almost overnight, it seemed, it cost something to be labeled "Christian."

So far, we may not have had to seriously count the cost of
following Christ. Some statistics estimate that for more than
2.5 billion people around the world, simply attending a church
meeting can mean harassment, arrest, torture, or death. For
Christians throughout much of Africa and the Middle East,
the cost of their commitment to Christ exacts a high toll. For
us in the United States, being a Christ follower might mean
being shunned by friends or finding ourselves humiliated by
the politically correct. Such persecution may yet take on more
serious consequences, as it has in the past. Will you be ready to
hold tight to your faith?

The early church counted the cost of following Christ. Today,
many of our brothers and sisters worldwide are doing the same.
They're ready for whatever comes. We need to be ready too.

*Lord, don't let me forget that my salvation
doesn't come without cost or sacrifice. Amen.*

Daily Choice

*"The robber comes only to steal and to kill and to destroy.
I came so they might have life, a great full life."*

JOHN 10:10

Some days it seems the negative outweighs the positive. People demand so much of our time. Bills demand so much of our money. Feelings of inadequacy surface quickly. It all caves in around us—it's just too much! But when God's words fall on our hearts, those thoughts of defeat are shown for what they really are: lies that delight the enemy who wants to destroy our souls.

But Christ comes to give life! Choosing life is an act of the will blended with faith. We must daily make the decision to take hold of the life Christ offers us. It's this Spirit-infused life that keeps us going; our greatest efforts often come up short. Accepting this gift from Jesus doesn't guarantee a perfect life; it doesn't even guarantee an easy life. But Christ does promise to sustain us, support us, and provide a haven from the storms of life in His loving arms.

Giving Lord, help me daily choose You and the life
You want to give me. Give me eyes of faith to trust
that You will enable me to serve lovingly, as You do.

Praise Him

Jesus said to them, "I tell you that if these did not speak, the very stones would call out."

LUKE 19:40

Jesus says that if His people do not praise Him, the rocks will cry out. We serve a God who must be praised. He is worthy of honor and praise. We serve a God who created the universe and everything in it. He is not a small *g* god. He is a capital *G* God. He is a great big God, and He deserves great big praise. How do we praise Him? We praise Him by telling Him of His greatness. When you pray, before you begin asking the Lord for things, try telling Him how wonderful you think He is. Speak scripture back to Him. Tell Him that He is the Great I Am and your provider. He is the Prince of Peace and the King of Kings. He is the Lord of Lords, the Savior, your Abba Father. Praise Him for you are wonderfully made. Praise Him for His presence that is always near. Then your heart will be filled with thankfulness, and you can move into a time of thanksgiving in your prayers. Certainly it is appropriate to ask God for things that others need or that you yourself desire, but God is honored when you begin with praise.

Lord, I praise You for who You are. You are the Creator of this beautiful world. You are the King of Kings, and yet You became a man and lived on earth. You died for me. I praise You for these things and so much more. Amen.

The Battle of the Mind

*We break down every thought and proud thing that
puts itself up against the wisdom of God. We take
hold of every thought and make it obey Christ.*

2 CORINTHIANS 10:5

What does it mean to take every thought captive to make it obedient to Christ? Prevent the first lie from taking root. Weigh every thought against truth. Partial truth still constitutes a lie. If a thought is not consistent with God's Word, do not give it credence. Dismiss it from your mind by not dwelling on it.

The battle rages: Who or what will control our minds? We have an enemy that wants to influence our thought life. He masquerades as a friend, whispering deception. But beware! He is no friend. He is the father of lies. We must constantly discern God's truth from Satan's lies. Deception is subtle. Once we buy into one lie, we are quickly led down a path riddled with more. Before we know it, we have drawn false conclusions and made decisions based on wrong information.

We cannot test our thoughts unless we know scripture. Even Satan knows truth. He twists God's Word to accomplish his purposes—our destruction. Saturate your mind with truth by reading the Bible. Meditate on scripture. Learn truth so you can recognize a lie. Then you will be victorious in the battle of your mind.

*Dear Lord, help me win the battle of my mind by
taking every thought captive to You. Amen.*

Always Thinking of You

What is man, that You think of him,
the son of man that You care for him?

PSALM 8:4

What are you thinking about today? Do you have a list of things you want to get done, people you need to call, or maybe a vacation you want to plan? Your thoughts fill up your days and keep you busy going and doing life.

Have you ever wondered what God thinks about? He thinks about you! You are always on His mind. In all you think and do, He considers you and makes intercession for you. He knows the thoughts and intents of your heart. He understands you like no other person can. He knows your strengths and weaknesses, your darkest fears and highest hopes. He's constantly aware of your feelings and how you interact with or without Him each day.

God is always with you, waiting for you to remember Him—to call on Him for help, for friendship, for anything you need. He wants to be a big part of your life. And if you include Him, He will open the doors to as much goodness, mercy, and love as you'll allow Him to bless you with.

Lord, help me to remember You as I go throughout
my day. I want to include You in my life and
always be thinking of You too. Amen.

I Lift My Eyes

*I will lift up my eyes to the mountains. Where will
my help come from? My help comes from the
Lord, Who made heaven and earth.*

PSALM 121:1–2

Have you ever been told to "keep your eyes on the prize" or "keep your nose to the grindstone"? These clichés are worldly pieces of advice that are meant to be helpful in the pursuit of success. However, when our eyes remain on the end result—the prize—we can miss much along the way. Or if we keep our heads down, focused on our work, we cannot be guided.

We all go through seasons when decisions can be the most crucial. Challenges, failures, doubts, and fears may cloud decisions and cripple us into inaction because the end result is unknown. Career paths, relationships, and financial decisions are only some of the areas that cause concern.

In all of those things and in all of life, we shouldn't keep our eyes fixed on the end result, and we shouldn't keep our heads down and simply plow through. Instead, we must lift our eyes to the Lord. If we fix our focus on Jesus, we will see that He is prepared to lead and guide us through all of life's challenges.

Lord, I lift up my eyes to You. Please help me and
guide me down the path of life. Let me never become
so focused on my own goals or so busy about my work
that I forget to look to You, for You are my help. Amen.

Spiritual Gifts

The Holy Spirit works in each person in one
way or another for the good of all.
1 CORINTHIANS 12:7

You are one of a kind, uniquely created by God. He has bestowed upon you at least one spiritual gift. Accept this gift, and don't try to be something you're not. If you don't know what your spiritual gift is, ask the Lord to reveal it to you. What are you passionate about? When do you feel the most alive and fulfilled? Look for opportunities to serve in that area.

As believers, we have received various spiritual gifts from the Holy Spirit. They are used to build up the body of Christ. All of the gifts are equally important, although some are more visible than others. Don't covet someone else's gift. Concentrate on developing your own. Pursue opportunities of service that emphasize your giftedness. Be willing to give up other endeavors in order to pursue God's call. You cannot serve everywhere.

Focus on exercising your spiritual gifts. As you learn and grow in these talents, you'll make a greater impact for the kingdom and fulfill God's purpose.

Dear Lord, reveal my spiritual gift. Help me use
it effectively to benefit the church body. Amen.

Child's Play

He said, "For sure, I tell you, unless you have a change of heart and become like a little child, you will not get into the holy nation of heaven."
MATTHEW 18:3

The famous biographer James Boswell recounted with fondness his memory of a boyhood day when his father took him fishing. Boswell gleaned important life lessons from his dad that day as they sat on the creek bank waiting for a bite on their fishing lines.

Having heard Boswell's fishing experience so often, someone thought to check the journal that Boswell's father kept to determine, from a parental perspective, what he recorded about the father-son excursion. Turning to the date, the inquirer found one sentence: *Gone fishing today with my son; a day wasted.*

Though hard to admit, have you ever felt the same? Like when you played catch with a nephew rather than catching up on housework, or when you took your child to the zoo although you had errands to run?

As our to-do list grows, it becomes harder to engage in child's play. But often what we need most is to enter the world of make-believe where clocks and adult responsibilities are as extinct as the toy dinosaurs with which children play.

Spending time with a special child in our lives affords us the opportunity to influence him or her for God's kingdom. So don't waste another moment; seize the day and play!

Father, help me to learn to play and enjoy the children
You have brought into my life. I want to influence them
for Your kingdom. Bless them and use me today. Amen.

The Light of Life

Your Word is a lamp to my feet and a light to my path.

PSALM 119:105

Imagine yourself camping in the woods with friends. There are no street or porch lights. The fire has been put out, and everyone has gone to bed. The darkness of night in the country has settled in, but you need to go from one tent to the other.

What would you do? Carry a flashlight, of course. Without it, you can't see the tree roots, twigs, rocks, or uneven ground beneath your feet. There could be snakes, raccoons, coyotes, or bears lurking in the dark. Only a complete fool would step out into the dark without a flashlight to illuminate the way.

The road of life sometimes has uneven ground, sharp turns, and dangers awaiting us. Foolishly, we try to walk it in the dark. Jesus said in John 8:12, "I am the Light of the world. Anyone who follows Me will not walk in darkness. He will have the Light of Life." Our light is the Living Word, Jesus Christ. He has revealed Himself in scripture, and His Spirit illuminates the scripture for us as we read it. With His Word, He guides our every step.

Father, thank You for the gift of Your Son,
who is the light of life. Give me the desire to
study the scriptures and know You as revealed
to me in them. By Your Spirit, bring the Word
to my mind in times of need and temptation.

Leave Your Bags Behind

*Give all your worries to Him
because He cares for you.*

1 PETER 5:7

Imagine that your best friend has announced she's treating you to an all-expenses-paid cruise. All of your meals are included, and she's even throwing in a brand-new wardrobe.

"Leave your bags behind," she tells you. "All you have to do is show up."

Can you imagine arriving at the cruise ship with suitcases full of clothes, shoes, and food? "Why are you carrying all this junk?" your friend would say. "I told you I had it covered—don't you trust me?"

All too often, this is how we approach God. He invites us to give Him our burdens, but we show up time and time again weighed down with bags so full we can't even carry them. So we drag them behind us wherever we go. They slow us down so that we're not productive, just burdened. Worry, anger, resentment, anxious thoughts. . .sometimes the list is long.

God has told us to give all of our cares to Him. He promises that He has them covered, and yet we still hang on. What baggage are you carrying today that you can give to the Lord?

*Father, thank You for the invitation to cast all my
cares upon You. Help me to let go of the things that are
weighing me down and to trust You to take them for me.*

A Place in Heaven

"There are many rooms in My Father's house. If it were not so, I would have told you. I am going away to make a place for you."

JOHN 14:2

At times, heaven seems far, far away. You gaze into the sky and try to imagine it—God on His throne, angels singing, no more tears, only joy, only praise for the Father. But you can't see it. It is not visible to the human eye.

Other times, heaven seems ever so close. Have you said goodbye to a loved one who was a Christian? You simply let them slip away, out of your grasp, from one world to the next, from earth to heaven. Heaven seems close in those moments, just beyond a thin veil, almost reachable, almost visible. If someone you love dearly and who recently talked and laughed with you has gone there suddenly, heaven feels a little closer.

There is much we do not know about heaven, but we know that our Jesus is there preparing a place for us. We are not aware of the exact date or time that we will leave this earth, but God is. The Bible says there is an appointed time for each of us to be born and to die. There is no question for the Christian about what happens after death. We will go instantly into the presence of the Lord. If you know Jesus as your savior, He is preparing a place in heaven—just for you.

Thank You, Jesus, for preparing a place for me in heaven with You where I will live eternally. Amen.

A Life of Joy

Fill us in the morning with Your loving-kindness.
Let us sing for joy and be glad all our days.
PSALM 90:14

Webster's dictionary defines joy as "emotion evoked by well-being, success, or good fortune." When was the last time you experienced joy? Was it last month? Last week? Today?

There are many joyful occasions: a birthday, an anniversary, a job promotion, a wedding, the birth of a baby. . .the list can go on. But do we need a big event to give us joy? Many ordinary moments can bring joy as well: getting a close parking spot at the mall, finding a ten-dollar bill in your pocket. . .again, the list continues.

First Thessalonians 5:16 tells us to "be full of joy all the time." That doesn't mean we need to take pleasure when things go wrong in life, smiling all the while. Rather, God wants us to maintain a spirit of joy, knowing that He has provided happy times and will carry us through the hard times.

Ever notice how a joyful spirit is contagious? When you're around someone who is full of joy, it's easy to find yourself sharing in that joy. Maybe you could be that person today, bringing smiles to others. When you find delight in the ordinary moments, they will catch the joy.

Heavenly Father, I thank You for being the source of my joy. Please help me to share Your joy with those whom I come in contact with today. Amen.

Fruitful Living

*But the fruit that comes from having the Holy Spirit in our
lives is: love, joy, peace, not giving up, being kind, being
good, having faith, being gentle, and being the boss over
our own desires. The Law is not against these things.*

GALATIANS 5:22–23

We've all had those days. Frustration mounts. Resentment surfaces. Anger brews. Our day is not going according to our plan. We might as well be beating our heads against the wall. What's the problem?

Because we are human, we tend to want to rely on ourselves to fix our problems. It's a constant battle. The apostle Paul describes this wrestling match in Romans 7:19: "I do not do the good I want to do. Instead, I am always doing the sinful things I do not want to do." Paul asks in verse 24, "Who can set me free from my sinful old self?" His answer? Jesus Christ!

We need to recognize the problem. Frustration, resentment, and anger are red flags. They are by-products of our sinful nature, proving that we've bypassed the help and peace God offers. We want life to go according to our plan and agenda, but God's way is so much better. Jesus came to rescue us from ourselves. He came to enable us to walk in the spirit by yielding control to Him. Once we do that, our lives will produce the spiritual fruit God wants us to grow. It's a better way to live!

Dear Lord, help me realize when I am
walking in the flesh. May I yield to
You so that I reap spiritual fruit. Amen.

Conquer That Mountain

"I am the Lord your God, Who teaches you to do well, Who leads you in the way you should go."

ISAIAH 48:17

Life is full of ups and downs—mountain and valley experiences. There are times when you can get stuck or grow frustrated trying to conquer one specific mountain. Maybe you find yourself facing the same obstacle for the second and third time. Sometimes those mountains can present very difficult lessons to learn, so you climb them again and again, trying to understand something about yourself vital to reaching your next level of life.

If you feel like you're repeating the same lesson, go deep into your heart and ask yourself the hard questions. Why am I climbing this mountain again? What did I miss? What do I need to know or learn before I can go to the next level? Then ask the Lord to give you answers and show you things you might have missed.

God gave you a life to fulfill with a specific purpose to complete. He wants to see you moving forward. With your heart and mind open, ready to receive clear direction, you can conquer the mountain this time! You have an amazing destiny to achieve.

God, I ask for Your wisdom and guidance in my life. Help me to see whatever it is I've missed, and help me to follow Your direction in all things. Amen.

A Faithful Example

"For sure your God is God of gods and Lord of kings, and He makes hidden things known. For you have been able to make known this secret."

DANIEL 2:47

King Nebuchadnezzar had a dream that neither he nor his magicians and sorcerers could explain. After each group tried and failed to tell the king about his dream, God revealed both the dream and its meaning to Daniel. He, in turn, explained the dream to the king. King Nebuchadnezzar was so pleased with Daniel that he promoted him to a high position in his court.

What a day that must have been for Daniel! After years of remaining faithful to God—even in a foreign, unbelieving land—he was able to prove God's might to the king.

Maybe you have a friend, coworker, or family member who has not yet put his or her faith in God. Perhaps you have been praying about it for many years. Don't give up hope! Daniel's faith allowed God to demonstrate His power to the king, and while the king did not immediately bow down to God, he saw that God was real and powerful.

Our faithful example is important. When we trust in God, those around us will see His power in us. Through our actions, others will come to know God and proclaim that He is a God of gods and a Lord of kings.

Dear Lord, be with my friends who don't know You.
Help me to plant seeds of faith in their hearts. Let
me trust that You will make them grow. Amen.

Add Love

*And to all these things, you must add love. Love holds everything
and everybody together and makes all these good things perfect.*
COLOSSIANS 3:14

Paul wrote a letter to the Colossians, a church he loved and had
spent time with, a group of people whom he knew needed this
advice. We need the same advice today. He told the Colossians
that, as God's people, they were dearly loved. He admonished
them to exhibit compassion, kindness, and humility. As if these
were not enough, Paul also told them to show gentleness and
to have patience with one another. He told them to bear with
one another and to forgive one another as the Lord had forgiven them. Then Paul said a peculiar thing, but it really makes
a lot of sense. He told them to *put on love*. But how does one
"wear" love?

Imagine a winter morning. You put on long underwear, then
a shirt, followed by a sweater, and on top of all that, you wear
a coat. It binds it all together. What enables you to forgive, to
show compassion, to be gentle? What can cause even the most
type-A personality to be patient with another believer? Love.
Only love. It binds it all together. It causes the Christian to look
and act and even feel different from the non-Christian. It is the
greatest of all the virtues. Don't start your day without putting
on love!

Father, let Your love show in all that I do
today. Help me to be quick to forgive others
as You have forgiven me. Amen.

Tough Love

*My children, let us not love with words or in talk
only. Let us love by what we do and in truth.*

1 JOHN 3:18

The relationship between speech and actions is seen throughout the Bible. Joseph's brothers *tell* Jacob they are sad that their brother is dead, yet they are the ones who staged his death and sold him into slavery. Saul *says* he loves David, but he tries over and over again to kill him. Pontius Pilate *declares* that he thinks Jesus is innocent, but he gives the order to crucify Him anyway. As the old adage goes, "Actions speak louder than words."

We are called to intentionally love one another, not with our meaningless words, but with our quantifiable actions. We discover that the command to love actively is much more difficult than loving with words. Loving with words requires little thought and no commitment. Loving with actions requires firm purpose and devotion.

Jesus is the embodiment of active love. He loved those who most thought were unlovable, talking to, touching, healing, and eating with them, and in the ultimate act of love, dying on the cross to save every one of us from our sin. The author of 1 John is asking us to love as Jesus loved. We must push our selfishness aside and give ourselves fully to others with active and truthful love.

Dear Lord, teach me to love like You love. Let me be
intentional, active, and willing to put aside my own
desires so that I can love others better. Amen.

Pleasing God

His joy is not in the strength of a horse. He does not find
joy in the legs of a man. But the Lord favors those who
fear Him and those who wait for His loving-kindness.

PSALM 147:10–11

Americans value achievement. We measure our country by its various accomplishments. Scientific discovery, space exploration, technological advancement, and world economic and political power all attest to the hard work and achievement of people building a nation.

As individuals, we measure our days by how much we get done. We take pride in checking items off our to-do lists. We email on our handheld devices while sitting in airports and talk on our phones while driving down the highway in an effort to maximize our time so we can get more accomplished in a day.

God does not place value on our achievements. He does not measure our days by how much we get done. He is not delighted by our efficiency or our excellence. This is pretty hard to believe because our culture places such value on self-reliance, but what pleases Him is our worship of Him. He wants our reverent fear, our wonder and awe at His great power and steadfast love. He desires our dependence. He enjoys our hope when we are looking to Him to meet all our needs.

Great God, who gave Your Son for all my sins, help
me to remember that I do not have to perform
for You. You have redeemed me and made me Your
own. You desire my worship and my hope. Amen.

A Life of Love

*Do as God would do. Much-loved children want to do
as their fathers do. Live with love as Christ loved you.
He gave Himself for us, a gift on the altar to God
which was as a sweet smell to God.*

EPHESIANS 5:1–2

Are you living a life of love? Ephesians 5:1–2 tells us Christ loved us and gave Himself up for us. John 15:13 tells us there is no greater love than when you are willing to lay down your life for someone else.

How can you apply this to your daily life? By putting others first! Think of others' needs before you worry about yourself. Be others-minded instead of selfish. Wholeheartedly loving another person is one of the most selfless things you will ever do.

Do you love people enough to lay down your life for them? Putting others first can be difficult to do, but when we are being "imitators of God," He fills us with His Spirit and His power, and through Him we can do all things.

Dear God, show me how to love people selflessly
and wholeheartedly. Help me to be willing to lay
my life down for someone else if necessary. Amen.

Heavenly Treasure

"Gather together riches in heaven where they will not be eaten by bugs or become rusted. Men cannot break in and steal them."

MATTHEW 6:20

You've got ten minutes to leave your home before it is destroyed by fire. What will you take with you? Once you knew your loved ones were safe, you would likely grab the things that remind you of them—photos, heirloom jewelry, a precious family Bible.

Questions like these have a way of whittling our priorities down to the bare essentials. Most of what we own is easily destroyed and just as easily replaced. There are, however, a few things really worth having, and Jesus reminds us that these are things on which we can't put a price tag. Relationships. Eternal life. The assurance that our loved ones will live eternally with Him.

What will you take with you? This isn't a rhetorical question. The practicality of Jesus' words reminds us that the way we live our lives each and every day should be guided by this principle. Invest yourself in the things that matter. Take a look at your calendar and your checkbook. Do they reflect your desire to store up eternal treasures?

Lord, You know it is easy to get distracted by earthly things–things that will ultimately be worth nothing. Help me to shift my focus to matters that have eternal significance and help me to invest my life in those things that will bring eternal dividends.

Seek Peace

Turn away from what is sinful. Do what is good. Look for peace and follow it. The eyes of the Lord are on those who do what is right and good. His ears are open to their cry.

PSALM 34:14–15

If something is worth searching for, it is often very valuable. Pirates search for treasure. A lady may search for just the right dress for a party or the perfect pair of shoes to match an outfit.

Children playing hide-and-seek search for the participant who is hiding. To find this hidden person and capture them is to win the game!

God's Word, in the Psalms, tells us to search for peace. Peace is more valuable than all of the wealth on earth. To lay your head on your pillow at night and know that you are at peace with God and with those around you is a tremendous blessing. True peace is known only by the Christian. The world offers counterfeit versions, but only God can give true and lasting peace that passes all understanding. Seek peace. Search for it. Protect its presence in your life at all costs. If you are on a path that does not bring you peace, you are on the wrong path. Ask God to give you the strength to say no to the things that curtail peace in your life. Peace is essential.

Father, help me to find peace. Reveal to me any area of my life that is not pleasing to You that I might rid myself of it. I want to be at peace with You and with those around me. Amen.

Who's in Control?

At the right time, we will be shown that God is the One Who has all power. He is the King of kings and Lord of lords.
1 TIMOTHY 6:15

Hannah was having second thoughts about her visit to Italy as a short-term missionary. Between the language challenges and cultural taboos, her jet-lagged brain was in overdrive. Things continued to worsen with each passing day.

On her second trip to the bureau where she had to finalize some legal papers for her stay, she stood in the pouring rain to keep her place in line. Like everyone else, Hannah stood in two inches of water. Once inside, the situation wasn't much better. The person she had to speak to wasn't there. He couldn't make it in; his car was under three feet of water. Hannah would have to make a third trip back. Disgruntled, she and her host left.

The street had become a lake. People were walking in thigh-high water. Everyone was trying to walk, wade, or swim their way to their cars and go home. Hannah and her host saw one man who wasn't about to let the flooding best him. He walked down the street clothed in his T-shirt and underwear, holding his pants above the garbage-strewn street river.

Hannah looked for a sign that read, Welcome to your mission field.

Sometimes when we go on what we're sure is a God-ordained mission, bad things happen. In spite of inconveniences over which we've no control, we can rest in knowing God retains control. Some days we just have to trudge our way through— and look for a laugh along the way.

In my frustrations, Father, remind me
that You're in control. Amen.

God Is in the Details

Give all your worries to Him because He cares for you.
1 PETER 5:7

Do you ever wonder if God cares about the details of your life?

Take a look at nature. God is definitely a God of details. Notice the various patterns, shapes, and sizes of animals. Their life cycles. The noises they make. Their natural defenses. Details!

Have you wandered through the woods? Towering trees. Their scents. The cool refreshment their shade provides. The different types of leaves and the tiny, life-bearing veins that run through them. How intricate!

What about the weather? It is filled with details from the hand of your God. The Creator sends raindrops—sometimes gentle and kind, other times harsh and pelting. He warms us with the sun, cools us with breezes, and yes—it is true—he fashions each snowflake, each unique, no two alike! The same way He designs His children!

Do you wonder if God cares about that struggle you are facing at work or the argument you had with a loved one? Is He aware of your desire to find that special someone or the difficulty you find in loving your spouse? He cares. Tell Him your concerns. He is not too busy to listen to the details. He wants to show Himself real and alive to you in such a way that you know it must be Him. The details of your life are not *little* to God. If they matter to you, they matter to God.

Thank You, Lord, for caring about the details of my life. It means so much to know You care. Amen.

Using Time Wisely

*So be careful how you live. Live as men who
are wise and not foolish. Make the best use
of your time. These are sinful days.*

EPHESIANS 5:15–16

Is your testimony something you review on a regular basis? It should be. This world is full of darkness, and God needs dedicated Christians who truly love Him to shed His light on lost souls.

Our primary desire should be to bring people to Jesus. This doesn't mean that all we ever do is talk about God, but when He gives us opportunities, we should take them. No matter what we are doing or saying, it should always honor God.

Our time on earth is limited, and we must use every minute wisely. We will give an account of all our time, whether we waste it or use it for God's glory. That is why it is so important to look often at how we measure up to God's expectations for our lives.

Jesus is our ideal. It really doesn't matter if we are better or worse than someone else. If we don't measure up to Christ, there is work to be done. We must let God work in and through us that we might wisely use the time He gives us to make a difference for Him.

O God, give me a desire to make every
moment I have count for You. Help me
be wise in how I conduct my life.

Put on the Armor

This is the last thing I want to say: Be strong with the
Lord's strength. Put on the things God gives you to fight
with. Then you will not fall into the traps of the devil.

EPHESIANS 6:10–11

As your relationship with the Lord grows closer, Satan will attempt to knock you off course. Has your soul ever felt oppressed for no particular reason? Satan is powerful and persistent, devising schemes that undermine the Lord's work in our lives. His attacks are more forcefully felt when we are on the front battle lines, fighting for the cause of Christ. He will go to great lengths to prevent the advancement of God's kingdom on earth.

Don't get discouraged. God has already won the battle! Christ claimed the victory by overcoming death, defeating Satan once and for all. He gives that victory to us.

Put on the spiritual armor Christ provides. We can't fend off Satan's attacks without it. We will triumph over him as we put on the belt of truth, breastplate of righteousness, helmet of salvation, shield of faith, and sword of the spirit. Don't face your adversary ill prepared. Put on the full armor of God and stand!

Dear Lord, remind me to wear the full armor You
have given me to ensure spiritual victory. Amen.

Difficult People

*He will save my soul in peace from those who make
war against me. For there are many who fight me.*

PSALM 55:18

There always seems to be that one person who opposes you.
Maybe it's the professor who won't permit you to make an A,
the coworker who has to put her fingers in every project you are
involved in, or the neighbor you just don't get along with.

Differences can really bring division between people. The
enemy of your soul, Satan, has long tried to point out our
differences—color of skin, political differences, gender, or religion. He'll use anything he can to divide people, specifically
believers.

It's difficult to embrace those who oppose you, but with the
Lord's help, you can make a friend in the most adverse situations. Find something about that person you can be positive
about. Show yourself friendly. The greatest gift you have to
give is love. Let the love of God shine through you—and God
will use you to change that person, or He will help you to find
a way to be at peace with your differences.

> Lord, I can't handle this difficult situation on my
> own. Please help me find a way to create peace
> and harmony and turn it for good. Amen.

Keep Short Accounts

"He that is faithful with little things is faithful with big things also. He that is not honest with little things is not honest with big things. If you have not been faithful with riches of this world, who will trust you with true riches?"

LUKE 16:10–11

Credit cards seem like such a simple and easy way to buy all we want. Sometimes, though, plastic helps us acquire not only a bunch of stuff but a mountain of debt as well. Good intentions can result in never-ending bills, interest charges, and minimum payments that barely chip away at the actual money owed. Buying on credit allows us to immediately fulfill our desires for things we want, but this isn't God's way. Instead, He desires us to be wise in our wealth.

When we prove to be faithful with our own finances, God will trust us with the bigger things in life. If we patiently wait for the blessings of life to come, we will reap the rewards of satisfaction, financial security, and the trust of others. Exercise godly principles by making sound financial decisions and faithfully honoring the gifts God gives.

Jesus, thank You for the rich blessings in my life. Please help me to be patient and wise with my finances. I want to be faithful with the little things so that I will be worthy of trust in the big ones. Amen.

Honor God with Healthy Habits

So honor God with your body.
1 CORINTHIANS 6:20

The statistics are grim. More than half of Americans are overweight or obese. Only about a third of us get the minimum recommended amount of exercise each day. Health problems that were once reserved for elderly people—like diabetes and high blood pressure—are now affecting us at younger and younger ages.

In spite of living in a society obsessed with diet and exercise, many of us are becoming more unhealthy. Yet the Bible says to honor God with our bodies. We often think of this verse in relation to sexual purity, and it certainly applies. However, we also have an opportunity to honor God with our bodies by taking good care of them—by getting enough rest and enough exercise.

Take a look in the mirror. You need at least eight hours of sleep each night so your body can function optimally. Do you make it a priority to get enough rest, or do you stretch yourself to the limit all week then try to make up for it on the weekends? Adults should get thirty to sixty minutes of physical activity most days of the week. Is there time in your day for fresh air and exercise, or do you spend long hours sitting at a desk in a stuffy building? It sounds like a cliché, but you only get one body—make it a priority to honor God with it.

*Father, thank You for blessing me with a body that does
so much for me. Please help me to make it a priority
to care for it in a way that honors You. Amen.*

Filled with Fear

"What I was afraid of has come upon me.
What filled me with fear has happened."

JOB 3:25

Job 3:25 tells us that for all the great stuff that was Job's before Satan ripped his life to shreds, deep down Job was always afraid of what might happen. When terrible times came to him—the loss of his children, his wealth, and his health—he says he expected it all along.

None of us looks forward to hardship. Some of us, quite frankly, don't expect it. Things are going well. Great family, great job, stick-by-me friends—why clutter our heads with the "what ifs"?

But then the "what ifs" intrude into our orderly world. There's a bad diagnosis. We lose our job. Or there's a natural disaster. And too often our response is like Job's.

"I knew it was too good to last."

Do we have a secret fear or dread? God knew Job's secret fears but still called him "right and good" (Job 1:8). God doesn't withhold His love if we harbor unspoken dread. He doesn't love us any less because of secret anxieties. The Lord "has loving-pity on those who fear Him, as a father has loving-pity on his children. For He knows what we are made of. He remembers that we are dust" (Psalm 103:13–14). God never condemned Job (and He'll never condemn us) for private fears. He encourages us, as He did Job, to trust Him. He alone retains control over all creation and all circumstances (Job 38–41).

Father, please stay beside me when
what I dread most comes to me. Amen.

Laziness vs. Rest

*"Come to Me, all of you who work and
have heavy loads. I will give you rest."*
MATTHEW 11:28

In our society, we are so very *busy*. Many people work seven days
a week. Even children's schedules are packed with lessons and
tutoring, special classes, and clubs. They dance and play sports.
They go, go, go. . .just like the adults in their lives. Why are we
all so busy? Are we running from the quiet? Are we afraid to
rest? We complain about the busyness but continue to pack our
calendars and to-do lists. Do we think we might appear lazy or
strange if we simply choose to stay home, to have quality time
with God and with our families?

Certainly, the Bible warns against laziness with such verses
as Ecclesiastes 10:18, which says: "When men are lazy, the roof
begins to fall in. When they will do no work, the rain comes
into the house." But Jesus Himself rested. He often went away
from the crowds to rest and to pray, to rejuvenate. We are
commanded to remember the Sabbath and keep it holy. This
involves rest. We are encouraged to be still and know that He is
God. Don't confuse laziness with rest. Just because you are not
busy one day or one evening does not mean you should experience unnecessary guilt. Find a balance between work and play,
busyness and rest. You will be better off for it in the long run.

God, help me to avoid laziness but to seek out
rest when it is needed in my life. Amen.

Unswerving Faith

Let us hold on to the hope we say we have and not be changed.
We can trust God that He will do what He promised.
HEBREWS 10:23

Do you remember your first bicycle? Maybe it was a hand-me-down from an older sibling or one found at a neighborhood garage sale. Or maybe you remember the joy of discovering a brand-new bike on Christmas morning. In your delight, you never wondered how Santa got it down the chimney!

Do you remember learning to ride your bike? What a process! While mastering putting it all together—the pedaling, the steering, the balance—did you ever lose control? When you started to swerve, it was a lost cause. Regaining momentum was practically impossible. Almost inevitably, the bike tipped over, and you ended up in the grass.

"Keep it straight!" parents call out when they see their child headed for yet another bike crash. "Look where you're going! Hold it steady!" Similarly, the author of Hebrews challenges us to hold *unswervingly* to our hope in Christ Jesus. Certainly, we fail to do this at times, but life is much better when we keep our eyes fixed on Him.

Sometimes just a whisper from Satan, the father of lies, can cause shakiness where once there was steadfastness. Place your hope in Christ alone. He will help you to resist the lies of this world. Hold *unswervingly* to your Savior today. He is faithful!

Jesus, You are the object of my hope. There are many
distractions in my life, but I pray that You will help me to
keep my eyes on You. Thank You for Your faithfulness. Amen.

Go with God

"Go and make followers of all the nations. Baptize them in the name of the Father and of the Son and of the Holy Spirit. Teach them to do all the things I have told you. And I am with you always, even to the end of the world."

MATTHEW 28:19–20

Have you ever had to make a presentation? Maybe you had the opportunity to teach a class at your workplace or church. Wasn't it a boost to have a coworker or friend there for moral support? Even if that person just nodded occasionally in the audience, assisted with passing out papers, or adjusted the laptop or projector for you, it was a blessing to not go it alone.

Having the moral support of a friend is great, but the promise of the Great Commission scriptures is even greater. The God of the universe gives believers a command in these verses, but He does not tell us to go and teach the Gospel on our own. He makes His intention very clear: He promises to be with us always.

Ask God to reveal to you the people in your life who need to hear the good news of Jesus. As He shows you lost friends and family members, share the Gospel through word and deed and claim God's promise to be with you.

Father, thank You for the joy of sharing Christ with others. Remind me that You accompany me as I follow Your command to go and make disciples. Amen.

Free at a Price

The Holy Spirit and the Bride say, "Come!" Let the one who hears, say, "Come!" Let the one who is thirsty, come. Let the one who wants to drink of the water of life, drink it. It is a free gift.

REVELATION 22:17

Have you noticed lately that a lot of "free" things have many strings attached? Search the Web, and you'll discover scores of ads that offer a supposedly free item *if* you'll do something. In our world, very few people really want to give anything away.

But Jesus gave His earthly life away without our asking Him to or paying Him beforehand. Love led Him to give all He could to draw some to Himself. Though He knew many would deny His gift, Jesus offered Himself freely.

The benefits are all on our side: new life and a relationship with our Creator. What can we offer the Omnipotent One? What could He require that we could fulfill for Him? Our Creator doesn't really need us. He simply chooses, out of His own generous nature, to give us new life.

As we drink deeply of the water of life, we recognize God's great gift. Grateful, we seek out ways to serve Him. But even if we gave all we had, we could never repay God. His gift would still be free.

Do you know people who could use the best, really free gift in the world? Tell them about Jesus!

Thank You, Lord, for giving me a really free
gift—the best anyone could offer. Amen.

The Open Door

"For everyone who asks, will receive what he asks for. Everyone who looks, will find what he is looking for. Everyone who knocks, will have the door opened to him."

LUKE 11:10

The whole process of looking for a job can be overwhelming—not just the first time but every time. From preparing and sending out your résumé to the interviews, the fear of the unknown can weigh heavily on you. If only someone would just give you a chance to show what you can do.

You don't have to be a bundle of nerves. You can rest assured that God has prepared a place for you. He has the right environment for you to flourish and grow in, as well as people in that environment who need what you have to offer to help the company succeed.

Be confident in who He created you to be. Trust Him to place you in the right place. You do your best, and He'll do His part. Ask Him for direction and guidance to lead you to the right people, places, and choices. Don't become discouraged if what you want and what He wants for you are a little different. He perfects everything that concerns you. Place yourself in His capable hands.

Heavenly Father, please open the door to that fulfilling job that You've created just for me, one that will meet all my needs. Direct me to the right place, and give me wisdom and favor. I'm trusting You! Amen.

God's Confidence

"Who has made man's mouth? Who makes a man not able to speak or hear? Who makes one blind or able to see? Is it not I, the Lord? So go now. And I will be with your mouth. I will teach you what to say."

EXODUS 4:11–12

Moses was raised in Pharaoh's palace, but he remained loyal to his own people, the Israelites. As a result of killing an Egyptian, he was forced to flee Egypt. Much later, Moses saw a burning bush that was not consumed. He decided to investigate, and suddenly, God began to speak. God called Moses to deliver the Israelites from Egypt, but Moses did not want to go.

Moses feared the rejection and scorn of both Pharaoh and the Israelites. Even when God allowed His reluctant servant to perform miraculous signs, Moses was still scared to go back to Egypt. After all, he was about to demand that the most powerful ruler in the world release more than a million slaves from bondage!

Like Moses, we might sometimes question God when He calls us to do something for Him. We don't think we're the best choice for the job. When we feel doubt setting in, we can find comfort in the words God spoke to Moses. We know He has given us all the abilities that we possess. God's confidence in us is not misplaced. *He* will help us speak, and *He* will teach us what to say.

Dear Lord, thank You for promising to help me do Your will. Teach me to trust Your confidence in me. Amen.

Display His Glory

*We have this light from God in our human bodies. This shows
that the power is from God. It is not from ourselves.*
2 CORINTHIANS 4:7

Many Christians struggle with the fact that they struggle. We forget our frailty. We don't remember that our spiritual growth is as much a work of Christ as our salvation. We find ourselves frustrated and disappointed because we fail to live up to our own high expectations of ourselves.

At the root of this thought pattern is our pride. We are trying to live out our faith in our own strength—but we can't. We forget that the Bible says we are clay pots. Our Father deliberately places the treasure of knowing Christ into a jar of clay.

Think of bright red geraniums filling clay pots in summer or an exquisite orchid planted in an ordinary clay pot. Picture fuchsia blooms, waxy green leaves, and soft petals that stand in contrast to the rough pot that contains the plant. Drop the clay pot on the patio, and it will break. Leave it out in extreme cold, and it will crack. Place it in a wet, shady spot, and moss will grow on its sides. The pot alone is not valuable, strong, or beautiful, but when filled with blossoms it becomes a joy to behold.

Father, help me not to think too highly of myself.
Help me to remember that I am made of
dust, but that You have placed the treasure
of Your Son in me to display His glory.

Wired for Fun

All the days of the suffering are hard, but a
glad heart has a special supper all the time.
PROVERBS 15:15

What do you do for fun? It seems that in our busy society, fun has been pushed out in favor of work accomplishments, acquiring stuff, and making sure our families are safe and cared for.

But God created us with a need for laughter and fun. Laughter relieves stress, bonds us with other people, and even promotes healing.

Some people love to play games with their friends for fun; others like to watch movies; and others love to shop or do physical activities. There's no right or wrong way to have fun—whatever gives you relief from stress and makes you laugh is fun to you.

If you're stumped for fun ideas, watch children for a while. They instinctively know how to create lots of fun out of a little bit of material and time. Follow their lead, and play with modeling clay, blow bubbles, or toss a ball around in your backyard with friends. You'll be glad you did.

Lord, thank You for making me with
a need for fun. Give me the heart of
a child when I start to get too serious.

Inside Out

Do not act like the sinful people of the world. Let God change your life. First of all, let Him give you a new mind.
ROMANS 12:2

Makeovers are fun. The effects of a new hairstyle, makeup, and wardrobe can be instantaneous and dramatic. Some makeovers are so good that it's almost impossible to recognize the person in the before photo. But no matter how trendy the haircut or how fashionable the clothes, it's always the same person underneath, and nothing can change the heart. This is the worldly formula for transformation: change what's on the outside and maybe the inside will feel better.

The Bible presents a much more effective alternative. Paul tells us that *true* transformation radiates from the inside out. The word *transformation* means *metamorphosis*. This process does not happen overnight. The process of transformation begins with the attitudes of our minds. Our attitudes determine our thoughts. Our thoughts influence our actions, and our actions reveal our character.

Allow God to influence and shape your thoughts, and your character will gradually look more and more like His. Soon you won't even recognize the person you were before. Now *that's* genuine transformation.

Father, thank You that in You I am a
new creature. Continue to transform and
change my character from the inside out.

The Same in a Changing World

*"The grass dries up. The flower loses its color.
But the Word of our God stands forever."*

ISAIAH 40:8

The world has changed so much in the past one hundred years. Electricity, indoor plumbing, airplanes and automobiles, computers, MP3 players, GPS, and countless other technologies have created an entirely new world. Perhaps you have flipped through a yellowed photo album with pictures of your great-great-grandparents and then looked at perfectly preserved digital photos on a computer. Or maybe you remember a day when you paid much less for that gallon of gas or cup of coffee than you did yesterday morning. The world is changing, but our God is not.

God is the constant in our lives. His Word was, is, and will always be the same. It's amazing to think that while we cannot imagine life without electricity, someone hundreds of years ago read the same Bible we read and was learning to trust in God just as we are learning to trust in Him. God's Word is for all people, regardless of the world they live in. God speaks to His people no matter where they are in life. Hundreds of years before the birth of Christ, Isaiah proclaimed that the Word of our God stands forever. Praise be to the Lord that we are still able to proclaim that same message today!

Dear Lord, thank You for Your unchanging Word. Thank You for Your love and for the comfort of knowing that You are the same yesterday, today, and forever. Amen.

God Cares about Your Disappointments

You have seen how many places I have gone. Put my tears in Your bottle. Are they not in Your book?

PSALM 56:8

There are disappointments in the Christian life. God has not promised us otherwise. When sin entered the world in the garden that day through a bite of fruit, disappointment was instantly included in the consequences. This is a fallen world. We live and move and have our being in a place that truly is not our home. One day and for all eternity, in heaven, everything will be perfect as it is supposed to be. We will spend our days praising God. There will be no more tears or loss. We will not be let down or hurt in any way. But here, and for now, there is disappointment. We must learn to live with it. We should embrace it even.

It is in the sorrows of life that God shows Himself so real and loving. He is near to the brokenhearted. The Bible says He "collects our tears." Have you gone through a divorce that you never dreamed would take place? Are you heartbroken over a child's decisions? Has someone hurt you or abandoned you at the time you needed him or her most? God is there in the midst of the hurt. He may not always take the storm away, but He will always ride it out with you. Take refuge in the Lord. He cares for you.

Thank You, heavenly Father, for caring when I hurt. Even in my disappointments, I can see You at work in my life. I love You, Lord. Amen.

Keep Praying

Jesus told them a picture-story to show that
men should always pray and not give up.

LUKE 18:1

A story is told of a foreign missionary with a wife and six children. While on furlough in the United States, he asked local church leaders to pray that the Lord would provide a car upon his return to the mission field. Although he gladly walked to the store or church, his heart ached with the desire to reach more people with the Gospel. When asked how long he had been praying for a car, he responded matter-of-factly, "Fifteen years." Imagine faithfully praying for something for fifteen years!

God answers our prayers in one of three ways: yes, no, or wait. "Yes" is the answer we most desire. However, sometimes out of divine wisdom, God's response is "no." Although it's not the coveted answer, at least the matter can be put to rest. But what happens when God requires that we wait?

Jesus encourages us to be faithful in prayer. We are to be persistent. We are to not give up. We are to continue bringing our request before Him. Our faith grows as we pray and wait upon His perfect timing.

Do not become discouraged. God hears every prayer you utter. He sees every tear that falls. Continue to ask. Continue to seek. Continue to knock. The Lord will answer. Trust and persevere.

Dear Lord, thank You for Your love and
faithfulness to me. May I persevere
in prayer as I trust You. Amen.

Joy vs. Happiness

*The missionaries were filled with
joy and with the Holy Spirit.*

ACTS 13:52

There is a popular children's song about joy often sung in Sunday school or church. It goes like this: *"I've got the joy, joy, joy, joy down in my heart to stay!"* While it was written for children, it bears a wonderful message for all of us.

The difference between happiness and joy is that joy *stays*. If you are a believer in Christ, He resides in your heart. No matter what your circumstances, you can maintain a joy that is deep in your heart. You are a child of God, and He will never leave you. You know you have the promise of eternal life. Happiness, on the other hand, is an emotion that comes and goes within minutes. Ever heard a baby crying loudly, but when they get what they want—a bottle, the mother, or a toy—the crying ceases immediately? Sadness has turned to contentedness. Temporary! Take the object of the baby's affection away, and the tears return. As adults, we are not that different from these young ones. The breakup of a dating relationship or news that we are going to have to move due to a job transfer can zap us of our happiness. Not so with joy! Joy remains. Peace and joy go hand in hand. The Christian never has to lack either.

Lord, thank You that even when I am not
particularly happy, I have joy in Jesus. I have
joy deep down in my heart because You have
saved me and made me Your child. Amen.

Christ Is Involved

*I am sure that God Who began the good work
in you will keep on working in you until the
day Jesus Christ comes again.*

PHILIPPIANS 1:6

When you accepted Jesus as Savior, that was just the beginning of His work in your life. Yes, salvation was complete through His grace. Your sins were forgiven, and your home in heaven was secured.

But Christ wants so much more for you. He wants you to grow in your faith. He wants to help you flee the temptations that you will inevitably face. He wants to give you strength to be joyful even as you go through trials. His ultimate desire is to help you become more like Him.

Do you allow Jesus to be as involved in your life as He wants to be? Unfortunately, a lot of people accept Him in order to get into heaven, but then they want little more to do with Him. Why not choose now to let Him be a part of everything you do and every decision you make? Go to Him in prayer. Seek answers from His Word and from the Holy Spirit. He will do a great work in your life. He will be faithful to complete what He started in you—and you will become like Him.

Dear Jesus, thank You for wanting to help me
be like You. Thank You for being involved in
my life and not leaving me to my own designs.

His Help for Our Holiness

*"Do not sin against My holy name. I will be honored among
the people of Israel. I am the Lord Who makes you holy."*

LEVITICUS 22:32

Jamie sighed as she read the word in her Bible: *holiness.* She'd
been a Christian for more than a decade, but she felt as far from
holiness as she ever had. "Lord," she prayed, "I want to please
You. But I'm always messing up! I feel like such a failure."

She cried as she mentally reviewed the sins she'd committed
in just the past day. But as she prayed, journaled, and confessed
her sins, God reminded Jamie of a sermon she'd heard the week
before. "God doesn't just ask us to be holy and then leave us to
figure it out on our own," the preacher said. "He's the one who
will make us holy if we daily surrender everything to Him."

As she closed her Bible, Jamie smiled. God always brought
the perfect words and scriptures to mind at just the right time.
It's not hopeless, she thought. *God is working on me and with me.
I'm not the same as I was last year, and I will keep growing if I stay
close to Him.*

"Make me like You, Lord," she prayed. "And thank You for
never leaving me to figure it out on my own."

> Holy God, I praise You for never leaving me on
> my own. You are changing me to be like You. I
> want to participate with–and not hinder–You.

When You Are Tempted

*You have never been tempted to sin in any different way
than other people. God is faithful. He will not allow you to be
tempted more than you can take. But when you are tempted,
He will make a way for you to keep from falling into sin.*

1 CORINTHIANS 10:13

Have you ever felt that temptation was just too great? Have you given in to it? You are not alone. It is not easy to resist temptation. Satan, the prince of darkness, is always seeking to devour God's children. He knows your personal weaknesses and uses them against you. The good news is that there is always a way out when you are tempted to sin. Every temptation that you have ever faced or will face in the future has been experienced by others. No temptation is new. Satan just recycles the same juicy bait and uses it again and again, generation after generation. Staying in God's Word and praying daily will help you to resist temptation. Being part of a Christian community will help with this also. As you bring down your walls and allow other believers to get close to you, they can pray for you and hold you accountable. Remember that no matter what temptations you are facing today, the payoff will be far greater if you resist than if you give in. Jesus stands ready to help you escape if only you will reach out and take His hand.

Lord, help me in this area today: (fill in this blank
with your area of greatest temptation to sin). I need
to see the way out. Thank You, Father. Amen.

Count the Cost

*If a man does things to please his sinful old self,
his soul will be lost. If a man does things to please
the Holy Spirit, he will have life that lasts forever.*

GALATIANS 6:8

In decision-making there is a cost factor associated with everything you do—and everything you don't do. Action or lack of action both cost you.

Take exercise for example. Regular physical exercise offers amazing benefits. It strengthens your body, boosts your immune system, and improves mental health. The cost to exercise includes the time you need to actually do it and the pain of putting your body through the motions to get in shape. But there is also a cost associated with not exercising, such as deteriorating physical and mental health.

When you make a decision, remember to take a look at the whole picture. What will it cost you if you act? What will it cost you if you fail to act? Everything you do—or don't do—carries consequences.

God made wisdom available to you to help you make good choices for your life. The next time you are faced with a decision, take a step back and count the cost!

Heavenly Father, thank You for making wisdom available to me. I ask You to show me how to count the cost in all my choices. Amen.

Puffed Up

So watch yourself! The person who thinks he can stand against sin had better watch that he does not fall into sin.

1 CORINTHIANS 10:12

It's easy to fall into the trap of thinking that we have conquered a sin and it will never bother us again. Be careful! First Corinthians 10:12 is a warning not to puff ourselves up with pride. Allowing ourselves to think that we have completely overcome sin is prideful. We can only overcome sin through the power of Christ, relying on His power daily.

This passage continues, "You have never been tempted to sin in any different way than other people. God is faithful. He will not allow you to be tempted more than you can take. But when you are tempted, He will make a way for you to keep from falling into sin" (1 Corinthians 10:13). This is a reminder that we are all human and are tempted. However, God promises to always provide a way out for us. It is only through Him that we can overcome!

Dear Lord, please help me not to be prideful.
Help me to rely on Your power each and every
day to overcome my shortcomings. Amen.

Rescued

God took us out of a life of darkness. He has put us in the holy
nation of His much-loved Son. We have been bought by His
blood and made free. Our sins are forgiven through Him.

COLOSSIANS 1:13–14

It was as if she had fallen into a deep, dark pit. Sleep, withdrawal, and numbness were her coping mechanisms when she was stuck in the ugliness of her sin. She was simply going through the motions, trapped in despair; helpless, it seemed, to make change within herself. She had dealt with these same battles years before—conquered them even. But her sins were again creeping through the chambers of her heart and mind like a dragon wreaking havoc on her spirit.

The message of the Gospel doesn't leave us trapped in our sin and misery without hope. God sent the rescuer, Christ, who plucked us out of the dungeons of despair and into His kingdom of light and strength to overcome the dragons of sin. It's by the Father's grace that we are not stuck in our habitual ruts and dead-end alleys, living without purpose and fulfillment. We walk in His kingdom—a kingdom that goes counter to the world's ideas. We are out of the pit, striding confidently in Him, enjoying life to its fullest.

> Glory to You, Jesus! You have rescued me from the
> pit and lifted me to Your kingdom of real life and
> victory. Help me to walk in that fact today. Amen.

Happy in Hope

Be happy in your hope. Do not give up when trouble comes. Do not let anything stop you from praying.

ROMANS 12:12

Romans 12:12 tells believers to be joyful in hope, patient, and faithful. This is a tall order. The good news is that believers can be strong, even in weakness, because of Christ living in us. We can do all things through Him—including being hopeful, patient, and faithful in prayer.

Hope is sometimes described as "the present enjoyment of a future blessing." Even if your situation is difficult now and doesn't improve while you are on earth, you are promised eternity with Him. He will make all things right in His time.

Patience is a virtue we teasingly warn each other never to pray for! Throughout our lives, we face trials both small and great. Whether your affliction is sitting in traffic or a cancer diagnosis, seek to be patient. Wait upon the Lord. Rest in Him, trust that He is in control, and lay your anxiety at the feet of your Savior.

Faithfulness in prayer requires discipline. God is faithful regardless of our attitude toward Him. He never changes, wavers, or forsakes His own. We may be faithful to do daily tasks around the house. We feed the cat, wash the clothes, and empty the trash. But faithfulness in the quiet discipline of prayer is harder. There are seemingly no consequences for neglecting our time with the Lord. Oh, what a myth this is! Set aside a daily time for prayer, and see how the Lord blesses you, transforming your spirit to increase your joyful hope, your patience, and your faithfulness.

Faithful God, find me faithful. Stir up the hope and joy within me. Give me the grace I need to wait on You. Amen.

May I Have a Towel, Please?

Jesus got up from the supper and took off His coat. He picked up a cloth and put it around Him. Then He put water into a wash pan and began to wash the feet of His followers. He dried their feet with the cloth He had put around Himself.

JOHN 13:4–5

Can you picture this scene? As Jesus and His disciples finished eating, He got up and wrapped a towel around His waist, poured water into a basin, and began washing their feet. Several jaws probably dropped to the floor as the disciples tried to comprehend what He was doing. Their feet, most likely dusty from walking on dirt roads, were being washed *by the Master*!

Jesus was giving us an example: just as He served the disciples in washing their feet, we should serve others. He humbled Himself and commanded that His disciples do the same. In verse 16, Jesus tells them, "A workman who is owned by someone is not greater than his owner. One who is sent is not greater than the one who sent him." This was a profound lesson in servant leadership.

Who can you serve today? While you may not know someone who could use a good footbath, there are many other ways to serve. Is there someone who needs a meal? Do you know of a shut-in who needs a ride to a doctor's appointment? Is there a coworker who is really swamped and could use a hand? Offer to help out, serving them in the name of Jesus.

Father, help me to be willing to serve others with a joyful spirit just as You did. Lead me to someone whom I could serve for Your glory. Amen.

Forgiving Others

He has taken our sins from us as
far as the east is from the west.

PSALM 103:12

Forgiveness. The word rolls off the tongue much more easily than it penetrates the heart. When someone has wronged you, it is natural to feel hurt. It is not easy to forgive a person who has wounded you. Forgiveness is no small thing. It is a tall order. The greater the offense, the harder you may find it to forgive. The model prayer that Jesus taught His followers includes this line: *"Forgive us our trespasses as we forgive those who trespass against us."* What was Jesus saying here? He was reminding us to emulate our Father's ability to forgive. Have we not all sinned and fallen short of the glory of God? Certainly! But our heavenly Father forgives us. He removes the dark stain of sin and says He will speak of it no more. It is gone. As far as the east is from the west. That is a long way! God does not keep bringing up your past sins. If you have asked Him to forgive you, He has. Pray for your heavenly Father to reveal to you just how much He loves you. As you experience His love and forgiveness, you will want to forgive others—regardless of the depth of the hurt they have caused in your life.

God, forgiveness is not always easy. Help me
to sense Your deep love for me. Remind me
of all that You have forgiven me of so that I
might be able to forgive others. Amen.

How to Please God

*O my God, I know that You test the heart
and are pleased with what is right.*
1 CHRONICLES 29:17

Of all the character traits we look for in a friend, a potential mate, a leader, and especially an auto mechanic, integrity sits at the top of the list. King David was a man of integrity (1 Kings 9:4). Even Jesus' sharpest critics said, "We know You are true" (Mark 12:14). Paul encourages teachers to "show them how to live by your life and by right teaching. You should be wise in what you say. Then the one who is against you will be ashamed and will not be able to say anything bad about you" (Titus 2:7–8).

Not everyone, however, appreciates the honesty that characterizes the person of integrity. Proverbs 29:10 tells us that "men who kill hate him without blame."

Even though we don't know a lot about Hanani in the book of Nehemiah, one thing we're told is that "he was a faithful man and honored God with fear more than many" (Nehemiah 7:2). What a high compliment! To have that said of us prepares us for whatever challenges come our way. Whether we're given a pat on the back—or a push out the door—for our personal integrity, we can be confident that our integrity pleases God.

Lord, make me a person of integrity so that I never bring
shame to Your name or pain to Your heart. Amen.

Reflecting God in Our Work

Whatever work you do, do it with all your heart.
Do it for the Lord and not for men.
COLOSSIANS 3:23

Parents often tell their children to do their best in school or to behave well when they visit friends' homes. Children are a reflection of their parents. When a mom and dad send their offspring out into the world, they can only hope that the reflection will be a positive one.

As believers, we are God's children. No one is perfect, and for this there is grace. However, we may be the only reflection of our heavenly Father that some will ever see. Our attitudes and actions on the job speak volumes to those around us. Although it may be tempting to do just enough to get by, we put forth our best effort when we remember we represent God to the world. A Christian's character on the job should be a positive reflection of the Lord.

This is true of our work at home as well. No one would disagree that daily chores are often monotonous, but we are called to face them with a cheerful spirit. God will give us the ability to do so when we ask Him.

Father, help me today to represent
You well through my work. I want to
reflect Your love in all I do. Amen.

Times of Trouble

*You have turned my crying into dancing. You have taken
off my clothes made from hair, and dressed me with joy.
So my soul may sing praise to You, and not be quiet.
O Lord my God, I will give thanks to You forever.*

PSALM 30:11–12

David knew times of trouble, and he also knew what it meant to
be relieved of trouble. He experienced want and he experienced
abundance. He hid in fear of losing his life to a king who he
knew hated him. . .and later, he danced with joy, praising God,
amazed at God's provision and protection. Can you relate? You
probably have never been chased by a king and his armies. But
every life is full of ups and downs. There will be times when all
you can hope to do is survive in the shelter of the Lord's wing.
You know He is there, but you cannot sense His presence. You
trust Him, but you don't know how in the world He will turn
things around. Just keep trusting. Just keep believing. Just keep
praying. David cried out to the Lord for mercy. Not just this
psalm but many others are filled with David's pleas to the Lord.
God is faithful to hear our prayers. Just as He turned David's
sorrow into joy, He can do the same for you.

Father, I ask You to turn my weeping
into laughter. Teach me to praise You
no matter my circumstances. Amen.

Faultless

There is One Who can keep you from falling and can bring
you before Himself free from all sin. He can give you great
joy as you stand before Him in His shining-greatness.

JUDE 24

Who is at fault? Who is to blame? When something goes wrong at work, at home, or at church, someone is held accountable. People want to know who is responsible, who made a mistake. The ones pointing fingers of accusation don't always care about the truth as much as they do about making sure they aren't blamed for the transgression.

Ever since God confronted Adam and Eve in the Garden of Eden, we have been pointing fingers at someone else instead of taking responsibility for our own actions. Shame and fear make us want to deny we have done any wrong even when we have done so accidentally or by mistake. We value what God and other people think of us. When we are at odds with God or others over a transgression, we often become depressed.

Jesus loves us so much despite our shortcomings. He is the One who can keep us from falling—who can present us faultless before the Father. Because of this, we can have our joy restored no matter what. Whether we have done wrong and denied it or have been falsely accused, we can come into His presence to be restored and lifted up. Let us keep our eyes on Him instead of on our need to justify ourselves to God or others.

Thank You, Jesus, for Your cleansing love and
for the joy we can find in Your presence. Amen.

An Unexpected Turn

"He has made my way safe."
2 SAMUEL 22:33

We always want to be in the right place at the right time. Life moves in a hurry, and with it, we thrust ourselves forward into each appointment or commitment. We get frustrated when we miss a turn or mistakenly veer down a wrong road.

What if you were to choose to put a different spin on the frustration of going out of your way? You can get bent out of shape and become frustrated because of the time you feel you have lost, or you can choose to believe that God makes your way perfect and He has kept you from harm's way. What if that wrong turn that you thought cost you ten extra minutes in traffic actually kept you from a fender-bender or something worse?

Instead of feeling lost and undone, consider that perhaps this was the path you were destined to take. A series of unfortunate events or a trip down an unexpected path can lead to a positive spin on your day. Be open to taking a different route today. It could open new doors of opportunity in unexpected ways.

Father, help me to relax, trusting that
You order my steps and make my
way perfect every day. Amen.

Water's Cost

*"To anyone who is thirsty, I will give
the water of life. It is a free gift."*
REVELATION 21:6

Drinking an ice-cold glass of water on a hot summer day is a wonderful experience. It seems that the thirstier we are, the better water tastes and the more of it we can drink.

Imagine attending a sporting event in the heat of the day. The sun beats down on you, you sweat like crazy, your senses become dull, and an overwhelming desire for a cold bottle of water gradually becomes the only thing you can think about. The players disappear, and the hard bleachers cease to matter; you would pay any amount of money for one sip of water.

Jesus, well aware of basic human needs, likens His message to water, "the water of life." Just as we cannot live without water, we cannot live without the Word of God. We are shocked to learn that this life-giving message, one we must have at any price and one to which we cannot assign value, costs us nothing. Jesus loves us so much that He gave up His life that we might partake of these invigorating waters. So drink up, and leave your money at home; the water of life is free.

Dear Lord, thank You for letting me drink for
free from the spring of the water of life.
Help me to remember Your sacrifice
and Your love for me. Amen.

Twenty Questions

"So you will know them by their fruit."

MATTHEW 7:20

Several friends laughed the night away as they enjoyed playing with a tiny electronic "Twenty Questions" game. The group would think of a common noun, such as a piano, mop, eyelash, or spoon, and then the gadget would begin asking questions:

"Animal, mineral, or vegetable?"

"Is it lighter than a duck?"

"Smaller than a microwave?"

"Can you put it in an envelope?"

"Can you hold it?"

"Would you find it at a school?"

Amazingly, the game could figure out what they were thinking of in almost every instance by asking fewer than twenty questions—simply by finding out characteristics of the object.

People are similar to this tiny computer. They don't have to be told who is a Christian. Every action answers their every curiosity: how people spend their time and money and set their priorities, how much they help the needy, whether they are patient when wronged, how generous they are, how they treat children, whether they gossip, how they show or fail to show love for people. Every action bears fruit, revealing whether individuals are true disciples of Jesus Christ. "A good tree cannot have bad fruit. A bad tree cannot have good fruit" (Matthew 7:18). The lives we lead *shout* whether Christ is front and center in our lives.

Lord, may my every action bear witness
of Your Holy Spirit's work, leading people
to a direct knowledge of the truth. Amen.

My Way or God's Way?

Good and right is the Lord. So He teaches sinners in His ways.
He leads those without pride into what is right, and teaches them
His way. . . . He will teach him in the way he should choose.

PSALM 25:8–9, 12

In today's culture, it is easy to follow "my way." We are bombarded with advertisements from TV, magazines, billboards, and the internet that tell us "It is all about me" and "We can have it all." We have access to people, information, and products 24-7. We have the internet, email, telephone, cell phone, fax, and pager that provide us with availability and resources. In buying anything, there is an overwhelming number of options to choose from. With all these distractions, it is not surprising that we have difficulty surrendering daily to God's way.

Nevertheless, God wants us to live life His way. Our good and upright God tells us that when we come before Him as humble, meek, needy, or afflicted, He will teach us what is right and just. God will teach us His way of living. If it is a decision that needs to be made, a course of action that needs to be taken, or a word that needs to be spoken, God will instruct us in a manner consistent with who He is. Therefore, it is of the utmost importance that we intentionally fall before the throne of God seeking His way, not our own. What way will you choose today?

Good and upright God, please allow me not to
be distracted in this world but to focus on You.
Teach me Your way, I humbly pray. Amen.

A Healthy Fear

*The fear of the Lord is to hate what is sinful. I hate
pride, self-love, the way of sin, and lies.*
PROVERBS 8:13

When we think about our fears, our minds and bodies almost always tense. Whether it's a fear of heights, spiders, public speaking, failure, or being alone, everyone has fears. In fact, it's considered perfectly natural to avoid what we fear.

Why does the Bible say we should "fear" God? In reality, to fear God is not the same as fearing the creepy-crawly spider inching up the living room wall. Instead, we fear God when we have a deep respect and reverence for Him.

Imagine that the president of the United States was paying your home a visit. The house would be extra clean, the laundry would be washed and put away, and the children would be instructed to be on their best behavior. Why? Because the visitor deserves respect.

Our lives should reflect a similar reverence for our heavenly Father every day—our souls scrubbed extra clean, sin eliminated, and love for our Creator bursting forth in joy. God wants speech and actions to match. Take time today to stand in awe of the One who deserves our greatest respect and love.

Lord, help my daily actions and speech
to reflect my respect for You. Amen.

Waiting

*Wait for the Lord. Be strong. Let your
heart be strong. Yes, wait for the Lord.*
PSALM 27:14

In our society, we wait in line to buy groceries, to make bank deposits, and to pick up our kids from school. We wait in classrooms, exam rooms, and even in rooms called "waiting rooms." Waiting is part of life. Because we dislike it, we seek to make things faster. With the invention of drive-through windows, we don't have to get out of the car. The meal is handed to us from a window as we drive by and pay. Microwaves have shortened cook times. We can even sign in online at an after-hours medical clinic to avoid waiting with all the other sick people. We can wait at home instead, where we are able to multitask!

Some things are worth waiting for. Would you agree? The right spouse is definitely worth the wait. Some people drive around for a few minutes waiting for that front-row parking spot to open up. Sometimes we wait for just the perfect moment to share some news, whether good or bad, with family members or friends.

Waiting for God to answer our prayers is easier said than done. God does not hurry. Nor is He ever late. He is always right on time to bless us, and He has our best interests at heart. Seek God's answers for your questions, and be patient. Waiting on the Lord will always pay off.

Help me, Lord, to be more patient. I know that
when You ask me to wait, You have a reason.
Thank You, Lord, for Your provision. Amen.

A Matter of Life or Death

*If you do what your sinful old selves want you to do, you will die
in sin. But if, through the power of the Holy Spirit, you destroy
those actions to which the body can be led, you will have life.*
ROMANS 8:13

A diabetic is dependent upon insulin. A cancer diagnosis
demands medical treatment. For the blind, a cane or a seeing-
eye dog is essential. These are matters of life or death.

The Bible teaches of another such matter. It is an ongoing war
within the believer that simply must be won by the right side! It
is spiritual life versus spiritual death.

The Holy Spirit indwells believers in Christ. Jesus Himself
taught His followers about this third part of the Trinity before
He ascended into heaven. He promised that a Helper would
come. This Helper, the Holy Spirit, came when Jesus went away.
The Spirit convicts us of sin. The Spirit, sometimes referred to
as our Counselor, also guides us in truth.

If you are a Christian, the Holy Spirit is your personal power
source. The strength to do what is right is within you if you
choose to live by the Spirit and not by the flesh. You will be
tempted to follow voices that tell you to do as you please or that
"it's okay if it feels right." You will experience anger and other
emotions that can lead you astray in life. But if you pay attention, your Helper, the Holy Spirit, will reveal the Father's ways.
It is a matter of life or death. Which will you choose?

Father, today I choose life. May Your
Holy Spirit lead me in truth. Amen.

Faith, the Emotional Balancer

*No one is made right with God by doing what the Law
says. For, "The man right with God will live by faith."*
GALATIANS 3:11

Our moods often dictate our actions. For instance, we schedule lunch with a friend for Saturday afternoon, but on Saturday morning we regret having made plans. Or we strategize what to accomplish on our day off but suffer from mental anemia and physical fatigue when the day arrives. So we fail to do what we had intended to do in a more enthusiastic moment.

Emotions mislead us. One day shines with promise as we bounce out of bed in song, while the next day dims in despair and we'd prefer to hide under the bedcovers. One moment we forgive, the next we harbor resentment.

The emotional roller-coaster thrusts us into mood changes and affects what we do, what we say, and the attitudes that define us.

It has been said that faith is the bird that feels the light and sings to greet the dawn while it is still dark. The Bible instructs us to live by faith—not by feelings. Faith assures us that daylight will dawn in our darkest moments, affirming God's presence so that even when we fail to pray and positive feelings fade, our moods surrender to song.

Heavenly Father, I desire for my faith not my
emotions to dictate my life. I pray for balance
in my hide-under-the-cover days so that I
might surrender to You in song. Amen.

Sibling Rivalry

*"Let there be no fighting between you and me. . .for we are
brothers. . . . Let each of us go a different way. If you go to the left,
then I will go to the right. Or if you go to the right, then I will go to the left."*

GENESIS 13:8–9

God led Abram (later Abraham) to the land of Canaan. Abram
responded by giving half of the land away.

Faithful, responsible Abram brought his nephew Lot with
him to Canaan. Problems arose because the land couldn't
support both men's herds. Abraham let Lot choose where he
wanted to settle. Lot, unlike his uncle, thought first of himself.
He chose the well-watered plain by the Jordan River.

Abram recognized the problem. Their employees were argu-
ing over the land. He proposed a radical solution. He gave
away what was rightfully his, and he let Lot choose first. Even
though he ran the risk of getting the less desirable land, he did
it anyhow.

Abram exemplifies the kind of love that should exist among
Christians. Jesus said we would be known by our love. But
loving others doesn't mean that disagreements will not arise.
From the Greek widows in the Jerusalem church to the quar-
relsome women at Philippi, early Christians had to learn how
to get along.

When faced with disagreements, do we dig our feet into the
ground and refuse to budge? Or do we put our desires second?
Much bitterness among Christians could be avoided if we said,
"You choose first. I will accept your decision."

Heavenly Father, You have adopted us into Your
family. Teach us to live together as brothers
and sisters, united in Your love. Amen.

Hold On

*"But hold on to the Lord your God,
as you have done to this day."*
JOSHUA 23:8

Life is the moment—the here and now—yet we spend much of our time outside of that moment worried about, focused on, and trying to figure out the next hour, the next day, week, or month. *Where will the money for this come from? Where will I be next year? How will my children turn out?*

Life comes at us fast, and we have to take each challenge as it comes. Sometimes there are so many variables to juggle that we just want to give up. Don't let go—hold on. The enemy of your soul *wants* you to quit. You've gotten this far in your faith believing that God will keep His promises and help you reach your destiny.

When you don't think you can take another step—don't! Just hold on. Tomorrow will give you a fresh start with the strength you need to go a little further and hold on a little longer. Take a deep breath, get a fresh grasp on your faith, and don't let go. God will help you get to your dream.

Lord, help me to hold fast to You. With You
by my side, I can make it through all the
circumstances of life no matter how tough they
seem. I trust You to help me hold on. Amen.

Running the Race

All these many people who have had faith in God are around us like a cloud. Let us put every thing out of our lives that keeps us from doing what we should. Let us keep running in the race that God has planned for us. Let us keep looking to Jesus. Our faith comes from Him and He is the One Who makes it perfect.

HEBREWS 12:1–2

The Christian life is a race. It must be run with endurance. It requires training and discipline. It is about putting one foot in front of the other, sometimes quickly, sometimes slowly, but always, always moving forward. When a runner stumbles in a 5K or marathon, what does he do? Does he just sit down right then and there and call it quits? If the race is not run with perfection, does he just throw in the towel? Of course not! Likewise, as you are running the race, when you get side-tracked or distracted, when you fall to temptation or take your eyes off the goal, ask Jesus to get you back on track. An old hymn puts it like this: "Turn your eyes upon Jesus. Look full in His wonderful face. And the things of earth will grow strangely dim, in the light of His glory and grace!" Look to Christ, the author and finisher of your faith. He will run right alongside you, encouraging you every step of the way.

Jesus, help me to keep my focus on You as
I journey through this life. It is not always
easy, but You are always with me. Amen.

Hold God's Hand

*"For I am the Lord your God Who holds your right hand,
and Who says to you, 'Do not be afraid. I will help you.'"*
ISAIAH 41:13

It is a typical Saturday in a suburban neighborhood. The sun is shining brightly. A dad runs alongside his six-year-old daughter's bicycle, holding on to the back to reassure her she won't topple. Cheering on the bike rider from the porch, the little girl's mother holds the hands of a toddler son and helps him climb up and down the porch steps. He does it again and again. It is a new accomplishment for him, and it is fun! A couple of doors down, a grandfather holds the hands of one of his twin grandsons. The boys are taking turns being swung around in the air. They laugh and grow dizzy, falling over in the soft green grass, but they always come back for more. Children reach out for a hand many, many times each day. It is good for them to have a hand to hold as streets are crossed or steep steps are climbed. Often, a child wants to hold a trusted adult's hand simply for comfort or companionship. God offers you a hand in much the same manner. You are His child. Take His hand today. He will walk with you wherever you go. If you let Him, He will even lead the way.

Lord, thank You for holding my hand as I face challenges
in my life. It helps to know You are with me. I will
not be afraid for my God goes with me. Amen.

"Doing Life" Together

*Iron is made sharp with iron, and one
man is made sharp by a friend.*
PROVERBS 27:17

Many churches encourage members to become part of a home group or community group. These groups are known by different names. One church refers to them (appropriately!) as *life groups.* While certainly there is nothing new about Bible study classes, which have been around for centuries, this idea of *doing life together* throughout the week is new to some believers. For some, studying the Bible, prayer, and worship have long been isolated to Sundays. Setting aside the Sabbath is a start, but God desires that Christians live and grow in community with one another throughout the week, not just when they enter the church building. Believers grow and challenge one another when they meet together regularly. We become closer to God when we open up and allow other believers to pray for us. Home groups in some churches have bonded so deeply that when a member is sick, other members will provide meals or care for the person's children if needed. As relationships are formed, it becomes possible to speak into one another's lives in love. Christians need one another. As iron sharpens iron, so one believer sharpens another. When you have been with brothers and sisters in Christ, it will show in your countenance and it will alter your interactions with those around you who don't know the Lord. There is no limit to the benefits of meeting together for prayer, encouragement, and the study of God's Word.

Father, help me to find a community of believers within my church with whom to connect and "do life." Amen.

Dog Breath

"These are smoke in My nose,
a fire that burns all the day."
ISAIAH 65:5

There is nothing like the sense of smell to give information that needs no explanation. Mothers learned a long time ago that smells like cigarette smoke can easily give away an experimenting preteen who was out "doing nothing" with friends. It only takes a few minutes of talking with someone to know if she ate Italian, Greek, or Chinese food for lunch. For decades, doctors have known that certain breath odors are associated with diseases like diabetes. Some think dog breath surpasses morning mouth in repugnance, but dogs may have something to say about that.

Dogs can detect cancer by smelling people's breath. For some years researchers have been studying how dogs can sniff out cancer. People who have used canines in human cancer detection postulate that it is the waste products produced by cancer cells that dogs can readily identify.

In the Bible, neither cancer nor spicy food stinks to God. Disobedience to His way and resting in our own self-righteousness repel Him. The cancer of sin is a stench to our gracious God. If we want to please Him, we must live lives of submissive love as Christ did—that's a pleasing fragrance to the divine sense of smell (Ephesians 5:2).

I pray, Lord, that my life will be
a sweet aroma to You. Amen.

The End in Mind

The people said to Joshua, "We will serve the Lord our God. We will obey His voice." So Joshua made an agreement with the people that day. And he made Laws for them in Shechem.

JOSHUA 24:24–25

The college chaplain stood at the podium and looked out across the seated students and faculty. It was the first day of classes and everyone was assembled together. Excitement mixed with nervousness was on the students' faces—especially the incoming freshmen. The chaplain glanced at his notes, cleared his throat, and then introduced his talk in six simple words: "Begin with the end in mind."

He went on to speak about the school's history and the beliefs they professed, but then he quickly went back to his introduction.

"Knowledge is good," he stated. "You'll be challenged and learn while you're here. But even if you have all the knowledge in the world, at the end of the day, what is the point of having it? Your job is to be a student, but your *first* job is to serve God—now."

As we go about our day doing whatever exciting or mundane activities we do, it is easy to lose focus and forget that our first priority is to serve God. In each action, our service and attitudes can reflect Christ—the Beginning and the End.

God, help me to reflect You in all I do. Amen.

Stop and Consider

*"Hear this, O Job. Stop and think about the great works of God.
Do you know how God does them, and makes the lightning shine
from His cloud? Do you know how the clouds are set in heaven,
the great works of Him Who is perfect in understanding?"*

JOB 37:14–16

On a late summer morning, as the sun streamed through the window, Charlotte sat at her desk and stopped for a moment. She heard a radio blasting a popular song through the hallway, muffled sounds of her daughter talking on her cell phone in her bedroom, the washing machine rumbling in the laundry room.

Today the sounds of an ordinary morning caught at her heart. Charlotte knew it wouldn't last. Change was coming. Her daughter would be leaving for college soon, and those noises would move with her. It wasn't that Charlotte couldn't accept change. It was just that for one moment she stopped, paused, and really soaked up the sweet ordinariness of family life. *Too rare, too rare.*

"Stop and think about my great works," God told Job. Then He pointed to ordinary observations of the natural world surrounding Job—the clouds that hung poised in the sky, the flashes of lightning. "Not so very ordinary" was God's lesson. Maybe He was trying to remind us that there is no such thing as ordinary. Let's open our eyes and see the wonders around us.

O Father, teach me to stop and consider the
ordinary moments of my life as reminders of
You. Help me not to overlook Your daily care and
provisions that surround my day. Amen.

Build for Today

"Build houses and live in them. Plant gardens and eat their fruit."
JEREMIAH 29:5

Skeptics sometimes accuse Christians of being so heavenly minded that they are no earthly good. Today few of us would sell all our earthly possessions and camp out on a hilltop, waiting for the Lord's return. However, we still often live in "Tomorrowland."

Tomorrow, we think, *we will serve God more fully, after our children are grown and we have more time. Tomorrow we will give more, after we have paid off the car and saved enough for a down payment on a house. Tomorrow we will study the Bible more, after we no longer work full-time.*

Jeremiah's audience, Jews deported from their homeland to Babylon, knew all about Tomorrowland. They said, "Soon God will return us to our homes. As soon as that happens, we will serve God." They lived with their suitcases packed, ready to return.

God sent a stern message through His prophet Jeremiah. "You're going to be there a long time. Put down roots where I have sent you."

God sends the same message to us. He wants us to live for today. We can't allow dreams for tomorrow to paralyze our lives today.

God's presence enables us to live in the present.

Dear Heavenly Father, You have given us the gift of today. You want us to plant gardens and make homes. Show us joy and fulfillment in the present. Amen.

Don't Be Anxious?

*Do not worry. Learn to pray about everything. Give
thanks to God as you ask Him for what you need.*

PHILIPPIANS 4:6

Today's world does not make worry-free living easy. With all our commitments and responsibilities, stress tends to overwhelm us. Instead of putting things into perspective, we let our anxieties spiral out of control. Often we rely on our own means to solve problems, accomplish interminable to-do lists, and balance overfull lives. When we trust in ourselves to deal with life's pressures, we become bogged down, weary, and disheartened.

In this verse, Paul urges his readers not to be anxious about anything. Instead, he writes that we should present all of our requests—with expressions of gratitude—to God. We find these words extremely challenging to integrate into our daily lives. *Don't be anxious? Be thankful instead?*

Paul was certainly familiar with trials. His words to the Philippians are actually written from jail. Undoubtedly, he could have succumbed to anxiety and worry. Yet he writes to the Philippians with thanksgiving and joy. Paul knows that we will experience hardship and adversity. However, he has experienced the solace that comes from trusting God with every aspect of life. While this way of life is admittedly a challenge, Paul assures us that relying on God for all of our concerns—and giving thanks all the while—is both comforting and rewarding.

Dear Lord, thank You for Your Word. Teach me
to look to You in times of trouble. Let me always
give thanks for my experiences. Amen.

What Riches Do You Possess?

Tell those who are rich in this world not to be proud and not to trust in their money. Money cannot be trusted. They should put their trust in God. He gives us all we need for our happiness.

1 TIMOTHY 6:17

Brick facades and sprawling landscapes adorned every house in the community. The neighborhood was known for their lavish living, and the neighbors socialized in the craft of one-upmanship. If one neighbor installed an in-ground pool, it wasn't long before the other neighbors did too. If one erected an elaborate gazebo, others were sure to follow.

A quote from Benjamin Franklin reads, "He does not possess wealth that allows wealth to possess him." The more we labor for "things," the more "things" take priority and govern our lifestyles.

God desires to bless us with possessions we can enjoy. But it displeases Him when His children strain to attain riches in a worldly manner out of pride or a compulsion to flaunt. Riches are uncertain, but faith in God to meet our provisions is indicative of the pure in heart.

Pride diminishes the capacity for humility and trust in God. We are rich indeed when our hope and faith are not in what we have but in whom we trust.

Heavenly Father, my hope is in You for my needs
and my desires. I surrender any compulsion
to attain earthly wealth; rather, may I be rich
in godliness and righteousness. Amen.

Pride vs. Humility

A man's pride will bring him down, but he whose spirit is without pride will receive honor.

PROVERBS 29:23

A great leader is known by his or her character. It is perhaps the things that one doesn't take part in that sets him or her apart. Great leaders are not prideful or boastful. They don't consider their accomplishments to be things they have done "in and of themselves," but they recognize the hand of God on their lives. Great leaders know that it takes a team to reach a goal. A great CEO treats the lowest man on the totem pole with as much dignity as he treats an equal. A great school principal knows that the teachers, assistants, bus drivers, and cafeteria workers make a huge impact on the students and the climate of the school. No one likes a bragger. It gets old hearing anyone go on and on about themselves. The Bible is filled with the teaching that the low shall be made higher and the proud will be brought to destruction. Take note of the areas of your own life where pride may sneak in and destroy. Replace pride with humility. Others will notice. You will not go unrewarded when you seek to be humble in spirit.

Father, root out any pride that You find in my heart and replace it with humility, I ask. Amen.

Work as Unto God

Whatever work you do, do it with all your heart.
Do it for the Lord and not for men.
COLOSSIANS 3:23

Whatever you do today, work as if you are working for the Lord rather than for man. What does that mean? For the employee, it means work as if God is your supervisor. He does see and hear everything you do. When you are tempted to slack off, remember that the Bible warns against idleness. When you are tempted to grumble about your boss, remember that God has put you under this person's authority—at least for this time. For the stay-at-home wife or mother, it means that even changing a diaper or washing dishes can be done for the glory of God. This verse has to do with attitude. Are you working in the right spirit? Work is not a bad thing. God created work. God Himself worked in order to create the earth in six days. And on the seventh, He looked at the work of His hands and He rested. Consider your work a blessing. If you are employed, remember today that many are without jobs. If you are able to stay at home with your children and keep your house, keep in mind that many are not able to do so for one reason or another. Whatever you do, work as if you are working for God.

Lord, help me to remember that I am working for You and not for man. You are my eternal reward. I want to please You in all that I set out to accomplish. Amen.

Where Do You Walk?

*I can have no greater joy than to hear that
my children are following the truth.*

3 JOHN 1:4

If the apostle Paul delighted in seeing his spiritual children walk in truth, how much more must God appreciate those who devotedly follow Him! He too wants those who love Him to walk in His ways.

Wouldn't all Christians naturally follow close on Jesus' heels? After all, doesn't the same salvation affect them all? Would anyone want to be a hair's breadth farther from Jesus than they need be?

In an ideal Christian world, that would be true—and it will be so in eternity. But while we remain on earth, sin easily tempts us. Our hearts are more prone to wander than we'd like to admit. Unfortunately, sin often sticks to us and holds us back from God.

That's just why believers must continually resist sin's hold and draw near to Jesus. He has opened the doors of forgiveness for every believer who habitually confesses the sticky sin that pulls her or him away from God. Again and again, we can turn to our Lord for a new lease on the new life.

As we habitually turn to God, sin's grip loosens. The goop sticks less, and God sticks more.

> Cleanse me, Lord, from the goop of sin,
> and help me stick to You alone. Amen.

In the Image of God

God saw all that He had made and it was very good.

GENESIS 1:31

God started with light, and His finishing touch was mankind. He created the heavens and the earth and everything in them. God was pleased with His creation. After He created the ocean and dry land, the plants and animals, He said that it was all *good*. But then He created man, and He said this was *very* good. Mankind is different from all of the rest of God's creation. We have intellect beyond that of animals. We have souls. We are made in the image of God. He is creative. We have a bit of creativity within us. Each of us is unique, and our creativity is displayed in a variety of ways. He is loving. We are capable of love. We are His children, and we are to reflect who He is. Just as a child looks somewhat like their earthly parents, we bear God's image. We are to look like our heavenly Father. When others listen to you, do they know that you are a child of the King of kings? When they look at how you carry yourself, do they see humility and confidence? You are a child of the Creator of the universe. Made in His image, you represent Him on this earth.

Father, I am created in Your image. I am Your
child. Help me to live like it today. Help me to
reflect Your light in a dark world. Amen.

Encouraging Those Around You

*Pleasing words are like honey. They are sweet
to the soul and healing to the bones.*

PROVERBS 16:24

Are you an encourager? Are your words pleasant and cheerful when you enter a room? Do you find yourself talking mostly about yourself, or do you focus on the other person in the conversation? The tongue is a powerful thing. Words can encourage or discourage, build up or tear down. As you go throughout your day today, seek to be one whose words are sweet to the soul and healing to the bones as the writer of Proverbs describes. If you are in the workplace, take time to greet your coworkers with a genuine "Good morning." Be sure to truly listen for an answer when you use the phrase "How are you?" rather than moving on as if your question were rhetorical. You will find that while kind words encourage the person who receives them, speaking them to others will also bless you. You will feel good knowing that you have lifted someone's spirits or shared in their sorrow. You will begin to focus on others rather than going on and on about your own problems or plans. It has been said that conversation is an art. Hone your conversation skills this week. Speak words of encouragement, words of life that remind the hearer they are special to you and, more importantly, to God.

*Father, help me to speak life today. May my
words be pleasant, sweet, and healing. May my
conversations be pleasing to You. Amen.*

What Next?

If you do not have wisdom, ask God for it. He is always ready to give it to you and will never say you are wrong for asking.

JAMES 1:5

Ever been lost in an unfamiliar place? Trees block street signs, and other streets aren't marked at all; construction causes confusing, squiggly detours. Embarrassment or even panic grows as the minutes pass.

In life, we hit unexpected detours that make us unsure where to turn next. They might be difficult decisions involving family, health care, jobs, or relationships at church. Maybe the weight is migrating from the tension in your shoulders to settle in your heart.

The good news is that our heavenly Father knows the way out of our confusion and will help us when we are at our most frantic. James tells us that God promises to give wisdom to those who ask for it in faith; He's "always ready to give it" and he will never reprimand you for asking. Sometimes it's intimidating to ask for advice from others, but God doesn't look down on us for admitting our weakness. He chooses to lavish His love and His gifts on error-prone people because they are a part of His family in Christ. We can entrust ourselves and our lives to our heavenly Father, knowing that through Christ, we have access to "all the riches of wisdom and understanding" that our Savior possesses (Colossians 2:3).

Dear heavenly Father, thank You that You have my days planned out for me and I am safe in Your hands. Please grant me wisdom when I am at a loss and help my spirit be sensitive to Your Spirit's leading. Amen.

Lady Wisdom Gives Directions

Does not wisdom call? Does not understanding raise her voice? She takes her stand on the top of the hill beside the way, where the paths meet.

PROVERBS 8:1–2

Wisdom. The very term sounds outdated, a concept hiding in musty, dusty caverns of the past. Has it anything to do with real life?

Many answer, "No, especially in a new millennium!"

But biblical wisdom, crafted by God before the earth existed, remains as fresh and powerful as its Creator. In the book of Proverbs, God personifies wisdom as a godly woman who does not hesitate to let her voice be heard. She stands atop a high hill "where the paths meet," at busy intersections, trying to help travelers find their way. But they rush past Wisdom, most talking into cell phones glued to their ears. Business meetings must start on time. Carpools must follow schedules. Bills must be paid. The travelers hardly notice Wisdom as they scurry past her. Focused on themselves, they make their deadlines and achieve their goals. Most do not realize they are completely lost.

Wisdom longs to make a difference in their stressful existence that leads to destruction. She never stops sharing her vital message: Whoever heeds God's instruction gains more than silver, gold, or rubies. His truth, His directions lead listeners to life.

Father, help us shake off the hypnotizing
effects of our culture's values and listen to Your
wisdom. Give us courage to share with others
who desperately need Your truth. Amen.

Not Flying Solo

*We are His work. He has made us to belong to Christ Jesus so
we can work for Him. He planned that we should do this.*

EPHESIANS 2:10

Sometimes when we think about doing "God's work," self-doubt can get the better of us. We tell ourselves that we aren't smart or skilled enough; we remember all our skipped prayer times and say, "The Lord wouldn't want to use me since I've been ignoring Him. Besides, my work probably isn't worth that much anyway in the big picture, *if* I don't completely mess up."

In Ephesians 2, Paul emphasizes that we weren't saved because of anything we had to offer, but we received God's gift of salvation through faith. He made us anew in Christ "so we can work for Him"; we can't brag about deserving salvation, and we can't brag about our good works being our big idea either! God planned them for us ahead of time to fit in with His perfect plan.

We may fear that our errors will "ruin" what God has going on. Consider that the work itself is a gift—the all-powerful Creator chooses to use us—ordinary believers—to accomplish mighty things. Throughout the Bible, we read stories of unremarkable people doing amazing things for the Lord because they trusted in His strength to do them. If God has work for us, we can have confidence that He will equip us for the job, no matter the challenges ahead.

Father God, please strengthen me to do the work You
have planned for me. Help me to depend on Your
ability and strength when I doubt myself. Amen.

Peace through Prayer

Do not worry. Learn to pray about everything. Give thanks to God as you ask Him for what you need. The peace of God is much greater than the human mind can understand. This peace will keep your hearts and minds through Christ Jesus.

PHILIPPIANS 4:6–7

Some days it is easy to be thankful. We nearly bubble over with thanksgiving. These are mountaintop days—a graduation day, a wedding, or a reunion with old friends. The day comes to a close, and we whisper a prayer. It flows easily off the tongue. "Thank You, God," we say, "for a perfect day."

There are days when thankfulness is not as natural, not as easy. These are valley days—in the hospital room, at the graveside, or when we are distraught about a relationship or work issue. It is in these times that the Father wants us to give Him our burdens through prayer. It seems impossible to be thankful for the pain, the confusion, or the longings in our lives. We can be thankful, though, that we have a loving heavenly Father who stands ready to help.

The peace of God cannot be explained. It cannot be bought. The world cannot give it to us. But when we release our cares to the Lord in prayer, His peace washes over us and fills our hearts and minds. What a comfort is the peace of God when we find ourselves in the valley.

Sovereign God, You are the same yesterday, today, and tomorrow. You are with me through the good and the bad. Draw near to me, and replace my worry with Your peace. Amen.

Savoring the Word

But Jesus said, "It is written, 'Man is not to live on bread only. Man is to live by every word that God speaks.'"
MATTHEW 4:4

Casseroles are veiled in gently rising steam; Jell-O salads wobble temptingly. Like a net, the smell of fresh rolls draws the guests to the table. Potlucks are meals of chance, roulette for the taste buds. The strategic guest fills her plate with a small bite of everything. There are surprises—what everyone thought was lemon meringue turned out to be a gelatinous banana pudding, while an untouched sauce swelled with savory, meaty flavors.

Studying the Bible's sixty-six books can feel like a potluck, and our reading habits might be picky too. The Psalms and Proverbs might be sweet and easy to read, but the book of Numbers might have the attraction of week-old dry bread. The "good stuff" gets scooped up and the other books are overlooked.

As unsavory as they might seem, don't be so quick to pass on challenging sections of the Bible. Jesus said that men and women live by *every* word that proceeds from the mouth of God, not just some of them. Unlike a hit-or-miss potluck dish, all of scripture is meant for the Christian's nourishment (Romans 15:4). Seek the Father as you chew on the book of Judges or contemplate the life of the prophet Ezekiel. All His Word is sweet when you can see Him in it.

Father God, thank You for Your entire Word. Please open my eyes to see You and Your goodness in the difficult passages and to spend time with You daily. Amen.

Phone Home

"Because when I called, you did not answer. I spoke,
but you did not hear. You did what was sinful in
My eyes, and chose what did not please Me."

ISAIAH 65:12

Cindy and her husband packed up their son for his first year away at college. The university their son chose was several states and over a thousand miles from home. They would not be seeing their firstborn for several months.

Cindy called her son, Matt, a day or so after he arrived on campus. She didn't hear back from him. She called again a day later. Still no response. By the third day with no word from the freshman, she left her final message.

"This is your mother. If you don't call back within the hour, your phone will be turned off."

Cindy got a call back within minutes.

Does God have to threaten shutting heaven to our prayers because we refuse to listen when He calls us? Do we turn on the television when we sense a need to pray for a missionary overseas? Do we continue loading the dishwasher when our daughter says, "Watch me, Mom"? Do we pick up a magazine when we should call a lonely friend or elderly aunt? Are we sometimes guilty of choosing what God doesn't delight in?

Tasks must be done and recreation does rest us, but prioritizing the important over the urgent shows our Father that we are listening for Him and to Him.

> Father, give me the hearing and the heart
> to recognize Your call to me. Amen.

Hold On!

*Do not let yourselves get tired of doing good. If we do not
give up, we will get what is coming to us at the right time.*

GALATIANS 6:9

Have you ever felt that God abandoned you? Have the difficulties in your life pressed you to physical and mental exhaustion? Do you feel your labor is in vain and no one appreciates the sacrifices you have made?

When Elijah fled for his life in fear of Jezebel's wrath, depression and discouragement tormented him. Exhausted, he prayed for God to take his life, and then he fell asleep. When he awoke, God sent an angel with provisions to strengthen his weakened body. Only then was he able to hear God's revelation that provided the direction and assistance he needed.

God hears our pleas even when He seems silent. The problem is that we cannot hear Him because of physical and mental exhaustion. Rest is key to our restoration.

Just when the prophet thought he could go on no longer, God provided the strength, peace, and encouragement to continue. He does the same for us today. When we come to the end of our rope, God ties a knot. And like Elijah, God will do great things in and through us if we will just hold on.

Dear Lord, help me when I can no longer help myself.
Banish my discouragement, and give me the rest and
restoration I need so that I might hear Your voice. Amen.

Sharper Than a Scalpel

God's Word is living and powerful. It is sharper than a sword that cuts both ways. It cuts straight into where the soul and spirit meet and it divides them. It cuts into the joints and bones. It tells what the heart is thinking about and what it wants to do.

HEBREWS 4:12

A Southeast Asian missionary translated Hebrews 4:12 as "the Word of God is living and active and sharper than any bush knife." His Indonesian colleague read the verse and wept, not because the translation was inaccurate, but because he was moved by the power of the metaphor. A bush knife was used to clear weeds from a field so that a farmer could plant and reap a harvest for his family. The bush knife needed to be sharp to cut away intrusive growth. He copied down the translation and quickly ran home to share the passage with his family.

Geoffrey, a member of a U.S. congregation, was asked how he would translate Hebrews 4:12 for today's culture. He replied, "The Word of God is sharper than a scalpel." What a perfect metaphor. The scalpel, used by doctors to remove harmful tissues and cancers, cuts with precision, just as the Word of God cuts with precision, removing damaging aspects of our interior spiritual life and allowing space for holy habits to replace ungodly ones.

Heavenly Father, use Your Word like a scalpel
to perform surgery on my heart. Cut away the
cancerous sin and make me holy within. Amen.

A Better Offer

*"Do for other people whatever you
would like to have them do for you."*

MATTHEW 7:12

"I need to cancel plans on Friday because I have the opportunity to go out of town with friends," Anne said. Marsha felt rejected, unloved, and inconsequential again as Anne canceled their weekly prayer and Bible study time because a better offer came along.

"At least," Marsha thought, "she didn't cancel on me this time because she needed to get her nails done."

How do you treat friends, colleagues, and acquaintances? Do you remain committed to your responsibilities? What are your priorities? Do you take on more than you can handle? Do you not give 100 percent to a task or relationship?

Jesus took responsibilities, commitments, and obligations seriously. In fact, Jesus said, "Let your yes be YES. Let your no be NO. Anything more than this comes from the devil" (Matthew 5:37). Satan desires for us to be stressed out, overcommitted, and not able to do anything well. Satan delights when we treat others in an unkind, offensive manner. However, God, upon request, will help us prioritize our commitments so that our "yes" is "yes" and our "no" is "no." Then in everything we do, we are liberated to do to others as we would have them do to us.

Lord, please prioritize my commitments to
enable me in everything to do to others as I
would desire for them to do to me. Amen.

Entering His Rest

And so God's people have a complete rest waiting for them. The man who goes into God's rest, rests from his own work the same as God rested from His work.

HEBREWS 4:9–10

What is the ideal way to practice the Sabbath? Christian brothers and sisters have given as many answers to that question as there are ways to spend the day. The Bible teaches that the Sabbath is for resting from the work and cares of the week just like the Father modeled for us when He created the world (Genesis 2:2–3).

In Hebrews, however, Sabbath-rest takes on another meaning. The writer of Hebrews exhorts his readers to "enter God's rest" and to "rest from their works." In the letter's context, this rest is a peace that goes *heart-deep*. Instead of fretting that we are not right with God, we point to Christ's perfect life and work, trusting in Him alone to be accepted in God's sight.

Just as God declared that His creation was perfect and complete ("very good") on the seventh day, Christ pronounced His saving work to be perfect and complete ("It is finished") on the cross. We can approach our Creator boldly and without fear of rejection, resting in the knowledge that we are fully pleasing in His sight because of His Son. We do not have to work to be worthy. We can rest in Him.

Dear heavenly Father, help me rest in the work Your Son did to save me. Deepen my faith so that Your peace and Your truth will answer my worrying heart when I fear I am unworthy to be Your child. Amen.

Well-Watered

"The Lord will always lead you. He will meet the needs of your soul in the dry times and give strength to your body. You will be like a garden that has enough water, like a well of water that never dries up."

ISAIAH 58:11

The county restrictions allowed for watering only twice a week. It just wasn't enough. His carefully tended acre—once lush, green, and profuse with color and variety—was now brown and crunchy underfoot. The blooms hung limp, pale, and dehydrated. He couldn't ignore the living word picture this was to his own spiritual life. For months now, he'd actually only watered her spirit with Sunday morning sermons. He too felt lifeless and dried up from the stresses that weighed on him—too many demands, a frenzied sprint from place to place, poor nutrition from grabbing unhealthy foods on the run, no margin to properly rest or enjoy life.

He needed a downpour of God's Word and the Holy Spirit's presence in his parched spirit. Not an occasional sprinkle but a soul soaking to replenish his frazzled body and weary mind. He knew this soaking came from consistent Bible study, the necessary pruning of confessed sin, and prayer time. These produce a well-watered garden, fruitful and lush, mirroring God's beauty, creating a life to which others are drawn to come and linger in His refreshing presence.

Eternal Father, strengthen my frame, guide my paths, and satisfy my needs as only You can. Make my life a well-watered garden, fruitful for You and Your purposes. Amen.

Reflecting (on) Christ's Beauty

All of us, with no covering on our faces, show the shining-greatness of the Lord as in a mirror. All the time we are being changed to look like Him, with more and more of His shining-greatness. This change is from the Lord Who is the Spirit.

2 CORINTHIANS 3:18

What are you thinking about? Careful. The act of contemplation is powerful. Why else would teachers chide students when their attention is anywhere but on the lesson? Their daydreams about recess won't fuel their brains for mathematics. Contemplation is a moral and transformative action too. Contemplating the difficulties of a relationship could sway a person's commitment; contemplating wealth (or the lack thereof) can create heart-sinking envy. We pay attention to what we care about; what we care about shapes and changes us.

Throughout scripture, Christians are called to "keep looking to Jesus" (Hebrews 12:1–2). Here in 2 Corinthians, Paul writes about contemplating Jesus' glory—the Greek word translated into English as "contemplate" means both "to meditate upon" and "to reflect." Dwelling on Christ's life *transforms us* into being more like Him.

Thinking on Jesus means to meditate on the truth we believe about Him. The Word shows us a Savior who gave up His holy, perfect life to restore the undeserving to Himself, who rose again victorious over death! The Holy Spirit enables us to reflect Jesus' loving, sacrificial character in "ever-increasing" measure as we know and love Him better. As God's children, let us know our Savior deeply and reflect Him more and more!

Father God, when my mind wanders, teach me to turn my attention again to Christ and His beauty. Let me know Him better so I can show Him better to others. Amen.

With a Song on His Lips

The Lord your God is with you, a Powerful One Who wins the battle. He will have much joy over you. With His love He will give you new life. He will have joy over you with loud singing.
ZEPHANIAH 3:17

Our relationships with our earthly fathers can greatly affect how we view our heavenly Father. Whether consciously or not, we take the earthly father we can see and try to puzzle out what our heavenly Father is like. Some women had attentive, loving fathers. If only this were the norm! Some fathers were absent, never known to their daughters. Other fathers violated the family's trust through abuse or neglect. Some fathers were caring but distant—emotional connection difficult or nonexistent.

Where our earthly fathers have fallen short, our heavenly Father does all perfectly and to the full. He is full of mercy, full of loving-kindness, absolutely just and right. He brings order where there is disorder, peace instead of confusion. He heals bodies and broken hearts, and He keeps all His promises.

Though the Father rules over the whole universe, He is also close to us. He does not love us at arm's length, His disapproval looming if we misstep. He *sings* and rejoices over His children; He *delights* in that we belong to Him. The love of our great God surpasses all earthly love in its perfection, its sacrifice, its provision, and its salvation. Regardless of our family backgrounds, our Creator perfectly loves and delights in us.

Father God, I am astounded that You delight in me and sing joyfully over me. Show me Your love and I'll sing back to You in praise! Amen.

Listening to God's Voice

"Today you have said that the Lord is your God, and that you will walk in His ways, keep all His Laws, and listen to His voice."
DEUTERONOMY 26:17

What would have happened had Moses been less than an excellent listener? Would Israel's tabernacle have ended up a cubit short on one side? Would Israel's burnt offerings have turned out medium-rare? Would Moses have written down only nine of God's Ten Commandments?

While Moses was on Mount Sinai, God gave him detailed instructions on how the children of Israel were to live and to worship. God gave Moses the law, including the Ten Commandments, a blueprint for the tabernacle, and the method by which He would receive Israel's sacrifices. Listening carefully was of utmost importance, for God told Moses to tell Israel: "Now then, if you will obey My voice and keep My agreement, you will belong to Me from among all nations. For all the earth is Mine" (Exodus 19:5).

Developing good listening habits is as important for Christians today as it was for Moses and all the other biblical patriarchs. It takes practice and time alone with God to hear His unique voice. God has much to say to us if we will listen carefully.

> Dear Lord, teach me to listen well so
> that I may learn obedience and not
> miss Your blessings in my life. Amen.

Yet Praise Him

*Why are you sad, O my soul? Why have you become
troubled within me? Hope in God, for I will yet
praise Him, my help and my God.*

PSALM 42:11

Many individuals and prayer groups use the acronym ACTS to guide their prayers. The letters stand for Adoration, Confession, Thanksgiving, and Supplication. Note that adoration comes first, before the believer confesses sin, thanks God, or asks anything of Him. God delights in His children's praise and adoration.

If you have cared for a child, you have probably received genuine adoration at times as well as times of appreciation in response to something you have done for her or him. Which warms your heart more? Certainly it means more to be held in high esteem simply because of who you are in the child's life than to be told "I love you" when you hand out dollar bills or promise a trip to the zoo!

Imagine how God feels when one of His children praises Him simply for who He is, even when their circumstances are far from perfect. Don't you suppose it feels like a tight hug around His neck? A "just because" sort of hug, not the "I got something from you" sort.

Praise God regardless. Praise Him *yet*, as the psalmist did. Adore Him today, for He is God.

Father, You are the great I Am, faithful and good.
I adore You. I choose to praise You whether You
alter my circumstances or not. Amen.

Don't Bite the Apple!

"First of all, look for the holy nation of God. Be right with Him. All these other things will be given to you also."

MATTHEW 6:33

Satan vehemently opposes God's will. As we desire to draw close to the Lord, Satan pulls in the opposite direction. He attempts to dissuade us from seeking the Lord at the beginning of each day. He whispers subtle lies, hoping that we will take the bite.

Temptingly, he says, "You can have a quiet time after you finish watching this episode" or "You can read your Bible tonight after work." If we choose to embrace those lies, we know how the scenario usually plays itself out. The quiet time or Bible reading never happens. Satan has deceived us once again. We have taken one step in his direction instead of the Lord's.

We must be on guard against Satan's covert tactics. Each morning upon rising, we must purpose to put the Lord first. When we do, the Lord prioritizes our day and stretches our time. He helps us accomplish what we must and let go of what we should. Satan is defeated. We experience victory. The Lord is glorified.

The Lord desires to walk close by our side throughout the day. In order for that to happen, we must seek Him first in the morning. Refuse to give credence to other options. Believe God's truth and don't bite the apple!

Dear Lord, help me seek You at the beginning of each day. Protect me from Satan's lies that would tempt me to do otherwise. May I bring glory to You today. Amen.

Basic Math

Jesus said, "The one who loves Me will obey My teaching. My Father will love him. We will come to him and live with him."

JOHN 14:23

If you disliked math in school, perhaps at some point you asked, *How will I ever use it in real life?*

A certain kind of relational math is fundamental to your daily life. The words and actions exchanged throughout your day add to or take away from your life and the lives of those around you. Are you a positive or negative force? Are those around you positive or negative influences in your life?

God's nature is to give—to add—to every life He encounters. As Christians, we are created in His image and should be positive influences on those around us each day. Look around you and determine who adds to your life and who takes away. You will probably find that you prefer to spend time with pleasant communicators. Words of anger, frustration, confusion, and jealousy take away from the spirit of a man, but words of affirmation and gestures of kindness add to every heart.

Think before you act. Consider your words before you speak. Will you be adding to that person or taking away with what you are about to say or do? Share the love God shows you with others.

God, help me to think before I speak so that I can be a positive influence on others. Amen.

Judged!

*There was a woman in the city who was a sinner. . . . She brought
a jar of special perfume. Then she stood behind Him by His feet
and cried. Her tears wet His feet and she dried them with her
hair. She kissed His feet and put the special perfume on them.*

LUKE 7:37–38

What a beautiful story of repentance. Though we don't know
her name, we relate to this woman's loving testimony. How we
would like to be able to anoint Jesus with our love.

Had it been up to the Pharisee who shares the story with
her, we probably wouldn't know about the sinful woman. This
man who had invited Jesus to dinner missed the point of her
actions and began judging her and the Master who accepted her
loving gift. *Surely*, assumed the Pharisee, *a prophet would know
this woman is a sinner.*

This first-century Jew isn't alone in leaping to judgment.
Many churchgoers fall into the same trap. New people come to
our church and don't follow the rules. Maybe they don't dress
like everyone else or don't use the right spiritual jargon. In an
instant, we doubt their salvation.

But if they don't know Jesus, isn't this the right place for them
to be? Standing near Him, an unbeliever may come to faith—if
the people in God's congregation are loving and nurturing.

We need not judge a casual acquaintance's spiritual life—
God can do that. All we need to do is love, and He will bring
blessings.

Thank You, Lord, that Your first reaction to me
was love not condemnation. Turn my heart in
love to all who don't yet know You. Amen.

Wisdom in Action

And my God will give you everything you need because of His great riches in Christ Jesus.
PHILIPPIANS 4:19

Money. You could always use more no matter how hard you work or how much money you make. It is one of the biggest stresses in the world today. People worry about job security, growing debt, gas and food prices, and how to get ahead.

Sometimes when Christians express financial concerns, they hear well-meaning believers say, "Oh, Jesus is all you need." Really? When you truly have a need and you're doing all you know to do, is that really what you need to hear? What about a little wisdom, a little knowledge, a little understanding of how to find and experience a great place of peace in the middle of your need?

God has promised to supply all your needs, but it takes action on your part. Searching for wisdom for your situation and asking God to direct you in the right decisions will lead you down a path of financial success. It may be as simple as skipping dinners in nice restaurants so you can save money to purchase living room furniture with cash. We can all make better decisions if we put wisdom into action.

Lord, show me the wisdom of making good
decisions financially. Help me to choose wisely
when and where to spend or save. Amen.

Even the Little Things

"Only fear the Lord and be faithful to worship Him with all your heart. Think of the great things He has done for you."
1 SAMUEL 12:24

No one likes sweeping dust bunnies out from under the fridge, scrubbing grout, or filing taxes. Sometimes the boss will assign a grueling task, or worse, an extremely tedious one. It's tempting to expend the minimum effort required and get on with the better things in life. This can happen in relationships as well—we manage the minimum amount of closeness and small talk without any real depth or connection.

However, as God's children, we are called to a higher standard. Not just to "get things over with," but to do all things to His glory. Practically, this means doing our best in whatever task or goal we pursue, knowing that He is the final inspector of our work, tasks both big and small.

So, should we scurry to scour the oven until the metal squeaks for mercy? No, we don't work out of fear or out of cold duty (though sometimes those are the motives that compel us), but because we desire to please God, knowing how much He loves us. The way we do the "little things" reveals for whom we labor—for us? For our employers, family, or friends? We may benefit from our efforts, but ultimately our work is for our Father.

Father God, You see all of my work. Please forgive me for when I have complained, and help me do my best in everything and do it out of joy in You.

Asking for It

Tell your sins to each other. And pray for each other so you may be healed.
JAMES 5:16

Forgiveness is hard enough to grant, let alone to request. Taking responsibility for your mistakes and asking for mercy from the person you've offended are not easy things to do. It is especially difficult when you didn't know you'd hurt the person in the first place and they had to approach *you*.

Most people would rather make excuses for their behavior than own up to it. However, asking for forgiveness is one of the most powerful testimonies of your faith that you can demonstrate. When we ask for forgiveness, we acknowledge we have trampled the dignity of another human being. We admit that we have hurt God as well by sinning against a person He deeply loves. In asking for forgiveness, we humble ourselves and throw ourselves on mercy—the mercy of the person we've hurt and our Father's mercy.

It is a gift to be forgiven. Sometimes forgiveness is withheld—a "reasonable" human reaction to sin but painful nonetheless. Even if the person in question refuses to forgive you, you must do all you can to make peace, and then leave it in the Father's hands—He can bring peace where peace seems impossible. Take heart: if you have confessed your sin to the Father, He has forgiven you and will never hold that sin against you.

Father, help me to be humble and ask for forgiveness
from those whom I sin against. Thank You
for Your forgiveness that frees me to admit my
weakness and foolishness to others. Amen.

Prickly Love

"I give you a new Law. You are to love each other.
You must love each other as I have loved you."

JOHN 13:34

Tumbleweeds have a reputation of being an annoyance. They grow with little water. When they are mature, they break free of their roots in a wind and blow whichever direction the breeze takes them. They are full of little stickers that can poke into you or your car's radiator. If you walk too close to them, you can also get small, painful barbs in your skin.

One woman riding her bike had an accident and landed in the middle of a large tumbleweed. The plant was still a bit green, and she'd never seen one so close. To her amazement, in the midst of all the prickly parts were tiny, beautiful flowers. After she extricated herself, she bent close to examine the beauty she couldn't have noticed without getting close to the irascible plant.

Oftentimes people we meet in the workplace, store, or even in church have prickly exteriors. They grumble, complain, or are disagreeable in a number of ways. Jesus commanded us to love one another. When we take the time to get close to a person who is difficult, we can often see some small piece of beauty amid the orneriness. The willingness to love as Jesus loves is worth the risk of getting pierced by a word or an attitude.

Jesus, show me how to love the unlovable.
Help me to understand their attitude and to
emulate You, not those around me. Amen.

For the Beauty of the Earth

He loves what is right and good and what is fair.
The earth is full of the loving-kindness of the Lord.

PSALM 33:5

Summer. The best citrus fruits are in season, berries ripen, backyard gardens burst with productivity. God has placed such beauty in the spaces where we live, in the smallest leaf and bud, in the intricacies of root systems and the earthworm's travel. The fireflies flicker on night-covered lawns, praising their Creator by doing exactly what He designed them to do.

God shapes His children as well as His creation. He knew us when we were inside our mothers, knows us now in whatever size or shape or situation we find ourselves. The same Creator who lovingly crafted His world's diversity and wonder knows the diversity of His people, the gifts and talents He has bestowed upon us.

He looks and says, "My child, I made you and you are loved." He sees what His hands have knit together and loves us beyond words. He built us with inherent dignity, with an eternal soul unlike any other upon the earth.

Believe that He loves you—all of you, not in spite of you or only parts of you. He loved you so much that He sent His Son for you. You are just as vibrant with His beauty as the most brilliant scene in all creation.

Father God, help me see myself with Your
eyes and see the beauty You have put
in me and in others. Amen.

Powerful Prayer

Be full of joy all the time. Never stop praying. In everything give thanks. This is what God wants you to do because of Christ Jesus.
1 THESSALONIANS 5:16–18

Ever fallen asleep during prayer? Or have you ever told a friend you'd pray for her request and then completely forgotten about it until she brought it up again? We've all been there. Squirming inside, you listen to her update, and say, "Oh, yes, I'll keep praying for that." What makes prayer so hard?

We might feel intimidated to talk to a holy God, even though He invites us to tell Him about our lives and ask for what we need. Self-reproach and doubt can get in the way too; sometimes our prayers sound ridiculous to our ears, or we have been praying for the same request for so long that it doesn't seem like God will answer it. Or, we are worn out simply by the thought of the energy, focus, and humility required for prayer.

However, prayer is a discipline where sweetness and hard work flow together. God commands us to pray continually because prayer is an exercise in trust. We ask the Creator of the Universe to act on our behalf in faith that He *will* act—it is our faith that makes our prayers effective, not our eloquence.

Whatever your prayer life is or has been, approach God in faith. He is always ready to hear us, and His Spirit will give us the strength to pray (Romans 8:26–27).

Father God, give me strength to pray. I want
to be closer to You and to rely fully upon You.
Thank You for always listening. Amen.

Holy, Wholly

Be holy in every part of your life. Be like the Holy One Who chose you. The Holy Writings say, "You must be holy, for I am holy."
1 PETER 1:15–16

Holiness is one of the most difficult concepts to grasp about God because it is so foreign to us. He is unable to sin, set apart in glorious light. However, we can easily understand why Isaiah fell on his face when he beheld the Lord, feeling his sinfulness weighing heavy upon him (Isaiah 6:5).

Just as the angel cleansed Isaiah's lips, Christ made us His righteous, holy people (1 Peter 2:9). Because Christ has given us His holiness, we don't have to earn it ourselves. For Christians, pursuing holiness isn't fulfilling a set of rules in order to be accepted before God. Instead, it is a heart-deep desire to model our lives after our Savior's perfect example.

Though we are holy in Christ, we still struggle with sin in this life. Where is the Holy Spirit convicting you to practice holiness? Do you have trouble being kind in your words, spoken or unspoken? Are your thoughts filled with peace and thankfulness, or do you struggle with envy? Does the way you treat others honor Christ, especially folks who disagree with you or are different from you?

Don't be discouraged by how you fall short. Our Savior rewards His children who pursue holiness; He will give you grace to learn to practice His ways faithfully.

> Father God, thank You that Christ's holiness covers
> me. Show me the sins I've ignored so that I can
> be holy in my actions as You are holy. Amen.

Equipped for Good Work

All the Holy Writings are God-given and are made alive by Him. Man is helped when he is taught God's Word. It shows what is wrong. It changes the way of a man's life. It shows him how to be right with God. It gives the man who belongs to God everything he needs to work well for Him.

2 TIMOTHY 3:16–17

Have you thought, *How am I to accomplish this work?* Have you ever felt inadequate for the task set before you?

God gives us the aptitude and ability to do the work He leads us to. However, we may find it challenging at times because God is using the tasks to draw us in a closer relationship to Him through His Word. We are told that all of God's Word, the Bible, has the purpose of teaching, admonishing, correcting or modifying our behavior, and instructing us to be right with the Lord. Regardless of the type of work, God is enabling us to do the work He has purposed for us.

Therefore, it is important that we spend time in God's Word. We are to participate in Bible studies, worship God with fellow believers, and have a daily time of prayer and devotions. It is through these activities that we will become proficient, equipped for the good work God has planned for us. God's Word tells us we can trust Him to make us capable, adequate, prepared to do the good work we are destined to do for His kingdom.

Lord, I praise You that Your Word can mold me into
a being capable of carrying out Your good works.
Help me to consistently study Your Word. Amen.

The Father's Voice

My Christian brothers, what good does it do if you say you have faith but do not do things that prove you have faith? Can that kind of faith save you from the punishment of sin?

JAMES 2:14 NLV

A young family set out on a three-day hike. The mother and father were avid hikers and were excited to share the experience of the mountain trails and campsites with their young son and daughter. The children marveled at the sights and sounds of the wilderness. At nightfall they sat around the fire after their meal. The young son explored the edges of the campsite, and his father warned him not to step outside of the light.

Curious, the boy traced the shadows on the trees and followed a night crawler to its hiding place under a rock. Suddenly, the son had lost sight of the campfire and of his family. He cried out in panic, "Daddy, I'm lost!" The father responded calmly, "As long as you can hear me, you're not lost." The father called out to him over and over again until the son had followed the sound of his voice safely back to the campsite.

Perhaps you've felt like that small boy, lost with darkness all around you. Your heavenly Father is always listening, and as long as you follow His voice, He will guide you back to safety and into His loving arms.

God, help me to listen for Your voice
and follow Your direction. Amen.

Changeable?

*Dear friends, I have been trying to write to you about what God
did for us when He saved us from the punishment of sin. Now
I must write to you and tell you to fight hard for the faith which
was once and for all given to the holy people of God.*

JUDE 3

God delivered your faith to you once and for all, and He'll never
back out on His covenant. But that isn't all there is to faith. You
have a part too as you contend earnestly to work out your salvation in a sin-filled world.

On the one hand, God is unchanging—His Word does not
alter, and His character never changes. Once you are His child,
He will never let go of you.

The changeable part of the equation is the human variable.
Each of us tries to follow Jesus, some with great success, while
others barely seem to know His name. Could it be that some of
us are more aware of our need to "fight hard" than others? Do
some of us keep our eyes on the prize more successfully?

If we depend on our own power to follow Jesus, we'll soon
get worn out and slip away. We're changeable by nature. But if
we put all our trust in Him, we latch on to the One who never
changes. In Him our earnest contention finds success.

Are you contending in your own power or the power of Jesus?
With the first, you'll only fail; with the other, you'll never lose.

Lord Jesus, help me contend
simply in Your power. Amen.

Heavenly Vision

*"God will take away all their tears. There will be no more death
or sorrow or crying or pain. All the old things have passed away."
Then the One sitting on the throne said, "See! I am making all
things new. Write, for these words are true and faithful."*

REVELATION 21:4–5

Longing for heaven is a learned longing. How could it be natural when so much beauty exists on this earth for us to see, taste, and touch? As wonderful as this short life can be, it will not compare to what awaits us—seeing the loveliness of the Savior with our own eyes and hearing His voice with our ears, knowing that we will never part from Him.

In His presence, all imperfection, pain, and sadness will vanish, and the earth will be remade. We will be reunited with our loved ones in Christ who were separated from us on Earth by death or distance. The expectation of that day helps us persevere through the hurt and brokenness of the present. Knowing that complete peace and joy lie ahead gives us courage.

Even now, Christ's work isn't on hold—He is making us new by renewing our hearts and strength; He is teaching us how to love as He loves in order to draw more people to Himself. Hold this world loosely, for it will fade in the light of the Savior's face. He who calls us Beloved is coming again soon!

Dear heavenly Father, thank You that You gave us
the hope of heaven when You sent Jesus. Give
me a heart that longs for heaven and longs
for Your presence even more. Amen.

Finding Your First Love

"But I have this one thing against you.
You do not love Me as you did at first."

REVELATION 2:4

If any church was zealous for Christ, it was the church at Ephesus.

Here was a church that was planted by the apostle Paul and pastored by Timothy. It was a church that did not faint from the work of the Gospel. The people of Ephesus *labored* for the Lord. But they became consumed by their labor and forgot that they were ultimately working for the Lord.

We are in danger of falling into the same trap today. As we pour ourselves into living a godly life, we can easily get consumed with the task. Soon we can forget the very One we want to model.

Why God would want to fellowship with us is a great mystery, but He does. He has gone to great lengths to do so. He sent His Son to the cross to make it possible. How can we neglect so great a love?

Today put aside life's never-ending demands. Open your Bible and return to your first love.

> "Out of myself to dwell in thy love,
> out of despair into raptures above. . .
> Jesus, I come to thee." Amen.

The Waves of Life

"Your strength will come by being quiet and by trusting."
ISAIAH 30:15

Opportunities abound, but do we have the confidence to meet the challenges that arise when the going gets tough?

Many times, we begin in confidence as we rest in the Lord, leaning on His strength. But we begin to falter when the waters rise or the wind picks up. We take our eyes off Christ, and the waves begin to take us wherever they will.

But God tells us that when we return to Him, when we focus on and rest in Him, our quietness and confidence will keep us strong. We can be like Esther, who, although facing a dire situation, put her confidence in God and garnered the courage to go before the king for the sake of her people, saying, "And if I die, I die" (Esther 4:16). This lone woman had more faith in her God than the disciples in the boat who, in the midst of a terrible storm, woke Jesus and said, "Teacher, do You not care that we are about to die?" (Mark 4:38).

These men were filled with fear because they didn't know who Jesus was. Do you? If not, learn about Him, and garner your confidence by reading, believing, and storing God's Word in your heart. (Start with Isaiah 30:15!) Do it today, and you'll find yourself confidently riding on the waves of life, making the most of every opportunity!

God, I believe in You, that You can help me take on any new challenge, any opportunity You put before me. Thank You, Lord. I sail through this life, keeping my eyes on You! Amen.

Look Up, Not Around

*We do not compare ourselves with those who think
they are good. They compare themselves with themselves.
They decide what they think is good or bad and
compare themselves with those ideas. They are foolish.*

2 CORINTHIANS 10:12

Humans tend to be competitive. It's a part of our nature that shows up at work, on the ball field, even at church. Human competition is also seen throughout the Bible, from Cain and Abel, Jacob and Esau, David and Saul, all the way through the apostles (Luke 22:24). Women are not immune to the pull of competition either (Luke 10:41–42), and often the busier we are, the harder we compete with those around us, as if the very act of winning will make our lives easier.

Nowhere does scripture condemn the drive to achieve a worthy goal. Ambition, in itself, is not a problem. It is how ambition manifests itself that Paul warns the Corinthians about. Are we striving to better ourselves for God, for our families, for our employers? Or has the goal become winning, looking better than others? Are we looking for worldly admiration only?

If we strive toward our goals in a way that causes other believers to stumble or violates the values God has set forth for us, then perhaps we should take a step back. After all, our final victory has little to do with what the world thinks about us.

Father God, Your standards are what I need to hold
before me. Grant me the wisdom to keep Your values
in mind as I aim for any higher goal. Amen.

Meat or Mush?

Anyone who goes too far and does not live by the teachings of Christ does not have God. If you live by what Christ taught, you have both the Father and the Son.

2 JOHN 9

Have you had to contend with "smorgasbord Christianity"? Suddenly, your minister leaves, and as your congregation seeks a new leader, a succession of preachers fills the pulpit week after week. And every week you're being fed a different kind of spiritual food.

Don't relax and figure you're on a spiritual vacation. This is the time to listen very carefully. You have no idea where these people come from theologically, and it might be easy to be led astray by a deep, mellow voice or empty but high-sounding words.

Spiritual ideas abound, but not all are sound. Sometimes it's easy to assume you're getting good meat when you're actually being served mushy, rotten vegetables.

How can you tell meat from mush? Compare the message to Christ's words. Is the preacher avoiding the Bible's tough commands, preaching ideas that are not biblical, or appealing to non-Christian ideas? Better beware.

Jesus gave us strong doctrines and good teaching to lead us into His truth. Faithful expositors cling to His Word. They offer meat and milk but no rotten teachings.

Eat well!

Keep me aware of Your truth, Lord.
I want to live on it not on mush. Amen.

Hindsight

Now that which we see is as if we were looking in a broken mirror. But then we will see everything. Now I know only a part. But then I will know everything in a perfect way. That is how God knows me right now.

1 CORINTHIANS 13:12

Hindsight is 20/20. From the vantage point of experience, we can reflect on former days with wisdom. With each passing twenty-four hours, time turns the page and today becomes yesterday. We cannot rewind the clock and relive the past. We are given but one opportunity to experience today.

One day our physical clock will stop ticking, and we will be ushered into eternity. Discarding the physical world, we will embrace the spiritual realm. We will see clearly and understand completely. No more confusion. No more questions. No more excuses. What will we know then that we wished we had known now? Based on that wisdom, how will we wish we had lived our life on earth?

Perhaps we would have spent more time developing our relationships with the Lord and others rather than being consumed by our homes or careers. Maybe we would have emphasized inner beauty instead of obsessing over calories, wrinkles, or hair. Possibly we would have served others rather than demanding that they serve us.

We don't have to look back with regret. We can live today with tomorrow in mind. We can gain spiritual wisdom by keeping our eyes on the Lord today. Let today count for eternity!

Dear Lord, help me live today in light of eternity. Give me spiritual wisdom so that Your priorities become my priorities. May Your will be done in my life today. Amen.

Blessing and Thankfulness

*In everything give thanks. This is what God
wants you to do because of Christ Jesus.*
1 THESSALONIANS 5:18

"Count your blessings, name them one by one. Count your blessings, see what God has done." As the hymn says, being thankful is a practice. We should take time to contemplate God's blessings to us, especially when there seems to be more trouble than peace in our lives.

No matter how difficult life becomes, God's gifts are still there, abundant and gracious. I knew an artist whose medical conditions caused such terrible pain that she could only stand and walk for a limited time each day. Despite her situation, she made a practice of tracing the threads of God's blessing in her life. If she ate a peach, she would thank God for the peach; the store that sold it; the store's employees; the truck driver; the orchard workers; the farmer who had cared for the trees; and for the soil, air, water, and sunlight. Her spirit radiated thankfulness in the midst of her suffering, even for something as small as a peach.

Our thankfulness is founded on God—He has promised to take care of our needs and to comfort us in our distress. Name what the Father has done for you, blessings big and small, in joyous and in troubled times. All good gifts are from Him (James 1:17). Can you trace the thread of His love in your life?

Dear heavenly Father, open my eyes to Your many blessings
so I may praise Your name! Teach my heart to focus on
Your goodness, no matter the circumstances. Amen.

Nature Rejoices

"You will go out with joy, and be led out in peace. The mountains and the hills will break out into sounds of joy before you. And all the trees of the field will clap their hands."

ISAIAH 55:12

The bumblebee-yellow float plane dropped off the young couple and their guide near a remote lake in the wilds of Alaska. It was their first Alaskan adventure vacation, and they expected to catch a lot of fish, but they hadn't realized how awestruck they would be as they drank in the majestic views that surrounded them. Standing in thigh-deep glacial waters, they cast their lines. A snowcapped volcano rose up on their left, and an ancient glacier reflected the sun on their right. The only sounds were those of nature itself—the rushing river, the wind in the trees, and an occasional whoop from the woman when she got a fish on her hook. They marveled at the pair of bald eagles that soared above them most of the day and the young bear that came out of the bush to investigate the strangers who had usurped his fishing rights.

We don't have to be outdoorsmen like our Alaska vacationers to appreciate and be inspired by the wonders of God's creation wherever we find ourselves. Wildflowers that grow alongside highways, a shed snakeskin—a found treasure that a boy brings to his mother—or the unusual cloud formations that dance in the sky before a storm inspire us to praise God, the Creator of all things. Nature declares the glory of the Lord.

Lord, the beauty in Your creation inspires me to sing Your praises. Praise be to God. Amen.

Space to Breathe

He who lives in the safe place of the Most High will be in the shadow of the All-powerful. I will say to the Lord, "You are my safe and strong place, my God, in Whom I trust."

PSALM 91:1–2

Summer is one of the busiest seasons of the year. Vacations, cookouts with friends, family visits, weddings, and other events pack the warm days tight as berries in a pie—and that's in addition to the everyday things that need doing.

Even joyous times can take a toll on us when we don't make any time for ourselves. It might sound strange to trust God with the "fun stuff," but because He loves us, He is interested in every part of our lives, even our overscheduled social calendars.

This season, set aside time to be still before the Father. Time is His gift to us to spend wisely for His glory. We may be tempted to invest all of our time in others, but we are called to rest as well as to serve. God calls us to quiet our souls and nurture our mental, emotional, and spiritual health. Take a moment and breathe deeply, go for a long walk, or watch the sunlight shift from morning to afternoon. Bask in His presence—wordlessly, in prayer, in His Word, whatever—draw strength from His presence. The fast-paced life will still be there when we get back.

Father God, thank You for being my refuge. I want to be close to You no matter how busy my schedule is. Please teach me to take time to be still before You. Amen.

Mountain-Moving Company

*"Because you have so little faith. For sure, I tell you, if you have faith
as a mustard seed, you will say to this mountain, 'Move from here to
over there,' and it would move over. You will be able to do anything."*

MATTHEW 17:20

We've all made the lament at some point, "If only I had enough
faith. . ."

". . .my parent/child/friend/husband wouldn't have died."

". . .I would have received that job offer."

". . .I would have enough money for everything in my budget
and more besides."

Any of those laments for greater faith pale when compared to
faith to move a mountain. After all, doesn't Jesus say that all we
need is faith the size of a tiny seed?

The problem with that line of thought is that we put the
emphasis on ourselves. If *we* have faith, our problems will go
away.

Jesus isn't prodding us to show more faith. He is pointing us
to the object of our faith—God. However small our faith, God
can move mountains. When we drop the seed of our faith into
the ground of His will, He will move the mountains out of our
way. He will show us the direction He wants us to take. He
may move the mountain; or He may carry us over, around, or
through it.

The next time a mountain looms ahead, God wants us to apply
to His moving company. He will take us to the right destination.

Lord God, You are the God of the impossible.
We trust You to move the mountains of our
lives and to move us through them. Amen.

Called to Be Storytellers

I will sing of the loving-kindness of the Lord forever. I will make known with my mouth how faithful You are to all people.

PSALM 89:1

In addition to being prayers and praise songs, some of the psalms also retell portions of Israel's history. The Israelites would sing them together to praise the past deeds of their Deliverer (e.g., Psalm 136). Today's worship songs don't list what He's done for us specifically like the Israelites' songs did, but we should definitely follow their example of remembrance.

Christians often use the word *testimony* to name the story of how they accepted Jesus as their Savior. Salvation is a great proof of God's love, but His work doesn't stop there. He daily fills our lives with His provision, nearness, and loving patience. When we recognize what He has done for us, we can be storytellers of His faithfulness, like the psalmist. We gather strength for the challenges ahead when we recall the victories He granted in the past, and our ongoing testimonies of His faithfulness display His love to those who don't know Him personally.

When you feel troubled, tell yourself *your* stories of His faithfulness. When did you feel His comfort when you called on Him for help? When has He provided for your needs beyond expectation? Just as He did then, your unchanging God will never stop caring for you.

Father, thank You that You've never stopped working in my life. When I am fearful, help me recall Your goodness and trust You more. Give me opportunity to tell others what You have done for me, so that they will come to trust You too! Amen.

Power-Packed and Personal

I will bow down toward Your holy house. And I will give thanks to Your name for Your loving-kindness and Your truth. For You have honored Your Word because of what Your name is.

PSALM 138:2

Of all the wonderful graces and gifts God has given humankind, there's nothing that touches the power and truth of that all-time bestseller, the Bible. Unlike many of God's gifts, the Bible is one thing we can touch, see, and hear.

God says the Bible we hold in our hand is something that will endure forever. "Forever, O Lord, Your Word will never change in heaven" (Psalm 119:89). "In Your light we see light," wrote the psalmist (Psalm 36:9).

Through God's Word we experience salvation (James 1:18). The Bible provides healing, hope, and direction (Psalm 107:20; 119:74, 133). If we want wisdom and the desire to do things the right way, God's Word equips us (2 Timothy 3:16–17).

From the scriptures, we can make sense of a confusing world. We can get a hold on real truth. God has given us His eternal Word to know Him and to know ourselves better. To know and obey the Word of God is to honor what God honors above all. "God's Word is living and powerful" (Hebrews 4:12).

Teach me to not only read but obey Your living, powerful Word every day, Lord God. Amen.

A Valuable Deposit

God is the One Who makes our faith and your faith strong in Christ.
He has set us apart for Himself. He has put His mark on us to
show we belong to Him. His Spirit is in our hearts to prove this.
2 CORINTHIANS 1:21–22

Payday may just be the best day of the week. Nothing beats knowing that a big hefty check was deposited into your account.

When we accept Jesus Christ as our personal savior, the Holy Spirit comes into our hearts and lives in us, showing us how to live a godly life. The Bible tells us God puts a deposit into our very own hearts. This incredibly valuable deposit guarantees we have a place in heaven someday.

When we commit our lives to Christ, He doesn't let us flail around in this mixed-up world without any help. We have the deposit of the Holy Spirit with us all the time, and He also gives us His Word and the help of other Christians to keep us strong in the Lord. So whenever you feel alone or overwhelmed with life, remember that God has anointed you, set His seal upon you, and deposited the Holy Spirit right inside your heart. That is the most valuable deposit of all!

> Dear Lord, thank You for depositing Your
> Holy Spirit in my heart to lead and guide
> me. Help me to listen. Amen.

Press On

No, Christian brothers, I do not have that life yet. But I do one thing.
I forget everything that is behind me and look forward to that which
is ahead of me. My eyes are on the crown. I want to win the race
and get the crown of God's call from heaven through Christ Jesus.

PHILIPPIANS 3:13–14

A runner never looks back. He presses on, straining toward the finish line, in order to win the race. This is God's Word for us through the apostle Paul in the book of Philippians.

Paul had previously been known as Saul, a relentless killer of Christians. One day while walking a dusty road, he was blinded by a great light. His life was forever changed after he met the living Lord. His name became Paul and his mission the preaching of the good news of Christ.

What a turnaround! Paul preached the Gospel as diligently as he had denounced it in his former life. Even being imprisoned didn't stop him!

If Paul didn't think he had arrived spiritually, then certainly we haven't either. The goal is to press on. *Keep on keeping on.* Wherever you go, let the name of Jesus be on your lips. Don't look back. There may be all sorts of sin and muck and mire in your past. Maybe you can relate to Paul, whose past was certainly tainted. But no matter what sins are in your past, remember, as Paul said, to "press on toward the goal to win the prize."

Father, help me to never look back at the mess my life
was before I met You. I want to look forward, just like
Paul. Your promise of eternity is the prize I strive
for. Thank You for Your grace and mercy. Amen.

Fearless

God is love. If you live in love, you live by the help of God and God lives in you. . . . There is no fear in love. Perfect love puts fear out of our hearts. People have fear when they are afraid of being punished. The man who is afraid does not have perfect love.

1 JOHN 4:16, 18

First John 5:3 says that if we love God, we will do what He commands. It sounds simple enough, but fear can creep in when we consider what it means to show Him complete devotion. Putting Him first in our lives might cost us more than we expect—in our relationships, in our jobs, in how we spend our money or time. We might worry about what others might think of us or fear that we can't accomplish what God calls us to do.

God's unconditional love frees us from fear—the fear of punishment, failure, or harsh judgment from our fellow men and women—because His opinion of us matters most. Through everything, He has promised to be with us and strengthen us. We may feel ashamed of our fear, but God is not angry. Instead, He gives us exactly what we need to strengthen our faith, whether it's the sign of a damp sheepskin (Gideon, Judges 6) or inviting us to touch His wounds (Jesus to Thomas, John 20:24–29).

Do not fear. Christ shows us the vastness of His love to drive out our worries and anxieties. When we rely on Him, we can accomplish *anything* He asks of us.

Father God, I want to step out in faith and
do what You command. Banish my fears by
showing me how perfectly You love me. Amen.

Light in the Dark

*The Light shines in the darkness. The darkness
has never been able to put out the Light.*
JOHN 1:5

A mother turns on the closet light in her toddler son's bedroom
before switching off his bedside lamp. Just a sliver of light from
that closet door is all he needs. He is not afraid of the dark, he
says, as long as there is a little light in the room. This small boy
knows that darkness cannot put out light. It cannot absorb it.
Even the flicker of a candle or the smallest nightlight will triumph over the darkness surrounding it.

The world around us can seem very dark at times, but so can
the circumstances of our lives. Is it really dark, or are we failing
to look toward the true Light?

Jesus said in John 12:46, "I came to the world to be a Light.
Anyone who puts his trust in Me will not be in darkness." He
also promised that He is always with us. Because we have Him,
we have light.

If we fail to perceive it, if we seem to be living in darkness,
perhaps we have turned our backs to the light of His countenance. Maybe we are covering our eyes with the cares of this
world. Clouds of sin may be darkening our lives, but He has not
left us. He promises us that in following Him, we will not walk
in darkness but have the light of life.

Lord Jesus, show me my blind spots. Where am
I covering my own eyes or walking away from
You? Turn me back to You, the Light of life.

What's in a Name?

*Live your lives as the Good News
of Christ says you should.*
PHILIPPIANS 1:27

Many families take pride in their family name. A name that has been around for a long time often commands respect; perhaps it is associated with money, power, or fine workmanship. When someone from the family enters the community, he often is expected to be careful to represent his family name well, behaving with dignity and honor, or he runs the risk of sullying the family name. In the same way, an employee must act in a manner that reflects well upon her boss or her company, or she risks damaging the reputation of the entire firm.

As Christians, we are called to conduct ourselves in a manner worthy of the Gospel. We must uphold the name of Christ while accurately representing the Gospel. Just like employees who lose their temper and reflect badly on their company, when we succumb to sin, we may tear down the Gospel we work so hard to advocate. Our conduct, no matter the situation, should worthily reflect the Gospel of Christ.

Dear Lord, thank You for Your Word. Please
help me to conduct myself in a worthy manner.
Let my life be a reflection of You. Amen.

Enter through the Narrow Gate

*"Go in through the narrow door. The door is wide and the road
is easy that leads to hell. Many people are going through
that door. But the door is narrow and the road is hard that
leads to life that lasts forever. Few people are finding it."*

MATTHEW 7:13–14

Although peer pressure is often associated with teenagers, adults also have to deal with this phenomenon. Human beings instinctively embrace a mob mentality. Following the crowd comes easy. Acceptance by others is important. From wearing the latest fashions to watching the most popular TV shows, we hate being viewed as weird. We'd rather blend in with those around us by getting lost in the crowd.

Jesus warns us that the crowd is traveling the road that leads to destruction. Paul describes the masses in Philippians 3:19 by saying, "Their god is their stomach. They take pride in things they should be ashamed of. All they think about are the things of this world." Believers are challenged to focus on the eternal— on things that have spiritual value. A choice is before us: embrace worldly values or adopt God's truth.

Dare to enter through the narrow gate. For it is through the narrow gate that true life is found. Embrace the life that God has for you by choosing the road less traveled.

Dear Lord, give me courage to enter through the narrow
gate and experience life as You intended. Amen.

The Lord's Loving-Kindness

O Lord, let Your loving-kindness be upon us as we put our hope in You.
PSALM 33:22

We hope that our sports team will win the big game and that Starbucks will bring back its hazelnut macchiato. We also hope that our jobs will continue to fulfill us and pay our bills and that God will answer a heartfelt prayer with a long-awaited yes.

Whatever we're hoping for, it's easy to think that God doesn't care about the details of our lives. However, just as a parent cares about everything that happens to her child, so God longs to share every part of our day. Why not talk to Him about all our needs and desires?

As we sip our morning coffee, we can jot down thanks for morning blessings such as flavored creamers and hot water for our shower. While we do our jobs, we can regularly bring our concerns (and coworkers) before God's throne. We could keep scriptures scribbled on sticky notes in our cubicle—or on our desk—to remind us to think with God's thoughts throughout the day instead of falling back on worldly patterns. When we lay our head on the pillow at night, we can voice the answered prayers that grace our lives, drifting off to sleep in gratitude at God's unfailing love.

Those small, simple actions add up to a day filled with hope and gratitude. . .and those days add up to a life well-lived.

Father God, thank You for Your unfailing love. Thinking
on that love, which I haven't earned and can't repay,
causes me to fall to my knees in hope, gratitude, and joy.

Jumping Hurdles

As for God, His way is perfect.
The Word of the Lord has stood the test.
PSALM 18:30

Sandy Allen prayed to be like the other girls, but she knew she never would. Throughout her childhood, she was ridiculed for her size and appearance. At over seven feet seven inches tall, Sandy holds the world record as the tallest living woman. She learned to confront adversity and accept her place in life. And with much determination, she learned to overcome the major obstacles she faced.

Obstacles appear in your path every day. The enemy of your soul wants to keep you from fulfilling your purpose and achieving your dream. You don't have to face challenges alone; you can depend on God to help you make it over the hurdles—tough decisions, physical pain, or financial insecurity.

Maybe there are times when you just don't think you can take one more disappointment or hurt. That's the perfect time to draw strength from God and His Word. Meditate on encouraging scriptures, or play a song that you know strengthens your heart and mind. Ask God to infuse you with His strength, and you'll find the power to take another step and another—until you find yourself on the other side of that challenge you're facing today.

> God, give me strength each day to face the
> obstacles I am to overcome. I am thankful
> that I don't have to face them alone. Amen.

A Covering of Faith

*Most important of all, you need a covering of faith in front
of you. This is to put out the fire-arrows of the devil.*

EPHESIANS 6:16

When Paul wrote to the church at Ephesus about the shield
of faith, he used the word *thureos,* which means "door." Roman
soldiers' shields were large, rectangular, and door-sized. In other
words, they covered every single part of the soldier's body. It's
the same with our faith. The salvation we've been given in
Christ covers us from head to toe. And because He is lavish in
love and steadfast in keeping His promises, we'll always have
enough for every situation we encounter.

The Roman soldiers' shields had one other distinctive quality:
they were made of several hides of leather sewn together. This
meant that every morning, a soldier would have to rub oil into
the shield in order to keep it pliable and to prevent it from
drying out and cracking. This daily renewal was the difference
between life and death. . .literally!

In our own faith walk, we must daily allow God's Holy
Spirit to refill and reenergize us. The Spirit replenishes our
joy, rebuilds our faith, and redirects our thoughts so that we
can live boldly and courageously for Jesus. This begs the question: What have we done today to oil our shields? Let's not get
complacent and allow distractions to deter us from our duty! In
Christ, we have a true shield that won't ever let us down. Praise
the Lord!

> Lord, thank You for Your Word and all the
> riches I find there. Give me the discipline
> to come to You regularly for refilling.

God Will Not Change

"For I, the Lord, do not change. So you,
O children of Jacob, are not destroyed."

MALACHI 3:6

Perhaps one of the most important truths that we need to recognize is that God doesn't change. Often we are guilty of trying to bring God down to our level so we can be comfortable in our worldly standards.

"God understands that society changes," we say. "If we are going to reach today's people, we must incorporate some of their behaviors."

Yes, God knows that society changes, and what is sad is that His people change right along with it. God, however, does not change. His standards for purity, friendship, entertainment—and the list goes on—are the same that He established from the beginning. It is true that He wants us to reach those around us, but His power is great enough that He can help us do so through godly behavior. Unfortunately, it is more often our desire to fit in than a true desire to win others that causes us to adopt the world's standards.

It is time for us to acknowledge that God remains the same. We must ask ourselves whom we want to please. It's not always easy to choose modesty over style. It can be difficult to turn down a social opportunity that is contrary to God's design. But when we choose God, the satisfaction is more rewarding.

Dear God, I know You had my best interest at heart
when You established Your standards. Help me
to flee the temptation to water down Your Word
for a mere moment of worldly pleasure.

Cultivating Contentment

I wait for the Lord. My soul waits and I hope in His Word. My soul waits for the Lord more than one who watches for the morning; yes, more than one who watches for the morning.

PSALM 130:5–6

What are you waiting for—a job, a relationship, physical healing, financial provision? Whatever answer to prayer you are longing for, remember that often it's in the waiting that God performs His perfecting work on our character. Joseph waited for many years, serving in Pharaoh's house (even ending up in jail) before God promoted Him. Abraham waited until he was a century old to see the child God had promised to him and Sarah decades before. God was still at work in both men's lives, though His actions and plans were hidden.

Maybe you've waited for God to come through, and so far, He hasn't. The word *advent* means "arrival or coming, especially one which is awaited." Like the silence the people of Israel endured for four hundred years between the last spoken prophetic word and the arrival of the Christ child, perhaps you've endured silence from God for so long that you think He's not there, not listening—or not inclined to come to your rescue.

No matter what you're going through, please know that God is for you, not against you. He aches with you. And He offers us a choice: be chained in fear or changed by grace.

Which will you choose today?

Father, forgive me for doubting Your love and mercy. Thank You that You are faithful and that You will provide for me. I believe. . .help my unbelief.

The Perfect Redeemer

He said, "Who are you?" She answered, "I am Ruth, your woman servant. Spread your covering over me. For you are of our family."

RUTH 3:9

Ruth was a woman of faith. After suffering the loss of her husband, she could have wallowed in grief and misery. Instead, she chose to follow her mother-in-law, Naomi, to a place where she knew no one, in order to honor her late husband (and, perhaps, the God he had introduced her to).

Ruth was also a woman of action. She worked hard to glean in the fields, toiling with intention and consistency. The owner of the fields, Boaz, noticed her work ethic and was impressed. Later, Ruth followed Naomi's advice and found Boaz at night while he was sleeping. Because he was a relative of hers and a man of integrity, he agreed to spread his covering over her as her "family redeemer." This meant he promised to marry and take care of Ruth (and Naomi).

Ruth's story has much to teach us. Just as Ruth moved on from grief to action, we can ask for God's help to move past our own losses and not get stuck in bitterness or anger. With His help, we can honor others and not wallow in self-pity or destructive habits. Also, as His strength and forgiveness cover our weaknesses and failures, we can find peace and joy. He is the perfect Redeemer who takes care of us so we don't have to worry about providing for ourselves.

My Rock and Redeemer, I praise and thank You for Your covering over me. You are a faithful provider.

Encouraging Words

Watch your talk! No bad words should be coming from your mouth.
Say what is good. Your words should help others grow as Christians.
EPHESIANS 4:29

"Sticks and stones may break my bones, but words will never hurt me," goes the old saying. It's not true, however. Words can—and do—hurt. Ask anyone who was bullied as a child. Discouraging, shaming words stay with a person for years, even decades.

As we spend more time texting and giving status updates—and less time talking—we also need to be aware that whatever we "say" online stays online for good (we can delete things, but others may have captured screenshots or printed our words). Did you rant on Facebook about a friend or political party? It's out there. That comment belittling a coworker? It's out there. When you left a nasty comment on a blog in a moment of anger? It's out there.

As Ephesians 4:29 says, the words we choose are important especially as the world becomes more disconnected and disinterested in the things of God. The way we talk, both online and off, can either attract people toward Jesus or turn them away from Him. Today, think about the language you use and the tone you're talking with. Are your word choices helpful? Are your phrases kind? Is the tone you're taking sarcastic? Cynical? Bitter? Ask God to help you think before you speak (or post).

> Father, may everything I say be helpful, kind,
> and encouraging to others, and thank You for
> forgiving me when I mess up, Lord—because I will.

Learn Contentment

*I am not saying I need anything. I have learned
to be happy with whatever I have.*

PHILIPPIANS 4:11

The time had come. The elderly woman, called Mamo by her grandchildren, could no longer live alone. She now required the medical supervision of a nursing home. On moving day, her family reluctantly pushed her wheelchair down the hall to her new room. As they entered, stark reality stared them in the face. Mamo's sparse furnishings included a bed, dresser, and chair. A semicomatose roommate occupied the other half of her room. Peacefully looking out her window, Mamo said, "How could I want anything more?" The amazing thing was, she meant it!

How do we find contentment like this? The secret is found on the plaque quoting Philippians 4:11 that hung above Mamo's bed. Contentment is learned and cultivated. It is an attitude of the heart. It has nothing to do with material possessions or life's circumstances. It has everything to do with being in the center of God's will and knowing it. Contentment means finding rest and peace in God's presence—nothing more, nothing less. It is trusting that God will meet all of your needs.

At the end of her life, Mamo could rest in God's provision completely. May we learn to say confidently, "The Lord is my shepherd, I shall not want." That is the secret of contentment.

Dear Lord, teach me how to be content in You,
knowing that You will provide all that I need. Amen.

A Promised Healing

*"See, I will make it well again, and I will heal them.
I will let them have much peace and truth."*

JEREMIAH 33:6

Are you longing to be healed of an affliction? Mary Magdalene suffered with seven demons before Jesus touched her and restored her to life. Scripture doesn't tell us much about how, when, or where Jesus healed Mary. It does tell us that Mary, along with several other women, provided for and supported Jesus so that He could do what God had called Him to do. After Jesus healed her, she became one of his most ardent followers.

This woman, who had been tormented by Satan himself, became a walking testimony of the power of the Light to dispel darkness: "The Light shines in the darkness. The darkness has never been able to put out the Light" (John 1:5).

Whether or not God chooses to cure you here on earth, one day He *will* restore you to total health. In heaven, our bodies will be perfect and no diseases will be allowed to touch us. We will live in peace and prosperity.

Such a promise should make us rejoice. Jesus will strengthen us for this life, whatever it may hold, and will one day turn on the light that will make the darkness scatter for all time. Hallelujah!

> Heavenly Father, thank You for Your promise
> of healing. Strengthen me as I walk this earth,
> and give me hope as I look toward heaven.

A Potent Paradox

Do not let sin have power over you.
Let good have power over sin!
ROMANS 12:21

There's an old adage that says, "Don't get mad, get even." Unfortunately, that's going expressly against what Romans 12:21 would have Christ followers do. So if revenge is out, what other ways of dealing with evil could we take? Well, we could either allow it to taint and dictate everything in our lives, or we could run and hide in fear. None of these ways seem very empowering, do they?

Jesus and New Testament writers give Christians many paradoxes. And the above verse is no different. Like the text about turning the other cheek (see Matthew 5:39), Romans 12:21 instructs God's people not to bow down to, hide from, or return evil for evil, but to conquer it by doing good. Amazingly enough, it works! And, as a bonus, it will not only stop evil (and evil doers) in its (their) tracks but will relieve the flesh-filled human desire of revenge.

What a glorious day it would be if, instead of taking revenge for or hiding from evil, every person in the kingdom faced the dark beast head on. Neither cowering in fear nor wallowing in self-pity, we can count on His power to step boldly, repay evil with a kindness, and move on. What a paradox! What a Godsend!

> Lord, it seems natural for me to want to return evil
> for evil. But I want to do the supernatural. Help
> me to conquer evil by doing something good!

Confession

The Lord has heard my cry for help.
The Lord receives my prayer.
PSALM 6:9

Where does faith like David's come from? How can he make such a bold and confident statement? Wrought with emotion, David cries out to God in Psalm 6. He feels punished by God. He describes himself as languishing, in need of healing, his bones trembling in terror. His soul is also afraid. He begs God for deliverance and says he is weary with moaning, flooding his bed with tears every night. He begs God for mercy and pleads for Him to save his life.

David's confession empties him. His weakness, sorrow, and fear gush forth. He reaches the end of himself. He sees that his only hope is God's steadfast love. Remembering that God's love never gives up or gives out, David is refreshed and renewed in spirit. His confidence in God is restored.

"Confession is good for the soul," says an old Scottish proverb. David shows us the truth of this. It is in our open, honest moments before God that we are restored. When we confess our weakness, we can receive His strength. When we admit our fear, He will calm us with His Spirit. When we give Him our sadness, He will turn the weeping to joy. Remembering Him, our faith and our confidence are restored.

Father, help me to come before You honestly
confessing my weak and helpless state. Thank
You for Your mercy and Your steadfast love.

Powered Up

God is able to do much more than we ask or think through His
power working in us. May we see His shining-greatness in the
church. May all people in all time honor Christ Jesus. Let it be so.
EPHESIANS 3:20–21

One day two blind men yelled out to Jesus. People tried to tell them to be quiet. But the men kept shouting, asking Him to have pity on them. Suddenly Jesus stopped in His tracks then asked them, "What do you want Me to do for you?" (Matthew 20:32). The blind men said they wanted to see. And so, God honored that request. But the men got so much more in return. Not only did they obtain their vision, but they were also given the eye-opening opportunity to follow this Man of Miracles!

God is asking each of us the same question: "What do you want Me to do for you?" He wants us not to let others dissuade us from telling Him exactly what we want—no matter how impossible or improbable the request may seem. He wants us to be specific yet also to dream big—for He is a limitless God, ready to do so much more than we could ever ask or imagine! He wants us to then begin expecting the unexpected as we continue to travel with Him down the road with a lighter, more joyful step.

> Lord, You have planted dreams within me.
> Power me up. Help me bring them to fruition
> beyond anything I could ever ask or imagine.
> To be specific, Lord, here's what I'd like....

Shut the Door

"When you pray, go into a room by yourself. After you have shut the door, pray to your Father Who is in secret. Then your Father Who sees in secret will reward you."

MATTHEW 6:6

We all have lists: things to buy, things to do, even a list for God. *Lord, I want. . .God, I need. . .and if You could please. . .*

He meets your needs because He loves you and wants to give you His best. Have you ever wondered what God wants? He wants you—your attention, affection, praise, and worship. He wants to be included in your life.

Prayer isn't just a time to give God our list, but a time to enjoy each other's company, just as you would if you were to take time with a close personal friend—and that's really who He is. In the busyness of life, we must be careful that our "quiet time" never becomes insignificant because it's limited to the needs we feel we must tell God about. We must remember our most precious desire—just spending time with Him.

Find a moment today, shut out the rest of the world, and discover truly how little anything else matters but God. No one knows the path He's chosen for you quite like He does. Let Him point you to the truth and bring about the results He destined for you before the beginning of time.

Father, forgive me for not taking time to spend with You. Help me to listen and include You in my life at all times. Amen.

Joy in the Ride

Many flowers will grow in it,
and it will be filled with joy and singing.

ISAIAH 35:2

What if we viewed life as an adventurous bicycle ride? With our destination in focus, we would pedal forward, but not so swiftly as to overlook the beauty and experiences that God planted along the way.

We would note the tenacity of a wildflower in bloom despite its unlikely location for growth. We would contemplate God's mercy and savor the brilliance of a rainbow that illuminated a once-blackened sky.

At our halfway point, we would relax from the journey, finding a spot in life's shade to refresh and replenish ourselves for the return trip. We wouldn't just live; we would explore, pausing along the way to inhale the fresh air and scent of wildflowers.

In life, however, sometimes the road gets rough, and we are forced to take sharp turns. When that happens, we miss the beauty that surrounds us. But if we savor the ride and keep moving forward despite the bumps in the road, then "joy and singing" will follow.

So when your legs grow weary and your pathway seems long, brace yourself, board your bike, and keep on pedaling. Joy awaits you just around the bend.

O Lord, pave my pathway with song, even
when the road is rough. Remind me to stop and
appreciate the scenery along the way. Only then
will I experience the joy awaiting me. Amen.

He Is Faithful

If we have no faith, He will still be faithful
for He cannot go against what He is.
2 TIMOTHY 2:13

Have you ever said you'll do something, knowing full well you probably wouldn't get it done? We humans have a knack for letting each other down; deals fall through, plans crumble, agreements are breached.

Sometimes we treat our relationship with God the same as we do with other people. We promise Him we'll start spending more time with Him in prayer and Bible study. *This time, it will be different—I'll stick with it*, we think. Soon the daily distractions of life get in the way, and we're back in our same routine, minus prayer and Bible study.

Even when we fail to live up to our expectations, our heavenly Father doesn't pick up His judge's gavel and condemn us for unfaithfulness. Instead, He remains a faithful supporter, encouraging us to keep trying to hold up our end of the bargain. Take comfort in His faithfulness, and let that encourage you toward a deeper relationship with Him.

Father, thank You for Your unending faithfulness.
Every day I fall short of Your standards, but You're
always there, encouraging me and lifting me up.
Please help me to be more faithful to You in the
big things and in the little things. Amen.

Seek First

"First of all, look for the holy nation of God. Be right with Him. All these other things will be given to you also."
MATTHEW 6:33

What do you seek? Wealth, harmonious relationships, an impressive home, power, a devoted spouse, a fulfilling career? The list can go on and on. We spend much time, energy, and resources chasing after what we think our hearts desire. Yet when we get what we want, are we truly content? Or do we simply pause until another tempting carrot is dangled before us?

Our Creator knows where we will find true contentment. Seeking the things of this world will never be enough. Our hearts yearn for more. Our souls search for everlasting love and inner joy. God meets our need in the person of Jesus Christ. If we attempt to fill the emptiness of our soul with anything or anyone else, it's like chasing after the wind. We will come up empty-handed and disillusioned.

Seeking His kingdom begins by entering into a relationship with our heavenly Father through the person of Jesus Christ. Accept Jesus as your Savior. Then honor Him as Lord in your daily life. Focus on God's priorities. Value people above possessions, eternal riches over earthly ones. When we seek first His kingdom and righteousness, we have obtained the most treasured possession. He will take care of the rest.

Dear Lord, may I have the desire to seek
You above everything else. Amen.

Firstfruits

Honor the Lord with your riches, and with the first of all you grow. Then your store-houses will be filled with many good things and your barrels will flow over with new wine.

PROVERBS 3:9–10

Perhaps you think this verse doesn't apply to you because you don't consider yourself *wealthy*. The only *produce* you have comes from the grocery store. *Store-houses* and *barrels of wine* may not be your top priority. But this verse applies. Read these words: *Honor the Lord. . . first of all.*

Our God is not a God of leftovers. He wants us to put Him first. One way to honor God is to give Him our "firstfruits," the best we have to offer. The truth is that everything we have comes from God. The Bible calls us to cheerfully give back to the Lord one-tenth of all we earn.

Giving to God has great reward. You may not have barns you need God to fill, but you will reap the benefit in other ways. When believers honor God by giving to Him, we can trust that He will provide for our needs. In Malachi 3:10, we are challenged to test God in our tithing. Start with your next paycheck. Make the check that you dedicate to God's kingdom work the first one you write. See if God is faithful to provide for you throughout the month.

Lord, remind me not to separate my finances from
my faith. All that I have comes from Your hand.
I will honor You with my firstfruits. Amen.

Feeling the Squeeze

The eye cannot say to the hand, "I do not need you."
Or the head cannot say to the feet, "I do not need you."
1 CORINTHIANS 12:21

We've all heard the term "the sandwich generation," referring to midlifers coping with teenagers on one end and aging parents on the other. Somehow, calling it a sandwich sounds too easy. The in-between filling seems to fit comfortably, like ham and swiss cheese nestled between two slices of rye bread. Sticking with the sandwich metaphor, a more appropriate term would be the "squeeze generation." Picture peanut butter and jelly oozing out of squished white bread. It is a challenging season of life.

So how do we keep our heads above water when every face we love is looking back at us with genuine, overwhelming needs? By learning to ask for help from family members, friends, the church, and even from resources available in the community.

It's a season in life when we need help. We can't do it alone. And perhaps that is a great blessing to realize. God never meant for us to do it alone! He designed us to live in community—family, friends, and church—helping and serving and meeting one another's needs. Paul told the believers at Corinth, "Our own body has many parts. When all these many parts are put together, they are only one body. The body of Christ is like this" (1 Corinthians 12:12).

There's nothing wrong with asking for help when you need it.

Lord, You promise never to leave us or forsake us. Thank You for providing helpers to come alongside of me. Amen.

More Than Words Can Say

"I will never leave you or let you be alone."
HEBREWS 13:5

Silence—for many people it can be quite uncomfortable. Televisions, stereos, and Spotify fill the void. Incessant conversation is the norm. Noise must permeate the air. What is it about silence that agitates us so? Perhaps pondering our own thoughts is frightening. Maybe we need constant reassurance from others that we are not alone.

We may desperately desire to hear from God, yet sometimes He chooses to remain silent. How do we interpret His silence? Do we become fearful, uneasy, or confused? We may feel that He has abandoned us, but this is not true. When God is silent, His love is still present. When God is silent, He is still in control. When God is silent, He is still communicating. Do not miss it. His silence speaks volumes.

Most couples who are deeply in love do not have to exchange words to communicate their love. They can experience contentment and unwavering trust in the midst of silence. The presence of their loved one is enough. That is what God desires in our love relationship with Him. He wants us to abide in His presence. Silence prohibits distraction. As we continue to trust Him amid the silence, we learn that His presence is all we need. God has promised that He will never leave us nor forsake us. Believe Him. Trust Him. His presence is enough.

Dear Lord, help me trust You even when You
choose to remain silent. May I learn how to
be content in Your presence alone. Amen.

Where Is Your Heart?

"For wherever your riches are, your heart will be there also."
MATTHEW 6:21

When others look at you, what kind of person do you want them to see? There may be many things you would wish to include in the list of adjectives that describe you. Maybe you aren't yet who you want to be, but you know you are a work in progress. Whatever the case, who you are is a very good indication of where your heart is.

For example, your attitude about your career is something people notice. Are you driven to succeed in order to obtain high position or salary? There's nothing wrong with desiring to succeed as long as you give God the glory and maintain a godly testimony. In fact, God could use a lot more God-fearing people running businesses and managing His finances.

If, however, you are willing to compromise God's standards in order to obtain position or wealth, your heart is not where it belongs. It is on corruptible things that will not last but that might destroy you if your attitude goes too far in the wrong direction.

Think about where your heart is in every decision you make. Ensure it is with those incorruptible things that matter. And as you direct your heart toward God, you will become the kind of person He wants you to be.

*Oh Lord, give me wisdom to direct my heart
to lasting treasure that will honor You.*

Humble Servant

Jesus knew the Father had put everything into His hands. He knew He had come from God and was going back to God. Jesus got up from the supper and took off His coat. He picked up a cloth and put it around Him. Then He put water into a wash pan and began to wash the feet of His followers. He dried their feet with the cloth He had put around Himself.

JOHN 13:3–5

Imagine the twelve disciples in the upper room. Among them is the Son of God, with all authority given to Him by the Father. He has come to earth as a man and soon will return to heaven to sit at the Father's right hand. He puts a towel around His waist, pours water in a bowl, and kneels down before His disciples. He begins to wash feet—one of the lowliest jobs of that day. The Lord of the universe, the Living Word who speaks things into being and commands all things, makes a deliberate choice to get down on His knees and serve others. He handles their dusty feet, getting dirty Himself in order to make them clean. In word and deed, He teaches the disciples to follow His example. His humility is rooted in the quiet confidence of His relationship with His Father.

Are we willing to make a deliberate step to humble ourselves to serve others? Would we do the lowliest job? Will we enter into the messiness of each other's lives?

Lord, help me to follow Your example.
Make me a humble servant.

Heavenly Appreciation

God always does what is right. He will not forget the work
you did to help the Christians and the work you are still
doing to help them. This shows your love for Christ.
HEBREWS 6:10

Sometimes it seems our hard work is ignored. We sell a record number of lattes at the local coffee shop only to be told that we need to sell more pastries, or we spend days working on a presentation that the boss barely acknowledges. Our hard work seems unimportant, and we feel unappreciated.

Unfortunately, our work in the church can often feel the same way. We dutifully assume the role of greeter every Sunday, or we consistently fill communion cups each week. We spend each Sunday afternoon visiting the sick among the congregation, or we cook and serve weekly Wednesday night meals. Yet our work seems to go overlooked, and we wonder what the point is of our involvement in the church.

When our work for Christ seems to go unnoticed by our church family, we can be assured that God sees our hard work and appreciates it. We may not receive the "church member of the month" award, but our love for our brothers and sisters in Christ and our work on their behalf is not overlooked by God. The author of Hebrews assures us that God is not unjust—our reward is in heaven.

Dear Lord, You are a God of love and justice. Even
when I do not receive the notice of those around me,
help me to serve You out of my love for You. Amen.

Private Prayer

After He had sent them away, He went up the mountain by
Himself to pray. When evening came, He was there alone.
MATTHEW 14:23

Jesus gave us a perfect example of prayer to follow. Not only can we learn *how* to pray from the Lord's Prayer, but we can also discover *where* to pray.

Although there is no magical place where we need to be to talk with Him, we should find a quiet, secluded location. He wants us to focus our thoughts on Him only—not the television program coming on in fifteen minutes, the ringing telephone, or the household chores that need to be done—just God, and God alone.

Look again at the verse above. Jesus went up into the hills. You certainly don't need to go that far—although it can be an option—but your place of prayer should be free of distractions. Night fell while Jesus was there, indicating that it wasn't a hurried time of prayer. He took the time to commune with His Father, giving Him priority.

We can pray at any time, in any place, but it will benefit you and honor God when you follow Jesus' example and find a special place to talk with Him.

Lord, thank You that You listen to me at any time I come to You. Help me to find someplace that can be for just You and me, where I can pour my heart out to You. Amen.

Mustard Seed Faith

*Now faith is being sure we will get what we hope
for. It is being sure of what we cannot see.*

HEBREWS 11:1

We exercise faith in the unseen on a daily basis. When we step
onto an elevator, we can't see the cables that keep us from falling.
It is rare to meet the chef face-to-face when dining at a restaurant. Yet we trust him to prepare our food. As we shop, we use
debit cards and place faith in the bank across town to back up
our payments.

Christians are called to spiritual faith. God is ever-present in
our lives though we cannot see Him with our eyes. Have you
found that trusting Him is easier to *talk about* than it is to *live
out in daily life*?

The Lord understands the limitations of our humanity. When
the disciples asked Jesus to increase their faith, His answer must
have been reassuring to them: "If your faith was as a mustard
seed, you could say to this tree, 'Be pulled out of the ground
and planted in the sea,' and it would obey you" (Luke 17:6). A
mustard seed is one of the tiniest of all seeds, yet even mustard
seed faith can accomplish great things.

Surely it was not happenstance that Christ chose a seed
as His example when teaching about faith. A seed has one
purpose—growth. As you trust in Him and find God consistently faithful, your faith will increase.

Father, I cannot see You with my eyes, but I know You
are there. I sense that You are at work in my life and
all around me. Increase my faith, I pray. Amen.

Too Good to Be True

The woman saw that the tree was good for food, and pleasing to the eyes, and could fill the desire of making one wise.

GENESIS 3:6

It sounded like King David's son Absalom was finally going to bury the hatchet.

Absalom carried a grudge against his half-brother, Amnon, for two years. When Absalom threw a party, he made a point to invite Amnon to the festivities. King David was a little suspicious about the whole situation, but he allowed Amnon to attend.

The whole thing turned out to be a ruse. Absalom did what he had intended for years. He got his revenge and killed his brother (2 Samuel 13). As David suspected and most of us know, if something sounds too good to be true, it probably is.

Eve faced this dilemma in the Garden of Eden. When Satan whispered that she could be more like God by partaking of the forbidden fruit, the thought may have crossed her mind that it was too good to be true. But instead of walking away, she decided to take Satan up on the offer.

When our conscience or our common sense tells us something doesn't sound right, we should heed the warning. It may keep us from throwing away hard-earned money. It may keep us from a relationship that's long on excitement but short on commitment. It may keep us from long-lasting, painful consequences of poor choices.

> Lord, give me wisdom in the simple
> and complex decisions I make. Amen.

Spirit and Truth

"The time is coming, yes, it is here now, when the true worshipers will worship the Father in spirit and in truth. The Father wants that kind of worshipers."

JOHN 4:23

Are you a true worshipper? Do you feel you live a life of worship?

God's Word tells us that if we are true worshippers, we will worship in spirit and in truth. John 4:24 continues and tells us that "God is Spirit. Those who worship Him must worship Him in spirit and in truth."

God is everywhere all the time, and He doesn't just want to be worshipped at church. Yes, church is a place to worship, but it is not the only place we can worship. We should be living a life of worship.

You can worship God on your way to work, during class, as you clean your house, and pay your bills. Worship is about living your life in a way that is pleasing to the Lord and seeking Him first in all things. Paying your bills? Ask God how He wants you to spend your money. That is pleasing to Him, and that is worship. In the middle of class? Be respectful of your professors, and use the brain God gave you to complete your studies.

If you are living your everyday life to please God, that is worship!

Father, help me to live my life in ways that please You. Let my focus be on worshipping You in everything I do. Amen.

A Living Hope

He died for us so that, dead or alive, we will be with Him. So comfort each other and make each other strong as you are already doing.

1 THESSALONIANS 5:10-11

What do we have to lose? Christians are either on earth or dancing on streets of gold in heaven with God. Do you see the power of that? Hearts that yearn for heavenly eternity radiate contagious hope and encouragement for others.

As a believer in Christ, you are in a position to give that hope and be that boost people need. Your well-placed words can build up when you share your life with needy hearts. Their world may be darkened by hopelessness, discouragement, or disillusionment. Your words of grace convey the reality of a life beyond what we see here on earth.

Your life has purpose, meaning, and a glorious future! Smile, look the lost squarely in the eye, and speak the truth of His love to them. As you go about daily life, look for opportunities to build up hope in others. Bring them along on this joyful journey.

Father, will You give me specific words of encouragement for those I am with today? May the hope within me be contagious, infecting them with Your life. Amen.

Prayer Reveals Our Dependence

Jesus came with them to a place called Gethsemane.
He said to them, "You sit here while I go over there to pray."
MATTHEW 26:36

Independent. Self-reliant. In control. These attributes are considered important in today's culture. Revealing weakness and depending on others is unacceptable. Sadly, these worldly mindsets often seep into spiritual matters. Christians don't want to be perceived as needy or weak. Yet, what did Jesus model? Did He desire spiritual independence?

Jesus was humble. He conceded that He needed help. He admitted His human weakness. He acknowledged His struggle in the Garden of Gethsemane. Confiding in His disciples, He revealed His anguish and pain. Then He turned to His heavenly Father. Jesus knew He needed God's help to endure the cross. Prayer revealed Jesus' utter dependence on God.

How much do you really need God? Your prayer life reveals your answer. If an independent attitude has crept into it, prayer may seem a ritualistic exercise. But if you realize your weakness and acknowledge your need, then prayer will become vital to your existence. It will become your sustenance and nourishment—your lifeline. Prayer reveals your dependence upon God. How much do you need Him?

Dear Lord, I truly need You. May my prayer life
demonstrate my dependence upon You. Amen.

Beyond the Thornbush

*"So I will put thorn bushes in her way. I will build a wall so
that she cannot find her way. . . . So I will lead her into
the desert and speak words of comfort to her."*

HOSEA 2:6, 14

Maybe, unlike Hosea's unfaithful wife, Gomer, about whom
this verse was spoken, you haven't walked away from God.
But life has become tough, with challenges outweighing the
smooth, peaceful days of easy faith. You feel hedged about with
thorns and may frequently ask, "God, what do You want of me?"
Frustration becomes your constant companion.

As you wait for God to show you the way, take heart. He
hasn't forgotten you. Though He may be redesigning your future,
He won't leave you in the dust. Just as the prophet wooed his
wife, God will draw you to Himself again. Sin may need to be
cleansed from your life or patience learned. But a new, bright
future doubtless awaits just beyond that thornbush. Simply obey
and wait for God to show you the way beyond its prickly points.

You'll be glad you stayed faithful.

Lord, I must admit I don't relish facing challenging
times. Help me to trust that You have a better
plan and all will be well in the end. Amen.

Saying Good Things

Give great honor to the Lord with me.
Let us praise His name together.

PSALM 34:3

It's so wonderful when people say nice things about you. It puts a smile on your face when someone notices you or the things you do. We all enjoy a word of encouragement and a little praise now and then. It takes a little thought to say something good about someone else, but it's worth it and much appreciated when it's heartfelt.

Now imagine how it must make God feel when you say good things about Him. He has given so much to us. He created a world for us and then gave His only Son to repair the breach between us and Him so we could have a relationship with Him.

There are so many ways to praise Him. Tell Him how much He means to you and how thankful you are for all He's done for you. Brag on Him to others in your life—sharing His goodness and love with them and expressing how faithful He's been to you. God's goodness makes it easy to find good things to say about Him. Make time to praise Him today!

Dear heavenly Father, I could never say enough good things about You, but I want to try. I am thankful for Your mercy and unfailing love. Your goodness is endless, and the way You express Your love to me is without measure. Thank You, Lord. Amen.

Eternal Treasure

"For wherever your riches are, your heart will be there also."
MATTHEW 6:21

For Melissa's parents, love meant providing for their children's physical needs. They had a comfortable home, drove late-model cars, and never had to worry about whether their children could have a college education.

Unfortunately, this also meant both parents had to work long hours. Throughout their childhoods, Melissa and her sister wanted nothing more than to take a walk in the evening or go on a picnic on the weekends as a family, having their parents' undivided attention. Sadly, Melissa's father died suddenly when he was in his early fifties, and Melissa never did receive the attention from him that she craved.

Fast cars, luxurious homes, travel, high-paying jobs, working hard to get ahead. . .these are the values that drive many people today. Most of us know logically that these things aren't the key to happiness, but it's easy to get caught in worldly trappings of success.

It's not that owning comfortable homes or driving nice cars is wrong, but as Christians we are called to live our lives differently. Jesus challenges us to place our value in things that have eternal significance and to make choices that have an impact on our spiritual lives—not just our physical lives. What investments are you making today that will have eternal significance?

Father, thank You for the promise that there is more
to life than material success. Help me to invest my
life in things that have eternal significance. Amen.

Standing Still

"The Lord will fight for you.
All you have to do is keep still."
EXODUS 14:14

The Israelites were panicking. They had just marched out of Egypt, leaving the tyrant king and slavery behind. Now they were stuck between the entire Egyptian army on one side and the massive Red Sea on the other side. Their leaders, Moses and Aaron, had seemingly led them to this dead end where death or captivity were the only options. They were scared, angry, and completely hopeless.

Moses knew exactly how the Israelites were feeling. But he remained faithful to God, even in the midst of his fear, and he commanded the Israelites to stop panicking and stand still. Then God held back the waters of the Red Sea, and the Israelites were able to walk across on dry ground! When the Egyptians tried to follow them, the waters rushed in and drowned them all.

Sometimes when we stress and panic, we rack our brains trying to figure out solutions to our problems. We find ourselves confronted with horrible options, and instead of standing still and praying to God, we become even more panicked. Moses' words still apply to us today. When we face our fears, we should be still, trusting in God and relying on Him to bring us through the struggle.

Dear Lord, please teach me to be still and to trust in You. Thank You for Your constant faithfulness. Amen.

By Obedience Blessed

*This is the good that will come to the
man who honors the Lord with fear.*

PSALM 128:4

Do you ever wonder if serving God is worth it? After all, acclaim tends to follow those who adopt the world's beliefs. Movie stars who bare their bodies in front of cameras make millions of dollars per film. Politicians who trade favors for votes inherit power and prestige. And people and companies who cheat on their taxes rack up even more wealth. Sometimes it seems nonbelievers prosper and those who serve the Lord suffer.

But God doesn't sit idly by while people flaunt their sinfulness and mock His righteousness. He sees everything—even those acts that the wicked prefer to keep secret.

And as the Psalms state over and over again, God delights in His faithful children. He sees their suffering, notices their obedience, and revels in their steadfastness. He will never leave the righteous.

Eventually, because He is a God of justice, love, and compassion, He will honor and reward His children. Either on earth or in heaven, the scales will be balanced. He will turn every bit of evil they've experienced into good. And because He made us for Himself, His presence will be His sons and daughters' greatest gift.

God, I praise You for being a God of justice and mercy.
Help me to keep my eyes on You and not on the world.

What a Rush!

"I tell you, it is the same way among the angels
of God. If one sinner is sorry for his sins and
turns from them, the angels are very happy."

LUKE 15:10

There's no feeling quite like an adrenaline rush. Experiences like riding a roller-coaster, bungee jumping, graduation, or getting a new job can result in the heart-pounding excitement adrenaline brings. It's intoxicating! And it always, always makes you want more.

Luke 15 tells us the angels experience that sort of rush when even one sinner repents and turns to God. Do we all feel that way? Are we driven to feel that same rush by witnessing to unbelievers and seeing sinners repent as they turn to God as their Savior? Challenge yourself to reach out and experience what the angels do when your lifestyle, words, and efforts cause an unbeliever to turn to God. There is no adrenaline rush that even comes close to that one!

Father, please give me boldness to reach out
to others and lead them to You. Give me the
words to say and make the hearer receptive to
whatever You lead me to say or do. Amen.

Priscilla and Aquila: God's Team

*He began to speak without fear in the Jewish place of
worship. Aquila and Priscilla heard him. They took him to
their house and taught him much more about the things of God.*

ACTS 18:26

Priscilla and Aquila, a Jewish couple, moved to Corinth because
Emperor Claudius expelled all Jews from Rome. There they met
the apostle Paul, a man who would change their lives. The three
shared the same vocation: tent making. They began to work
together. As they cut, stitched, and sold their wares, Paul followed Jesus' revolutionary pattern of teaching women, instructing both Aquila and Priscilla. These close friends sailed with
him to Ephesus. When Paul had to leave, he trusted Priscilla
and Aquila to nurture the fledgling church there.

When Apollos, a follower of John the Baptist, began to
speak in an Ephesian synagogue, the couple took him home
for dinner. Together, husband and wife shared the full Gospel
with Apollos and helped him grow spiritually. Apollos became
a strong advocate for Jesus Christ and helped spread the Gospel.

Priscilla and Aquila found it natural to welcome Apollos
into their home for fellowship and instruction. Later, back in
Rome, they would host another developing church, working as
a team to build Christ's kingdom.

Priscilla's challenging life reminds us that we can grow spiritually and share our faith amid business deals, meals, and meetings. In the everydayness of life, God does extraordinary things!

*Lord Jesus, thank You that Priscilla thought outside
the box. You used her to fan the flame of the Spirit
in the early church. Please use me as well. Amen.*

Make Every Effort

*Work hard to live together as one by the help of
the Holy Spirit. Then there will be peace.*

EPHESIANS 4:3

The church renovation project was near completion. For more than two years, the committee labored together with minimal conflict, swallowing minor differences and dislikes for the sake of forward movement on the project. Subtle discord sneaked in the back door of conversations, crept into emails, and lingered after backhanded comments were made. Soon rumbles were abundant. "Well, if the leaders just would have done. . ." Leaders defended themselves by saying, "Well, if the team could stop squabbling, we could. . ." The conflict was ripe with dissension—the antithesis of what Christ wants for the body of Christ.

Regrouping, the members devoted time to prayer. The Word reminded them to make every effort to preserve the unity, be diligent, work hard, and strive earnestly for oneness. Harmony with others isn't always easy. Differences can chafe at patience. Grievances may need to be delayed until a proper time. Restraint from pressing one's own agenda may need to be exercised. A willed choice of acting in love is needed instead of a rash response that may feel good at the time but further divide the group. Only when peace is restored can believers experience how good and pleasant it is to dwell in unity.

Prince of Peace, help me to make unity my
focus. Enable me to make every effort to preserve
oneness with fellow believers. Then with one heart
and one mouth we can glorify You. Amen.

A Spiritual Balm

May the Lord answer you in the day of trouble! May the name of the God of Jacob keep you safe. May He send you help from the house of God, and give you strength from Zion. . . . May He give you the desire of your heart, and make all your plans go well.

PSALM 20:1–2, 4

The psalms of David often speak directly to our hearts. When he writes, "May the name of the God of Jacob keep you safe," we are filled with the assurance that God is defending us. There is a hedge surrounding us that no demon's arrows can pierce. Nothing can get through God's shield. Nothing!

David's words of God's support, refreshment, and strength buoy our flagging spirits. We drink them in, and they quench our thirst for confidence, enabling us once again to hold our heads up high in God's power, determined to allow Him to work through us, with us, for us. We have a faith that can move mountains!

And the words "May He give you the desire of your heart, and make all your plans go well" give us an optimistic outlook. As we walk in God's will, He will give us opportunities to help make our plans successful. We are given the assurance of having our heart's desire. He provides all that we need and more.

These words are a spiritual balm to be applied daily for sustenance, growth, confidence, and peace. Apply every few hours if necessary. And pray them over the lives of others. Share the joy of God's Word!

God, through Your Word, my heart, soul, and spirit are nourished. Thank You for the precious gift of Your psalms, a balm to my spirit, a joy in my life! Amen.

One Day at a Time

Honor and thanks be to the Lord, Who carries our heavy loads day by day. He is the God Who saves us.
PSALM 68:19

There's a reason why the Lord's Prayer teaches us to ask for daily bread. We tend to forget about yesterday's provision in the crunch of today's needs. God calls us to a childlike faith, one that basks in the provisions of the moment and forgets yesterday's disappointments and tomorrow's worries.

Think about small children. A toddler may cry when another child knocks him down and takes away his ball. The tears disappear when his mother hugs him and gives him a kiss. His joy in the expression of his mother's love obliterates his disappointment about the toy. Later he returns to the ball with fresh enthusiasm. He lives in the moment.

God always provides for us. Benefits overflow the shopping carts of our lives every single day. But He only gives us what we need for today, not for tomorrow. He knows that we need those benefits like a daily vitamin. By tomorrow, even later today, we may forget all that God has done for us. The Bible verse that spoke to us this morning feels empty by afternoon.

God gives us blessings every day so that we still have what we need after we have spent ourselves on life's disappointments.

Father, You give us bread daily. We praise You for Your constant care and ask that You will train our eyes to focus on Your blessings, not on our failings. Amen.

Comforting Close

The Lord is near to those who have a broken heart.
And He saves those who are broken in spirit.

PSALM 34:18

Janice walked into the room full of people, still shaken from the death of her father. Her mind was filled with the memory of his laughing face; her hand yearned for his touch. Barely a day went by when she wasn't welling up with tears at some reminder of him. *When will this pain end?* she wondered.

As Janice continued across the room, she realized that everyone had stopped talking. She looked up, and the others turned away as if they were embarrassed, not knowing what to say or do.

Janice longed for someone to say something, anything. To act normal whether she smiled or cried. She needed so much comfort. To whom could she turn? Then Janice heard a voice. *"Turn to Me, child. I am here. I am always here. Take My hand. I long to comfort you."*

When others turn away from us, we know we can always rely on our eternal Father, the One who will never leave or forsake us. He is close to us in the best and the worst of times. He rescues us when we are crushed. Take His hand. Rest in His arms. Let Him love you.

God, thank You for always being there. Heal my broken heart, my crushed spirit. Hold my hand in Yours. With every breath I take, may I know You are right here beside me, loving me. Amen.

Nothing but the Truth

"God is not a man, that He should lie. He is not a son of man, that He should be sorry for what He has said. Has He said, and will He not do it? Has He spoken, and will He not keep His Word?"

NUMBERS 23:19

Balaam, a professional enchanter, had been summoned by Balak, the worried king of Moab. Balak feared the huge company of Israelites who had just wiped out the Amorites. Now they were pitching their tents in his country! Balak figured that Balaam could provide the supernatural help needed to get rid of them.

However, Balaam and his donkey had just encountered God's angel holding a sword. The donkey understood, but it took Balaam a while to comprehend God's warning. He meant to bless Israel not curse them. Balaam told his employer, "Even if you give me your house full of silver and gold, I must say what God wants. I must bless Israel!"

When the desperate king took him to three different places to perform a curse on Israel, Balaam's message did not change—because it was God's message: He would bless His people. Those who worshipped idols, including Balak and the Moabites, would fall.

Unlike the words of human beings, God's words can be trusted. What a comfort to know He who has promised us salvation, strength for daily living, and a glorious future means what He says!

Holy Lord, in a day when truth is hard to find, You won't change Your mind about me. Thank You! Amen.

Infinite and Personal

"Am I a God Who is near," says the Lord, "and not a God Who is far away?". . . . "Do I not fill heaven and earth?"
JEREMIAH 23:23-24

Back in the 1950s, the Union of Soviet Socialist Republics sent up its first satellite, *Sputnik*. At that time, Communism held Russia in its tightfisted grip. Everyone who was anyone in the USSR was a Communist and an atheist. Not long after *Sputnik*, the Russian cosmonauts circled Earth. After their return to Earth, one cosmonaut made this announcement to the world: "I saw no God anywhere."

When U.S. astronauts finally made it into space some months later, one remarked, "I saw God everywhere!"

Our worldview determines the way we see reality. The cosmonaut didn't expect to see God, and he didn't. The astronaut didn't see anything more or less than his Russian counterpart, but he came away with an entirely different response. God says that He is both close at hand and over all there is. The late theologian and philosopher Francis Schaeffer called Him the infinite-personal God.

Whether your day is crumbling around you or is the best day you have ever had, do you see God in it? If the "sky is falling" or the sun is shining, do you still recognize the One who orders all the planets and all your days? Whether we see Him or not, God tells us He is there. And He's here too—in the good times and bad.

Lord, empower me to trust You when it's hard
to remember that You are near. And help me to
live thankfully when times are good. Amen.

The Master's Needs

"If anyone asks you, 'Why are you letting it loose?'
say to him, 'Because the Lord needs it.' "

LUKE 19:31

Jesus gave His disciples strange instructions: "Go into the town ahead of you. There you will find a young donkey tied. No man has ever sat on it. Let it loose and bring it to Me. If anyone asks you, 'Why are you letting it loose?' say to him, 'Because the Lord needs it' " (Luke 19:30–31). The owners did ask what they were doing, and the disciples repeated what Jesus had said. The owners agreed, and Jesus rode that colt into Jerusalem.

Did the owners recognize the disciples? Had Jesus told them to expect the request? Even if they already followed Christ, giving up the animal took generosity and courage. They offered it willingly because the Master needed it. Jesus' need became their priority.

Today Jesus continues to ask for the unexpected. He may ask us for our things, our time, or our talents. He asks us to align our use of what He has given us with His priorities.

We can't predict when or how Jesus will call on us to serve Him. Maybe He calls us to use our vacation time to go on a mission trip. Perhaps He wants us to give new clothes to the homeless shelter. He may ask us to volunteer in the nursery during the worship service.

What does the Master need? That should become our priority.

Master of all, we invite You to be Master of our
hearts, of everything we possess and are. Teach
us to make Your priorities our own. Amen.

Busy Waiting

*"Not one of these men of these sinful people will see
the good land I promised to give your fathers."*
DEUTERONOMY 1:35

For forty years, those woeful Israelites wandered through the desert to reach the Promised Land. How often they must have stared down at a valley or looked to the mountain summits, dreading the thousands of steps required to get there. Scholars have determined that forty-year journey should have taken only three days—at the very most two weeks.

Imagine the mechanics of moving more than two million people through the desert. They must have had an organized method for moving so many bodies. Each person probably had duties and responsibilities. Their wandering existence must have become normal, even routine.

But that generation of Israelites had no real purpose to their lives. They were busy people but faithless. No Bible verses applaud their lives. It's as if they never lived at all. Despite witnessing miracle after miracle, they never saw those tests as opportunities to trust God in a deeper way. What wasted lives!

And what a lesson to the rest of us! Are we trusting and depending on God in deeper ways throughout our full and busy days? Or are we merely moving from one spot to the next, productive but not purposeful—busy waiting?

Lord, I don't want to wander aimlessly, unaware of how purposeless my life is. I want my life to count! With single-hearted devotion, may I look to You in all things. Amen.

Be Quiet

Be quiet and know that I am God.

PSALM 46:10

From the minute the alarm clock goes off in the morning, we are busy. Many of us rush off to work or begin our tasks around the house without even eating breakfast. Most of us keep hectic schedules, and it is easy to let the day pass by without a moment of peace and quiet.

In Psalm 46:10, the command to *be quiet* is coupled with the result of *knowing that He is God*. Could it be that in order to truly recognize God's presence in our lives, we must make time to silence ourselves before Him?

Sitting quietly before the Lord is a discipline that requires practice. Just as in our earthly relationships, learning to be a good listener as we converse with our heavenly Father is important. If prayer remains one-sided, we will miss out on what He has to say to us.

Although God may not speak to us in an audible voice, He will direct our thinking and speak to our hearts. Stillness allows us to dwell on God's sovereignty, His goodness, and His deep love for us. He wants us to remember that He is God and that He is in control, regardless of our circumstances.

Be quiet. . .and know that He is God.

God, so often I do all the talking. Quiet me before
You now. Speak to my heart, I pray. Amen.

Thinking of Others

Nothing should be done because of pride or thinking about yourself. Think of other people as more important than yourself. Do not always be thinking about your own plans only. Be happy to know what other people are doing.

PHILIPPIANS 2:3–4

The apostle Paul, along with Timothy, founded the church at Philippi. Paul's relationship with this church was always close. The book of Philippians is a letter he wrote to this church while he was imprisoned for preaching the Gospel.

Paul knew the Philippians had been struggling with jealousy and rivalry. He encouraged them in his letter to think of others. He reminded them that this was the attitude of Jesus, who took on the role of a servant and humbled Himself for us, even to His death on the cross.

In the final chapter of Philippians, we read the well-known verse that says, "I can do all things because Christ gives me the strength" (Philippians 4:13). We can do *everything* through Christ Jesus who gives us strength. That includes putting others before ourselves. That includes replacing "I deserve. . ." with "How can I serve?"

When you start to look out for "number one," remember that your God is looking out for you. You are His precious child. As you allow Him to take care of you, it will free up space in your heart and allow you to look to the needs of others.

Father, You have made me to be a part of something much larger than myself. Focus my attention on those around me and not only on my own needs. Amen.

Refreshing Gift

Your love has given me much joy and comfort. The hearts of the
Christians have been made happy by you, Christian brother.
PHILEMON 7

Unsure whether he could continue in the race, the runner looked ahead. A small stand wasn't far down the road. He could see the line of cups at the edge of the table—drinks set out to refresh the runners. The sight encouraged him enough to give him the needed confidence to finish the race.

Encouragement is a wonderful gift. Simple gestures mean so much to those around us. We don't have to make big, splashy scenes to give someone a boost. Our smile can lift someone who is discouraged. A sincere thank-you or a quick hug conveys a wealth of love, gratitude, and appreciation. We all have the opportunity to make small overtures to those around us.

Jesus always took the time for those who reached out to Him. In a crowd of people, He stopped to help a woman who touched him. His quiet love extended to everyone who asked, whether verbally or with unspoken need.

God brings people into our path who need our encouragement. We must consider those around us. Smile and thank the waitress, the cashier, the people who help in small ways. Cheering others can have the effect of an energizing drink of water so that they will be able to finish the race with a smile.

Jesus, thank You for being an example of how to
encourage and refresh others. Help me to see their
need and to be willing to reach out. Amen.

Help in the Midst of Trouble

"We do not know what to do. But our eyes look to You."
2 CHRONICLES 20:12

King Jehoshaphat's army was in big trouble. Several of the surrounding nations had declared war on Israel, and a battle was imminent. King Jehoshaphat was a good king, and he immediately called on his people to fast and pray. God answered the prayers of Jehoshaphat and his people by causing the enemy armies to attack each other. As the Israelites marched into battle singing praises to God, they found that not one of the enemy had survived.

So often in this world, we come face-to-face with experiences that are overwhelming to us. We may not be surrounded by enemy armies on all sides, but it sometimes feels that way. Life is full of situations that seem insurmountable. Like Jehoshaphat and the Israelites, God desires that we rely on Him for all our needs, great or small. When we are beset with fear and worry, when we do not know what to do, we must look to God for help.

Trust that God will hear your prayers. Depend on Him to listen and answer. Believe that God will not allow you to be overcome by your trials; instead, He will faithfully and lovingly bring you through to the other side.

Dear Lord, thank You for Your faithfulness. When I am overwhelmed, let me look to You for guidance and help. Help me to trust and depend on You today. Amen.

Mutual Delight Society

He brought me into a big place. He saved
me, because He was pleased with me.
2 SAMUEL 22:20

Did you know you are part of a mutual delight society? If you're a Christian, God delights in you, and you delight in Him too (Psalm 37:4). Over and over, scripture refers to this two-sided enjoyment. How could anyone, believer or not, have missed it?

Sadly, non-Christians don't understand this mutual-delight organization. They think Christians spend their time moping and complaining or sitting in church. All they can see are the things Christians don't do and no longer enjoy or the things they, as unbelievers, wouldn't like doing. The faithless miss out on the larger picture: sin is no longer fun for those who delight in God. It's more wonderful to live for Him than engage in the sin.

If a sliver of the light of Christian joy pierces the unbelievers' lives, Satan blocks it so they can't see what they might be missing. He can't let them know that loving God can be fun!

The one who delights in God has God delighting in them too. His plans for their future are beautiful because they have experienced His salvation. No good thing will He deny them (though their definition of a good thing and His may differ at times).

Do you delight in God? Then share the news. Help others join this mutual delight society today.

Thank You, Lord, for inviting me
to share Your delights. Amen.

Give Thanks

"Give thanks to the Lord. Call on His name. Make known His works among the people. Help them remember that His name is honored."

ISAIAH 12:4

Common courtesy grows more uncommon in our society with the passing of each generation. Finding someone who puts others first and uses words like *please* and *thank you* is like finding a rare gem. Most people hurry to their next task with little thought of others crossing their paths.

Every favor and earthly blessing that we experience is given to us by God. It is nothing we have accomplished in our own right. All that God has done since the beginning of creation, He did for humankind. You are His greatest treasure.

Give thanks to God today for giving you life—the very air you breathe. He has given you the ability to make a living, to feed your family, and to give to others. He is a good Father—He won't withhold anything good from you.

What has God done for you lately? What doors of opportunity has He opened? Give Him the credit, tell others of His goodness, and thank Him! It blesses God to hear you express your gratitude, and it will do your heart good as well.

God, I am thankful for all You have given me and for who you made me to be. Help me to have a grateful heart and to express my appreciation to You in everything! Amen.

No-Compromise Lifestyle

"Turn from your sinful ways and obey My Laws. Keep all the Laws which I gave your fathers, and which I gave to you through My servants and men of God."

2 KINGS 17:13

Obedience is a long walk in the same direction. Flirtation with sin is like wandering in aimless circles. Each public or private action, no matter how large or small, plays a key role in moving you either toward or away from personal integrity, intact marriages, healthy friendships, joyful and productive collegiality, and harmony in your relationship with God.

Disobedience is an age-old problem. Just read through 2 Kings. Over and over, kings did evil in the sight of the Lord and suffered grave consequences (see, e.g., 15:5). Amid a long string of evil kings, we periodically read with relief about kings who did do "right in the sight of the LORD." However, they still failed to remove the "high places" or altars of sacrifice to foreign gods (see, e.g., 15:3–4). So, as it turns out, the "almost good" kings were only "almost obedient," and "almost obedient" behavior doesn't cut it with the Lord.

Though the Lord saved His people from Egypt, providing guidelines for living and remaining patient, He warned His people over and over again against offending Him. He defined righteous behavior and forbade worship of idols. However, the people "stiffened their necks" and stubbornly would not listen. The consequence was that the Lord removed His people from His sight (2 Kings 17:7–18). God requires a no-compromise lifestyle.

O Lord, forgive me. You know the evil in my heart, my shortcomings, my failures. Help me live a life of integrity and moral purity, a no-compromise lifestyle. Amen.

Just Say No

*So give yourselves to God. Stand against the
devil and he will run away from you.*

JAMES 4:7

The antidrug slogan "Just say no" sounds easy. Yet if that is the case, why are so many people addicted to drugs? For the same reason we struggle with sin. Temptation is great. We are weak. An adversary is out to destroy us, but our hearts will be encouraged as we focus on greater truth.

Jesus defeated Satan at the cross when He died and rose victorious. He imparts that same resurrection power to us. But although the battle has been won, Satan attempts to convince us otherwise. Jesus called Satan the "father of lies" because lying is Satan's primary weapon. We must learn to recognize his subtle attacks on our thoughts. We must choose to listen to God's truth instead of embracing Satan's lies.

Bank tellers learn how to detect counterfeit money by handling large amounts of real money. In the same way, we need to immerse ourselves in God's Word and prayer, which show us how to discern God's voice and recognize the counterfeit. When confronted by our enemy, we need not retreat in fear. We can resist him and stand firm by God's power. Satan must flee in defeat. Let's "just say no" to Satan and say yes to the Lord!

Dear Lord, thank You for the truth of Your Word.
Help me resist the devil by embracing You. Amen.

Weary Days

Why are you sad, O my soul? Why have you become troubled within me? Hope in God, for I will praise Him again for His help of being near me. O my God, my soul is troubled within me. So I remember You from the land of the Jordan and the tops of Hermon, from Mount Mizar.

PSALM 42:5–6

It's easy for life's responsibilities and commitments to drag us down. Each day seems like a repeat of the day before. The morning alarm becomes our enemy, and the snooze button becomes our considerate companion. Our hard work often goes unappreciated. Nothing feels accomplished. Our soul yearns for something more.

If we accept it, God's constant goodness can be our delight. In the mornings, instead of our groaning and hiding beneath the pillows, God desires for us to communicate with Him. His voice could be the first one that we hear each day. As we roll over and stretch, we can then say, "I love you, God. Thank You for another day of life."

Our willingness to speak with God at the day's beginning shows our dependence on Him. We can't make it alone. It is a comforting truth that God never intended for us to trek through the hours unaccompanied. He promises to be with us. He also promises His guidance and direction as we meet people and receive opportunities to serve Him.

Getting started is as simple as removing our head from beneath the pillows and telling God good morning.

Lord, refresh my spirit and give me
joy for today's activities. Amen.

Release the Music Within

*He who obeys the king's law will have no trouble, for
a wise heart knows the right time and way.*

ECCLESIASTES 8:5

Miss Lilly is a talented woman. Without the luxury of taking
one lesson, she plays the violin with grace and ease. Her oil
paintings exude warmth, character, and charm. And her ability
to retain information would challenge a twenty-year-old college student. But in her eighty years, Lilly has merely dabbled
in the gifts God has entrusted to her.

"Never had the time, and too late to start!" she insists, as she
discusses her unfulfilled dreams and what she would do differently if she could "do it all over again." So her talents are
undeveloped, unused, and unappreciated by a world waiting for
Lilly's God-given abilities to touch, bless, and stir them.

It has been said that many people go to their graves with
their music still in them. Do you carry a song within your heart,
waiting to be heard?

Whether we are eight or eighty, it is never too late to surrender our hopes and dreams to God. Wise people trust that God
will help them find the time and manner in which to use their
talents for His glory as they seek His direction.

Let the music begin.

*Dear Lord, my music is fading against the constant
beat of a busy pace. I surrender my gifts to You
and pray for the time and manner in which I can
use those gifts to touch my world. Amen.*

No Unfinished Business

I have everything I need.
PSALM 23:5

An elderly man was admitted to the hospital after experiencing symptoms of a heart attack. His doctor was making preparations for surgery to repair some of the damage to his heart when the elderly man spoke up and said, "I don't want surgery. I want to go home!"

The doctor laughed, thinking he was a little "out of his head," when the elderly man's daughter spoke up. "Doctor, my dad is a Christian." And pointing up, she continued, "He wants to go to his heavenly home."

The doctor was silent for a moment and then said to the daughter, "Well, you'd better get the rest of the kids in here for any unfinished business with their dad." The elderly man looked at the doctor and smiled, "I have had a wonderful life filled with God's goodness and love. I have five children, and we have no unfinished business between us. There are no regrets, unspoken words, or needs for forgiveness. My children all know I love them. They all have a strong relationship with the Creator of heaven and earth. One day we will all be together again."

Lord, help me to live each day with a pure heart and love for others so that I can rest each day knowing that I have no unfinished business. Amen.

The Dream Maker

*"No eye has ever seen or no ear has ever heard or no
mind has ever thought of the wonderful things God
has made ready for those who love Him."*

1 CORINTHIANS 2:9

Dreams, goals, and expectations are part of our daily lives. We have an idea of what we want and how we're going to achieve it. Disappointment can raise its ugly head when what we wanted—what we expected—doesn't happen like we thought it should or doesn't happen as fast as we planned.

Disappointment can lead to doubt. Perhaps questions tempt you to doubt the direction you felt God urging you to pursue. Don't quit! Don't give up! Press on with your dream. Failure isn't failure until you quit. When it looks like it's over, stand strong. With God's assistance, there is another way, a higher plan, or a better time to achieve your dream.

God knows the dreams He has placed inside of you. He created you and knows what you can do—even better than you know yourself. Maintain your focus—not on the dream but on the Dream Maker—and together you will achieve your dream.

God, thank You for putting dreams in my
heart. I refuse to quit. I'm looking to You to
show me how to reach my dreams. Amen.

Say What?

*Obey the Word of God. If you hear only and
do not act, you are only fooling yourself.*

JAMES 1:22

Have you ever been introduced to someone and immediately forgotten the person's name? Similarly, have you ever tried to talk to someone who is engrossed in a television show? "Yeah, I'm listening," the person replies in a less-than-attentive voice.

James seems to be in a similar situation. He is frustrated by those who pretend to listen and yet do not apply what they have heard. Like a person who sits through a speech and afterward cannot list the main points, so the people to whom James writes have heard the Word of God and cannot—or will not—apply it.

So often we find ourselves tuning out the minister on Sunday morning or thinking about other things as we read our Bibles or sing hymns of praise. We look up at the end of a sermon, a stanza, a chapter, and we don't know what we've heard, sung, or read. We pretend to hear, but we are really letting the Word of God go in one ear and out the other. Our minds must be disciplined to really listen to God's Word. Then we must do the more difficult thing—*act* on what we've finally heard.

Dear Lord, please teach me to be attentive to Your
Word. Help me to act on the things You teach me
so that mine becomes a practical faith. Amen.

A Sacrificial Life

*"No one can have greater love than
to give his life for his friends."*

JOHN 15:13

Jesus, our Lord, took the form of a human and humbled Himself in coming to earth, not to be served but to serve (Philippians 2:6–8). In fact, Christ showed His love for us in that while we were still sinners, He died for us (Romans 5:8). We may not be called to literally lay down our lives for someone, but we all are called to lay down our lives in sacrificing our needs and desires for others.

Christ modeled for us daily how to live this sacrificial life. Is there someone in your life today who needs a word of encouragement, a listening ear, or God's truth spoken over her or him? Does someone need a meal prepared, an errand run, a lawn mowed? What physical acts of service can you do for someone in need today?

Serving others may mean that you won't be able to accomplish all the tasks you have on your to-do list. It may mean that you miss lunch because you are running an errand during your lunch break. It may mean that you go to bed late. Whatever the acts of love are, you can be assured that you are modeling this sacrificial life of laying down your own life for the good of others. In living this sacrificial life, you can be certain that Jesus is saying, "You have done well. You are a good and faithful servant" (Matthew 25:21–23).

*Lord Jesus, in an effort to follow Your example,
show me for whom I can lay down my life today. Amen.*

Pack Up!

Now the Lord said to Abram, "Leave your country, your family and your
father's house, and go to the land that I will show you. . . . I will bring
good to you. I will make your name great, so you will be honored."

GENESIS 12:1–2

"Honey, we're moving!" Kayla's husband called to tell her. His company had offered him a big promotion—in another state. Her response? Fat, sloppy tears. She hoped her weeping would change his mind.

Kayla ended up loving her new home.

In God's wisdom, He likes to shake us up a little, stretch us out of our comfort zone, push us out on a limb. Yet we resist the change, cling to what's known, and try to change His mind with fat, sloppy tears.

God seems to have a fondness for change. His first words to Abram were, "Get packing. Say good-bye to your pals in glitzy Ur. I have something better in mind for you" (my paraphrase).

Are you facing a big change? It might not be a change of address. It could be running for a seat on the school board or going on a short-term mission trip. God wants us to be willing to embrace change that He brings into our lives. Even unbidden change. You may feel as if you're out on a limb, but don't forget that God is the tree trunk. He's not going to let you fall.

Holy, loving Father, in every area of my life,
teach me to trust You more deeply. Amen.

Giving God Your Burdens

Give all your cares to the Lord and He will give you strength.
He will never let those who are right with Him be shaken.

PSALM 55:22

When we have a problem, our first thought is to contact a friend. In our world today, with so many technological advances, it is easy to communicate even with people who are far away. Just a hundred years ago, people waited days to receive a message from another town!

Certainly God desires that we help to bear one another's burdens and that we seek wise counsel. The trouble is that in doing so, often we fail to take our burdens to the One who can do something about them. We are called to release our cares to our heavenly Father. A cause with an effect is implied in Psalm 55:22—*If* you cast your burden on Him, *then* He will sustain you.

Sustain is defined by Webster's as a verb meaning "to strengthen or support physically or mentally" or "to bear the weight of an object." Does it sound inviting to have the sovereign God of the universe strengthen and support you? Would it help if He bore the weight of your current trial? Our sovereign God is there when heartaches are taking their toll. He doesn't have a cell phone or an email address, but He is always just a prayer away.

Lift the worries that weigh on my mind and
heart today, Father. I can't bear them alone any
longer. In my weakness, You are strong. Thank
You for Your promise to sustain me. Amen.

Disaster!

I will be safe in the shadow of
Your wings until the trouble has passed.

PSALM 57:1

Natural disasters bring about a host of responses from people. Understandably, many individuals weep and mourn. Others look for the silver lining or even some humor in devastation. That was the response of Charlie Jones.

He found his office underwater. Records, machinery, data, personal items—all of it—ruined by flooding. He didn't cry. He didn't scream. He didn't curse. He said he did what most grown men in his situation would do.

He began to suck his thumb.

In that moment, he said later, he heard the voice of God.

"It's okay, Charlie. I was gonna burn it all anyway."

We find little good in the premature loss of things that harbor dear memories for us. But God's Word is filled with promises of renewal and restoration. We may not see it today or next month or even ten years from now. Nevertheless, our Lord's name is Redeemer. He alone can and will redeem the valuable, the precious, the everlastingly worthwhile.

If we find no comfort in the words God whispered to Charlie, we have a sure Word of God that we can hold on to in our tears. "He suffered with them in all their troubles" (Isaiah 63:9).

Lord, You are in control of all things. When I'm overwhelmed with terrible events in my life, draw me close to You for the help I so desperately need. Amen.

Darkness into Light

We are glad for our troubles also. We know that troubles help us learn not to give up. When we have learned not to give up, it shows we have stood the test. When we have stood the test, it gives us hope.

ROMANS 5:3–4

When anything unexpected, painful, or trying comes our way, our first reaction is to run from it. Whether it's an illness, job loss, strained friendship, or even the everyday challenges that sneak up, we want to find the quickest way out.

Imagine a person who is afraid of the dark watching a sunset. The sky darkens and the light fades. Facing their biggest fear, the person attempts to chase after the sun. But the earth is moving too quickly, and no one could ever avoid night completely.

Fortunately, we have a loving God who promises to stay beside us through the darkness. Even though night does come, the quickest way to see the morning is to take God's hand and walk through the hard times. In the morning, the sun rises and the darkness fades, but God is still there.

God never promised that our lives would be easy, but He did promise that He would always be with us—in the darkness and all through the night.

God, thank You for being a constant source of comfort and dependability in my life. Amen.

An Empty Promise?

Never stop praying.
1 THESSALONIANS 5:17

"I'll pray for you." Much of the time this is an empty promise.

From the pulpit a pastor once apologized to his congregation for using that empty promise as a way to end long conversations or to fill the void when he had run out of good advice. One day he realized that he rarely actually followed through with prayer. His habits proved either that he didn't have much faith in prayer or that he didn't love and serve his people as he was called to.

While that must have been a very difficult admission for that sweet, old pastor, it also must have been deeply cleansing and freeing to admit to his human inadequacies. Also, the people who were affected naturally would have been convicted of their own lack of prayer commitment and the insincerity of their own empty promises to pray.

We need to see prayer as the greatest gift we can give, not as a last-ditch effort. Promising that you will keep others in your prayers means that you will continue to pray for them, without ceasing, until you hear of a resolution to their problem. "I'll pray for you" are words that offer hope and life to people who are hurting.

Dear Jesus, please forgive me for all the times I promised prayers in vain, never intending to follow through. Thank You for being bigger than my weaknesses and for meeting needs despite my failures. Call to mind the people I need to bring before Your throne each day. Amen.

Steadfast Love

Give thanks to the Lord for He is good!
His loving-kindness lasts forever!
PSALM 107:1

When the sea of life batters us, it's easy to forget the Lord's goodness. Caught up in our own storms, tunnel vision afflicts us as we view the troubles before us and may doubt the Lord whom we serve. Though we might not consciously separate ourselves from Him, deep inside we fear He won't act to save us—or that He won't act in time.

That's a good time to stop and give thanks to God, who never stops being good or ends His love for us. Our situations change, our love fails, but God never varies. He entirely controls all creation, and His character never changes. The darkest circumstances we face will not last eternally. Life moves on and alters. But God never deserts us.

Even when our troubles seem to be in control, they aren't. God has not changed, and our doubts cannot make alteration in Him. If we allow faith to take control, we will realize that and turn again to Him.

Facing troubles? Give thanks to the Lord. He is good. He hasn't deserted you, no matter what you face, and His goodness will never end. He won't fail us.

Thank You, Lord, that Your love never changes. I can depend on it, though my life seems to be crashing around me. Nothing is larger than You. Amen.

Light in the Darkness

"I will lead the blind by a way that they do not know. I will lead them in paths they do not know. I will turn darkness into light in front of them. And I will make the bad places smooth."

ISAIAH 42:16

In the dim moonlight, we can sometimes find our way in the darkness of our homes. In familiar places, we know the lay of the land. At best we will make our way around the obstacles through memory and shadowy outline. At worst, we will lightly stumble into an armchair or a piano bench. When all else fails, we know where the light switch is and, blindly groping in the darkness, we can turn on the light to help us find our way.

But when we walk in the darkness of unfamiliar places, we may feel unsettled. Not sure of our bearings, not knowing where the light switch is, we become overwhelmed, afraid to step forward, afraid even to move. At those times, we need to remember that our God of light is always with us. Although we may not see Him, we can rest easy, knowing He is ever-present in the darkness of unknown places, opportunities, and challenges.

God will never leave us to find our way alone. Realize this truth and arm yourself with the knowledge that no matter what the situation, no matter what the trial, no matter how black the darkness, He is ever there, reaching out for us, helping us find our way. Switch on the truth of His light in your mind, and walk forward, knowing He is always within reach.

Lord, be my Light. Guard me in the darkness of these days. Make my way straight and the ground I trod smooth. And if I do stumble, catch me! In Jesus' name, I pray. Amen.

Say You're Sorry

"Tear your heart and not your clothes." Return to the Lord your God.

JOEL 2:13

"Tell your sister you're sorry," Lynn instructed her younger daughter.

Blue eyes glaring, the four-year-old mumbled the ordered command. "Sorry."

How many times in a week do moms tell their children, "Say you're sorry"? And how many times does the "sorry" come out sounding like anything but an apology? There's sorrow for sin, and then there's sorrow for getting caught in sin. There's begrudging contrition, and then there's genuine repentance.

Pastor and Bible teacher David Jeremiah tells of unintentionally cutting off a woman in traffic. He could see she was angry. When he pulled into a fast-food drive-through, she was still behind him. So he did something she probably never expected. He paid for her order.

When God commands us to repent, He doesn't want a mumbled apology. He doesn't even want demonstrative tears—unless they come from a repentant heart. The scripture above from Joel shows true repentance. Repentance for sinning against God involves a willful action, a changing of direction. It's doing it God's way, going in God's direction. We can't always undo or fix all our wrong actions. But when it's in our power to do so, the Lord gives us specific guidelines. When we do our part, He does His because He "is full of loving-kindness" (Joel 2:13).

> Forgive me, Lord, for my sin against You and others. Help me to right those things I can right and not to repeat the same errors. Amen.

Too Busy for God?

"You can speak for Me," says the Lord. *"You are My servant whom I have chosen so that you may know and believe Me, and understand that I am He. No God was made before Me, and there will be none after Me."*

ISAIAH 43:10

Have you had thoughts like the following? *I am way too busy to spend time with the Lord today. I could have thirty more minutes today if I just skip my quiet time and get to work early.* Many of us feel uncomfortable admitting this, but how often do we skip our quiet time? How often do we think we are too busy to partake in fellowship with other believers one day a week? How often do we fail to participate in a Bible study because there is "homework" to complete?

When we are not engaging in the activities that draw us closer to the Lord, we are hindering ourselves from our true calling. God tells us that our purpose in life is to be His witnesses. We have been chosen to serve Him alone. God intends for us to be witnesses and to serve Him so that we may know and believe Him. God draws us into that intimate relationship of knowing Him through these Christian activities of quiet time, Bible study, and church attendance. As we deepen our relationship with the Lord, we will understand that we can trust and believe Him and then reflect Him to others through the many responsibilities He gives us.

Lord, thank You that I am chosen to serve as Your witness in order to know and believe You. Particularly during busy days, draw me into Your constant fellowship. Amen.

The Great Gift Giver

Whatever is good and perfect comes to us from God.
He is the One Who made all light. He does not
change. No shadow is made by His turning.

JAMES 1:17

Do you know a true gift giver? We all give gifts on birthdays and at Christmas, when we receive wedding invitations, and when a baby is born. But do you know someone with a real knack for gift giving? She finds all sorts of excuses for giving gifts. She delights in it. A true gift giver has an ability to locate that "something special." When shopping for a gift, she examines many items before making her selection. She knows the interests and preferences, the tastes and favorites of her friends and family members. She chooses gifts they will like—gifts that suit them well.

God is a gift giver. He is, in fact, the Creator of all good gifts. He finds great joy in blessing you. The God who made you certainly knows you by name. He knows your tastes and preferences. He even knows your favorites and your dreams. Most important, God knows your needs.

So in seasons of waiting in your life, rest assured that gifts chosen and presented to you by the hand of God will be worth the wait.

God, sometimes I am anxious. I want what I want,
and I want it now. Calm my spirit and give me the
patience to wait for Your perfect gifts. Amen.

Troubled Bones

Be kind to me, O Lord, for I am weak. O Lord, heal me for my bones
are shaken. My soul is in great suffering. But You, O Lord, how long?
. . . The Lord has heard my cry for help. The Lord receives my prayer.

PSALM 6:2–3, 9

We associate creaking, aching bones with aging, but they can strike at any age. Even children may suffer from rheumatoid arthritis; and sports injuries, cancer, and accidents do not spare the young.

We have not all broken a bone. But we do all know the deep-down pain of troubled bones. Illness and exhaustion carry physical pain. Broken relationships or the death of someone close to us weighs down our souls. Debts loom over us. Whatever the cause, we ache with a pain beyond words. Rest that refreshes the spirit as well as the body seems out of reach.

In the midst of that trouble, we wonder if God knows and hears us. With David, we cry, "How long? We can't take any more."

That cry is the starting point. God loves us, and the Holy Spirit carries our prayers to Him "with sounds that cannot be put into words" (Romans 8:26). God will answer every prayer at the right time according to His will.

The next time troubled bones keep us awake at night, we can take them to God in prayer.

Lord, our bones are troubled. We cry, "How long?" We
know You have heard our prayers. We ask that You
will give us peaceful rest in that assurance. Amen.

Forgiveness Hurts

"Forgive us our sins as we forgive those who sin against us."
MATTHEW 6:12

No one likes being wronged. Whether it's being cut off in traffic by a careless driver, gossiped about by a thoughtless friend, or hurt more deeply, we all have unresolved pain. A common feeling is to want the other person to experience the same pain we felt. Sometimes we follow through on our retaliation; other times no action is taken, but quiet festering and imagining take place in our minds. We want payback!

Unknown to us, the other person may not realize (or even care) that the wrong had such an effect on us. Sometimes we try to be the "bigger person" and resolve the issue. Other times that person might not want to address the issue, let alone claim any responsibility.

So what do we do? God says that we can do our part to examine the situation, acknowledge our responsibility, and attempt to move forward even if we don't receive an "I'm sorry." We may not forget the issue, but our stress, anxiety, and anger will be lessened because the issue will no longer be our focus. We will once again have the opportunity to live in and enjoy the present rather than concentrating on the past.

God chose to save us by sending His Son. The world reacted to this by abusing and killing Him. The next time hurt springs up, remember that God can especially relate to our feelings of being wronged.

Lord, thank You for forgiving my sins. Help me to forgive and love others as You love me. Amen.

Lead Goose

Moses' father-in-law said to him, "What you are doing is not good. You and the people with you will become tired and weak. For the work is too much for you. You cannot do it alone."

EXODUS 18:17–18

The V formation of flying geese is a fascinating example of aerodynamics. Each bird flies slightly above the bird in front of it, resulting in a reduction of wind resistance. It also helps to conserve the geese's energy. The farther back a goose is in formation, the less energy it needs in the flight. The birds rotate the lead goose position, falling back when tired. With this instinctive system, geese can fly for a long time before they must stop for rest. This is an example of God's wisdom displayed in the natural world.

We often find ourselves as a lead goose. We have a hard time recognizing signs of exhaustion in ourselves. Even harder is falling back and letting someone else have a chance to develop leadership skills. Deep down we think that no other goose could get the gaggle where it needs to go without getting lost or bashing into treetops.

Jethro, Moses' father-in-law, came for a visit as the Israelites camped near the mountain of God. Jethro found Moses to be on the brink of exhaustion. "You will wear yourself out and these people as well," he told Moses. Jethro recommended that Moses delegate responsibilities. Moses listened and implemented everything Jethro suggested, advice that benefited the entire nation of Israel.

Dear Lord, help me to know when to fall back
and rest, letting someone else take the lead.
Teach me to serve You in any position. Amen.

Lay It at the Cross

"Come to Me, all of you who work and have heavy loads. I will give you rest. Follow My teachings and learn from Me. I am gentle and do not have pride. You will have rest for your souls. For My way of carrying a load is easy and My load is not heavy."

MATTHEW 11:28–30

Does life sometimes get you down? Often when we experience difficulties that weigh us down, we hear the old adage "Lay it at the cross." But how do we lay our difficulties at the cross?

Jesus gives us step-by-step guidance in how to place our difficulties and burdens at the foot of the cross. First, He invites us to come to Him; those of us who are weary and burdened just need to approach Jesus in prayer. Second, He exchanges our heavy and burdensome load with His easy and light load. Jesus gives us His yoke and encourages us to learn from Him. The word *yoke* refers to Christ's teachings, Jesus' *way* of living life. As we follow His teachings, we take His yoke in humility and gentleness, surrendering and submitting ourselves to His will and ways for our lives. Finally, we praise God for the rest He promises to provide us.

Do you have any difficulties in life, any burdens, worries, fears, relationship issues, finance troubles, or work problems that you need to "lay at the cross"? Jesus says, "Come."

Lord, thank You for inviting me to come and exchange my heavy burden for Your light burden. I praise You for the rest You promise me. Amen.

Leadership's Responsibility

When a nation sins, it has many rulers, but with a man of understanding and much learning, it will last a long time. A poor man who makes it hard for the poor is like a heavy rain which leaves no food.

PROVERBS 28:2–3

God raises up individuals in families, at work, at church, and in government to become leaders. The decisions they make and the instructions they give have an impact on people's lives.

Everyone has been placed in some kind of leadership role. The president of the United States and a homemaker certainly have different responsibilities, but in God's eyes, each has important and specific tasks that have an influence on others. When we think about our jobs, our thoughts might center on weariness, lack of time, or day-to-day boredom. Rarely might we recognize that our job was specifically given to us for this specific time. No one else does exactly what we do the way we do it.

Whatever our jobs are, we are responsible. How we behave and what we believe not only influence us but those we come into contact with. What influences a good leader is a person who, like Christ, is willing to humble themself rather than oppress.

Lord, give me seeing eyes and
hearing ears to guide others. Amen.

Keeping a Clean Heart

Since we have these great promises, dear friends, let us turn away from every sin of the body or of the spirit. Let us honor God with love and fear by giving ourselves to Him in every way.

2 CORINTHIANS 7:1

Her new home had white ceramic tile floors throughout. Upon seeing them, visiting friends and family often asked, "Won't they show every speck of dirt?"

"Yes, but at least I can tell if I need to clean them," replied the new homeowner, explaining her thinking that the better she could see the dirt, the better chance she had of keeping them sparkling clean.

"So how often do you have to clean them—once a week?" her friends asked.

"More like every day," she replied, laughing at their horrified faces.

Keeping a clean heart requires similar diligence and regular upkeep. While Jesus Himself cleanses us from all unrighteousness, as believers we need to be on the lookout for temptations and situations that might cause us to fall into sin in the first place. Reading the Bible reminds us that God is holy and that He expects us to strive for holiness in our thoughts and actions. As we pray daily, God shows us areas in our character or behaviors that are displeasing to Him and that need a thorough cleaning.

Like the homeowner who enjoyed knowing her floors were clean, there is joy and peace knowing our hearts can be clean too.

"Make a clean heart in me, O God. Give me a new spirit that will not be moved" (Psalm 51:10). Amen.

Take Five

*Then the Lord God made man from the dust of
the ground. And He breathed into his nose the
breath of life. Man became a living being.*

GENESIS 2:7

How would you describe your physical and mental state today?
Are you rested and refreshed, or do you feel weary, worn down
by the unrelenting demands and pressures of doing life? We
tend to think that the longer and harder we work, the more
productive we will be. But when we become fatigued spiritually
and emotionally, we eventually reach a point of exhaustion.

You *are* in control and you *can* stop the world from spinning.
Even if you know that it is impossible to take a day off, it helps
tremendously to make time for a personal "time out."

Pause from whatever you are doing for just a few moments
and breathe deeply. Shut your office door, close your eyes, or
pause for a second or two in the bathroom. Ask God for a sense
of calm and clarity of mind to deal properly with your next
assignment. Take time to unwind from a stressful day by a few
minutes of "me time" in the car as you drive home. If your com-
mute is short, pull over for a few minutes and let the weight of
the day fall off.

Sometimes the most active thing we can do is rest, even if for
only a short time.

> Father, help me not to push myself so hard. Help
> me to remember to take five and breathe. Amen.

Creation's Praise

For You made the parts inside me.
You put me together inside my mother.

PSALM 139:13

God didn't spend seven days creating things and then put His creation abilities on the shelf. He is continually creating wonderful things for His people. He created each of us with a special design in mind. Nothing about us is hidden from Him—the good parts or the bad.

Before you had a thought or moved a muscle, God was working out a plan for your existence. Maybe He gave you brown hair and a sweet smile or good genes for a long life, or He gave you dark hair and clever fingers that are artistic. Perhaps He gave you a musical voice that worships Him daily in song. Whatever His gifts, He designed them just for you to bring ministry to His hurting world.

When we look at the seven days of Creation, let's thank God that He didn't set things working and then walk away. Adam and Eve were important to Him, but so are we. He has personally created everything in this wonderful world—including us.

Do we need any more reason to praise the Lord who brought into existence every fiber of our beings?

Thank You, Lord, for detailing every piece of my
body, mind, and spirit. I'm glad nothing that
happens to me or in me is a surprise to You. Help
me use all Your gifts to Your glory. Amen.

Reach Out and Touch

*For she said to herself, "If I can
only touch His coat, I will be healed."*

MARK 5:28

We should never underestimate the power of touch. In our busy lives, as we rush from one appointment to another, skimping on affection with our families and loved ones can become routine. We wave good-bye to our children without stopping for a hug. Husbands head off to work with the barest brush of a kiss.

We do our loved ones a disservice, however, when we skip touching them. Touching communicates our affection but also our affirmation and sympathy. You can encourage people—or comfort them—with a simple touch. The Bible records Jesus touching many people, comforting and healing them. He also let people touch Him, such as the sinful woman who touched and kissed His feet (Luke 7:38).

In Mark 5, however, the true power of a simple touch is beautifully portrayed. This woman who had suffered for so long believed so strongly in Jesus that she knew the quickest touch of His hem would heal her. She reached out, and her faith made her well.

So hold those you love close. Hug them, and let them see a bit of Jesus' love in you every day.

*Lord, I turn to You when I need comfort. Let me also
offer those around the comfort of a loving touch. Amen.*

Behave Yourself!

I will be careful to live a life without blame. When will You come to me? I will walk within my house with a right and good heart.

PSALM 101:2

Home is where the heart is.

Home is a refuge, a place of rest.

Home is the smell of fresh-baked bread, the sound of laughter, the squeeze of a hug.

Because home is a place of comfort and relaxation, it is also the place where we are most likely to misbehave. We would never think of yelling at family members in public, for example, but if one of them pushes our buttons *just once* at home, we will instantly level her or him with a verbal machine gun.

David himself knew the danger of walking unwisely at home. He was home—not in battle—when he saw Bathsheba on the rooftop. His psalm cited above reminds us that we must behave wisely all the time, but especially at home.

Because more is caught than taught, our family must see mature behavior from us. We must model integrity—we must keep our promises and act the way we want those around us to act. Hypocrisy—"Do as I say, not as I do"—has no place in the home of a mature Christian who has been made complete in Christ.

May God grow us up into mature people, and may we walk accordingly, especially at home.

> Father God, how often I fail at home. Make me
> sensitive to the Spirit so that I will recognize
> when I am straying from the path of maturity.
> I'm the adult here; help me to act as one. Amen.

Difficult People

*Christian brother, you were chosen to be free. Be careful that
you do not please your old selves by sinning because you
are free. Live this free life by loving and helping others.*

GALATIANS 5:13

In the classic movie *An Affair to Remember*, Deborah Kerr
asks Cary Grant, "What makes life so difficult?" to which he
responds, "People?"

Yes, people tend to make our lives difficult. But they also
make life worth living. The trick is not to let the biting words
or nefarious deeds of others become glaring giants that make us
flee or weigh us down with hate and resentment.

The only way David stood up to the giant Goliath was by
turning his problem over to the Lord and relying on His
strength and power. Then, acting in faith, David prevailed with
the weapons at hand—a slingshot and one smooth stone.

Sometimes, like David, we need to turn our skirmishes with
others over to the Lord. Then, by using our weapons—God's
Word and a steadfast faith—we need to love and forgive others
as God loves and forgives us.

Always keep in mind that, although we may not like to admit
it, we have all said and done some pretty awful things ourselves,
making the lives of others difficult. Yet God has forgiven us and
continues to love us.

So do the right thing. Pull your feet out of the mire of unfor-
giveness, sidestep verbal retaliation, and stand tall in the freedom of love and forgiveness.

The words and deeds of others have left me wounded and
bleeding. Forgiveness and love seem to be the last thing
on my mind. Change my heart, Lord. Help me to love
and forgive others as You love and forgive me. Amen.

Created vs. Creator

"Be careful not to lift up your eyes toward heaven and see the sun and moon and stars, all the things of heaven, and be pulled away and worship them and serve them. The Lord your God has given these things to all the nations under the whole heavens."

DEUTERONOMY 4:19

The sun, moon, and stars are not to guide our lives, regardless of the power their light seems to have over us or the horoscopes people have concocted. God placed those lights in the sky with the touch of His little finger and could turn them off again, if He so chose, with less effort than it would take to flip a switch. They are beautiful creations, but they do not compare with the Creator!

Once in a while nature takes our breath away. We marvel at snowcapped mountains or get caught up in the colors of a sunset. Our heavenly Father is like a loving parent on Christmas Eve who arranges gifts beneath the tree, anticipating the joy those gifts will bring to his children.

When God fills the sky with a gorgeous sunset, it is not just about the colors and the beauty. Those colors reflect His love. He paints each stroke, each tiny detail, and mixes purples with pinks and yellows so that you might *look up*! When you look up to find the bright lights that govern our days and nights, or the next time you see a sunset, remember the Creator and give Him glory.

Father, thank You for the beauty of Your world. Remind me to stand in awe of the Creator, not the created. Amen.

Eye Care

*For the Lord of All says, "The Lord of shining-greatness has
sent Me against the nations which have robbed you in battle.
For whoever touches you, touches what is of great worth to Him."*

ZECHARIAH 2:8

The apple of the eye refers to the pupil—the very center, or heart, of the eye. Consider the lengths we go to in order to protect our eyes. We wear protective glasses in some workplaces. We close our eyes or squint in windstorms or bright light. When dust blows, we turn our heads or put up our hands to keep the dirt from ending up in our eyes.

When we do get something in an eye, the ache and discomfort are instant. Tears form, and we seek to get the particle out as quickly as possible to stop the pain. If we are unable to remove the offending bit, we often become unable to do anything but focus on the discomfort.

To think that we are the apple of God's eye is incredible. Consider the care He must take for us. He will go to great lengths to protect us from harm. When something or someone does attack us, God feels our pain. He is instantly aware of our discomfort, for it is His own. When the storms of life come, we must remember how God feels each twinge of suffering. Despite the adversity, we can praise God for He is sheltering us.

Thank You, God, that You are so
aware of what is happening to me.
Thank You for Your protection. Amen.

Take Time to Take Time

Remember how fast my life is passing.
PSALM 89:47

You stroll a sandy, white beach as a warm breeze sweeps across your face. Broken waves froth against your bare feet, and seagulls soar above. You breathe in the fresh sea air. . .and then reality interrupts the daydream.

"Time and tide wait for no man," reads one quote. As surely as the tide rises and falls, time passes swiftly. Like a wet bar of soap slipping through our fisted hand, we lose grip on time as good intentions fall prey to crowded schedules. Our busy pace deters us from taking a walk on the beach, having lunch with a friend, or making a date with our significant other.

King David recognized the brevity of life when viewed through the window of eternity. Often we fool ourselves into thinking that we have plenty of time; meanwhile, months and years pass by seemingly without notice.

Is time passing you by? Have you allowed other things to rob you of much-needed time apart? It's never too late to grab a new bar of soap, cling loosely, and take that much-deserved walk on the beach.

Dear Lord, time flies, and I've let it pass me by. I want to use the time You've given me more effectively. I want to enjoy life. Help me to take time out for myself and for others. Amen.

Lost and Found

*"He that sent Me is with Me. The Father has not left
Me alone. I always do what He wants Me to do."*

JOHN 8:29

We lose things on a daily basis. Each year we probably spend hours looking for things—keys, sunglasses, lipstick, or even the saltshaker that normally rests next to the stove. We know these items don't sprout wings and walk off but have been set somewhere and forgotten by you or someone you know.

You are God's most prized possession, and while He'll never forget where you are, sometimes we walk off from Him. We lose ourselves in the things we need to do, the places we need to go, and the people we need to see. Our calendars fill up with commitments we're obligated to keep. We often commit to too many things and exhaust ourselves trying to stay ahead of our schedules.

The further we displace ourselves from God—not necessarily on purpose—the more we become lost in our own space. While we're doing life on our own, we can forget that He is standing there waiting to do life every day with us. If you feel distant from Him today, look up. He's waiting for you to find your rightful place with Him.

God, I never want to become so busy that I lose sight
of You. Show me what things I should commit to
and what things are for someone else to do, so
that I am available to You and ready to serve in
the capacity You've prepared me for. Amen.

The Practice of Praise

Praise the Lord, O my soul. And all that is within me, praise His holy name. Praise the Lord, O my soul. And forget none of His acts of kindness. He forgives all my sins. He heals all my diseases. He saves my life from the grave. He crowns me with loving-kindness and pity.

PSALM 103:1–4

Trials come to all of us, and when they do, it's easy to forget all that God has done for us in the past. Often our adverse circumstances sabotage our efforts to praise God in every situation.

The psalmist practiced the power of praise as he acknowledged God's faithfulness to forgive, heal, and restore. He blessed the Lord with his whole heart because he trusted in God's divine plan.

Positive acclamations of our faith produce remarkable results. First, praise establishes and builds our faith. It decrees, "No matter what is happening, no matter how I feel, I choose to praise God!" Second, praise changes our perspective. As we relinquish control, praise redirects our focus toward God rather than on our problems. And third, praise blesses the heart of God. It brings God joy for His children to acknowledge His presence and power through praise.

The Bible admonishes us to praise God in every circumstance, saying, "In everything give thanks. This is what God wants you to do because of Christ Jesus" (1 Thessalonians 5:18). To bless the Lord in all things is to receive God's blessings. Begin the practice of praise today!

Heavenly Father, You are worthy of all my praise. I thank and praise You for my current circumstances, knowing that You are at work on my behalf. Amen.

Changing Direction

*Then God spoke to them in a dream. He told them not to go back
to Herod. So they went to their own country by another road.*

MATTHEW 2:12

Wise men, having seen a shining star in the east, headed to
Jerusalem, where they asked King Herod about the birth of the
King of the Jews. Herod, a cruel and crafty tyrant, sent the wise
men to Bethlehem, telling them to search for this Child and,
after finding Him, to come back and bring him word.

So the wise men left Herod, continued to follow the star, and
eventually were led to Jesus' house, where they presented Him
with their gifts. Then, being warned by God in a dream not to
go back to Herod, they returned home by another way.

Do *we* listen to God that well? Are we able to change direction at God's prompting? Or are we bent on following the route
we have set before us and then are somehow surprised when we
come face-to-face with a Herod?

We would do best to become wise, daily presenting ourselves
to Jesus, asking Him to lead us on the right path, and keeping
a weather eye on the heavenly sky. Then, alert for God's direc-
tional promptings, we will avoid the Herods of this world.

By following God's direction—in a dream, His Word, your
quiet time, or conversations with others—you will be sure to
stay on the right path and arrive home safely.

Jesus, I present myself to You. Show me the right
path to walk with every step I take. Keep me away
from evil, and lead me to Your door. Amen.

Nothing to Lose

Saul said to David, "You are not able to go and fight against this Philistine. You are only a young man, while he has been a man of war since he was young."

1 SAMUEL 17:33

Goliath, a pagan Philistine, defied Israel's army and challenged it to send a single man to fight him to decide who would rule the land. As the Israelites observed his giant body and fearsome war equipment, they quaked in their sandals. How could they win?

Victory lay in the hands of a visionary shepherd, David, who recognized that the battle was not his but God's. The intrepid shepherd stepped forward to accept the challenge.

"Wiser" heads warned the youth of danger. King Saul counseled against fighting the Philistine warrior then tried to deck the shepherd out in his own armor. But David had a better armor—the Lord God.

Sometimes we clearly hear the call of God to move ahead into spiritual battle. Others warn us against it, and their counsel seems wise. But God's call pulls at our hearts. Who are we listening to? Are these counselors godly people or discouraging, worldly wise Sauls, with at best a tenuous connection to God?

If God is fighting your battle for you, trust in Him, seek godly counsel, and follow His call implicitly. You have nothing to lose.

If You lead me, Lord, I cannot lose. Show me Your path and give me courage. Amen.

Follow Your Heart

*"I was forty years old when the Lord's servant Moses
sent me from Kadesh-barnea to spy out the land.
I returned with news for him as it was in my heart."*
JOSHUA 14:7

Sometimes when we speak our hearts, we come against opposition. This is nothing new. The same thing happened to Caleb when he and the other Israelites were sent to spy out the land of Canaan. When the spies came back to Moses and the people, everyone but Joshua and Caleb gave a bad report. Those driven by fear said there was no way Israel could take possession of the land. The current tenants—giants, to be exact—were too strong for God's people to overcome.

Yet Caleb and Joshua, the men whose spirits witnessed with God's Spirit, knew the truth of the matter. They alone stood against the bearers of bad report. They spoke the truth in their hearts—truth that was met by the tears and mourning of the Israelites who feared the giants, were disgusted with their leaders, and rejected God.

Don't let naysayers mislead you. Walk uprightly and speak the truth in your heart (see Psalm 15:2). Although the going may get rough—with giants and unbelievers obstructing your path—by following your heart and God, you will never lose your way on your journey to the land of milk and honey.

God, give me the courage to speak from my heart. Stand
beside me, lead me in the right direction, and grant me
Your wisdom as I step out from among the crowd. Amen.

In the Light

Jesus spoke to all the people, saying, "I am the Light of the world. Anyone who follows Me will not walk in darkness. He will have the Light of Life."

JOHN 8:12

The hurricane forced the family to huddle inside without electricity for a second consecutive day. If days were dreary, nights seemed eternal. Not knowing how long they would be without electricity, they conserved flashlight batteries, candles, and oil for the lamp. Even walking posed a challenge without tripping over the dog or whacking a chair leg. Games and conversation by candlelight soon lost their appeal. Reading strained the eyes. By eight o'clock there was nothing else to do but go to bed and sweat for hours on end, praying for sunshine the next morning.

The basics of life were difficult and burdensome. When the dark clouds finally lifted, sunlight streamed in and power was restored. Despite the mess outside, their spirits were revived.

Jesus said followers will never have to walk in darkness again but will have a life in the light. No more stumbling—we have His guidance. No more dreariness—we have His joy. No more heaviness—we have freedom to bask in the warmth of His forgiveness! His light of life is a vibrant life lived confidently because we can see the path before us through eyes of faith.

Light of Life, thank You that we do not hover in
darkness any longer. In You we walk boldly in
the light of life, forgiven, free, and vibrant. Amen.

Comfort Food

Everything that was written in the Holy Writings long ago was written to teach us. By not giving up, God's Word gives us strength and hope.
ROMANS 15:4

A big mound of ice cream topped with hot fudge; a full bowl of salty, buttery popcorn; grilled cheese sandwiches and warm chicken noodle soup fixed by Mom—comfort food. There is nothing like a generous helping of things that bring the sensation of comfort to a worn body at the end of a long day or to a bruised mind after a disappointment. Those comfort foods soothe the body and mind because, through the senses, they remind us of happier and more secure times.

Romans 15:4 tells us that the scriptures are comfort food for the soul. They were written and given so that, through our learning, we would be comforted with the truths of God. Worldly pleasures bring a temporary comfort, but the problem still remains when the pleasure or comfort fades. However, the words of God are soothing and provide permanent hope and peace. Through God's Word, you will be changed, and your troubles will dim in the bright light of Christ. So the next time you are sad, lonely, or disappointed, before you turn to pizza, turn to the Word of God as your source of comfort.

Thank You, Father, for the rich comfort Your Word provides. Help me to remember to find my comfort in scripture rather than through earthly things that will ultimately fail me. Amen.

Power Up

The Holy Spirit raised Jesus from the dead. If the same Holy Spirit lives in you, He will give life to your bodies in the same way.
ROMANS 8:11

God is the same yesterday, today, and forever. His strength does not diminish over time. That same mountain-moving power you read about in the lives of people from the Old and New Testaments still exists today. The same power that caused the walls of Jericho to fall, an ax to float, and a dead girl to live again is still available today. The force of God that formed the world, brought the dry land above the waters of the sea, and raised Jesus from the dead is available to work out the details of your life.

It's natural to want to do things on our own. We all want to be independent and strong. When faced with a challenge, the first thing we do is try to work it out in our own skill and ability—within our own power. But there's another way.

We don't have to go it alone. Our heavenly Father wants to help. All we have to do is ask. He has already made His power available to His children. Whatever we face—wherever we go— whatever dreams we have for our lives, take courage and know that anything is possible when we draw on the power of God.

Father, help me to remember that You are always
with me, ready to help me do all things. Amen.

A Pure Heart

Keep your heart pure for out of it are the important things of life.
PROVERBS 4:23

Do the words of Proverbs 4:23 instruct us to isolate ourselves, building walls around our hearts like fortresses to keep others out? Should we avoid letting others touch our lives and get close to us? Certainly this is not what God would want! We are designed for fellowship with other believers and even for an intimate, loving relationship with a spouse. Guarding our hearts, however, is an important command that many people in the twenty-first century often fail to heed.

When we fall into relationships or activities that are unhealthy or that consume us, our hearts lose their focus and get wounded along the way. Even good things can become idols in our lives. An idol is anything that we allow to come before God. The Lord is always there to take us back and to help us heal, but He would much prefer to help us make wise decisions on the front end. If we seek God first in all things, He can protect us from pitfalls.

Christians are meant for a close walk with God, talking with Him daily, reading and applying His Word. This walk suffers when our hearts are given carelessly to other things or people in our lives. We must, therefore, *keep our hearts pure* in order that we may live the abundant lives God desires for us.

> Father, help me to love freely but also to
> guard my heart. Walk and talk with me
> today. Guide the steps that I take. Amen.

I Have Arrived

*"Who knows if you have not become
queen for such a time as this?"*

ESTHER 4:14

You may have experienced a time in your life when you thought, *I'm precisely where God destined me to be at this point in my life.* Did you feel as if you had arrived—or that you had found the very thing you were created to do?

Maybe you felt complete after the first week at a new job. Perhaps you found your niche in volunteering at church or for a worthy organization. In that season, God equipped you to fulfill your purpose, but even greater moments are awaiting you.

There is coming a day in which each one of us will truly be able to say, "I have arrived!" When we reach heaven and are able to worship God face-to-face, then we will be able to say that we are doing what we were destined to do—worship the very One who created us.

Then we will look around and say, "I have arrived!"

Heavenly Father, thank You for giving me a dream and a destiny. I want to serve You in the very purpose You created me for—today and into all of eternity. Amen.

Location, Location, Location

He who lives in the safe place of the Most High will be in the shadow of the All-powerful. I will say to the Lord, "You are my safe and strong place, my God, in Whom I trust."

PSALM 91:1–2

Where do you live? Where are you living right now, this instant?

If you are abiding in Christ, moment by moment, you are constantly safe under His protection. In that secret place, that hidden place in Him, you can maintain a holy serenity, a peace of mind that surpasses all understanding. If you are trusting in God, nothing can move you or harm you.

If money problems, physical illness, time pressures, job woes, the state of the world, or something else is getting you down, check your location. Where are you? Where is your mind? Where are your thoughts?

Let what the world has conditioned you to think go in one ear and out the other. Stand on the truth, the promises of God's Word. Say of the Lord, "God is my refuge! I am hidden in Christ! Nothing can harm me. In Him I trust!" Say it loud. Say it often. Say it over and over until it becomes your reality. And you will find yourself dwelling in that secret place every moment of the day.

God, You are my refuge. When I abide in You, nothing can harm me. Your Word is the truth on which I rely. Fill me with Your light and the peace of Your love. It's You and me, Lord, all the way! Amen.

Reality Check

Your heart should be holy and set apart for the Lord God. Always be ready to tell everyone who asks you why you believe as you do. Be gentle as you speak and show respect. Keep your heart telling you that you have done what is right. If men speak against you, they will be ashamed when they see the good way you have lived as a Christian.

1 PETER 3:15–16

Researchers sometimes conduct behavioral studies on groups of people. The hope is often to observe the similarities and differences in individuals' character, attitude, and behavior and learn from them.

To make the study effective, subjects are not always told they are being watched but instead think they are simply in a holding room, waiting for the study to begin. The study's conductors often are watching and listening from behind mirrors or walls.

Findings show that people's speech and attitudes often are different in public than they are in private. When in public, people seem to put on faces and attitudes that don't reflect their real selves.

Every day we are being watched—both by the Father and by the people around us. Our attitudes and speech often are weighed against beliefs we profess and the hope we claim. Take time to search your heart and your motivations. If your speech and attitude aren't Christ-centered, re-aim your heart to hit the mark.

Lord, help me to be a good representative for You. Amen.

Board God's Boat

He said to them, "Come away from the people. Be by yourselves and rest." There were many people coming and going. They had had no time even to eat.

MARK 6:31

Are you "missing the boat" to a quieter place of rest with God? You mean to slow down, but your church, work, and family responsibilities pile higher than a stack of recyclable newspapers. Just when you think a free moment is yours, the phone rings, a needy friend stops by, or your child announces she needs you to bake cookies for tomorrow's school fund-raiser.

The apostles ministered tirelessly—so much so, they had little time to eat. As they gathered around Jesus to report their activities, the Lord noticed that they had neglected to take time for themselves. Sensitive to their needs, the Savior instructed them to retreat by boat with Him to a solitary place of rest where He was able to minister to them.

Often we allow the hectic pace of daily life to drain us physically and spiritually, and in the process, we deny ourselves time alone to pray and read God's Word. Meanwhile, God patiently waits.

So perhaps it's time to board God's boat to a quieter place and not jump ship!

Heavenly Father, in my hectic life, I've neglected time apart with You. Help me to board Your boat and stay afloat through spending time in Your Word and in prayer. Amen.

Choosing What Your Life Looks Like

All those who are led by the Holy Spirit are sons of God.
ROMANS 8:14

"He's Got the Whole World in His Hands" is a song that generations of children have sung for years. The lyrics of this song say that God is in control and that whatever is going to happen in our lives will happen no matter what.

The truth is, you were created in God's image with a will, and that means you have the right to choose your own life, whether it's what God desires most for you or not.

Jesus said, "Not my will, but Yours, Father!" He chose to live God's dream for His life over His own. Each day you also decide what your life looks like. The Spirit of God stands ready to lead and guide you, but you must choose to follow His lead to reach the destiny He planned for you.

He has the whole world in His hands, but daily choices belong to you. Choose to live in His will, making decisions based on His direction. Knowing His will comes from a personal relationship and from time spent with Him in prayer and in the Word. Jesus knew the path laid before Him, and you can too. Choose today.

Heavenly Father, thank You for making a way to
form me to be Your child. I choose Your dream,
Your destiny for my life. Help me to make the right
choices for my life as I follow You. Amen.

Be Strong and Courageous

"Have I not told you? Be strong and have strength of heart! Do not be afraid or lose faith. For the Lord your God is with you anywhere you go."
JOSHUA 1:9

In Joshua 1:9, God demands Joshua to "be strong and have strength of heart," a phrase that is repeated five more times in the book of Joshua. When God repeatedly demands something, we would do well to pay attention. But are we listening to God, or are we letting the fears of this world paralyze us?

Many things in this world can terrify us—the state of the economy, terrorist threats, the current crime rate, another car swerving into our lane of traffic—the list goes on and on. But we are to take courage and be strong. We are *commanded* to do so.

Someone has calculated that the words *fear not* appear exactly 365 times in the Bible. How wonderful to have this affirmation available to us every day of the year! Praise God that with Christ the Deliverer in our lives, we are no longer threatened by the world around us. He has overcome all! Now all *we* need to do is believe it!

Believe that God is with you every moment of the day. Believe that He has the power to protect and shield you from the poisonous darts of the evil one. Believe that He has overcome the world. Believe that with Him by your side, you can be stronger than the world's most powerful army. Believe that you have the courage to face the unfaceable. Nothing on this earth can harm you.

Today, Lord, I will not fear. No matter what comes against me, I am strong and courageous, able to overcome any foe—because You are by my side! Amen.

Scripture Index

OLD TESTAMENT

NEW TESTAMENT

Notes